Stochastic Sorcerers: Diffusion Models

Jamie Flux

https://www.linkedin.com/company/golden-dawn-engineering/

Collaborate with Us!

Have an innovative business idea or a project you'd like to
collaborate on?
We're always eager to explore new opportunities for growth and
partnership.
Please feel free to reach out to us at:

https://www.linkedin.com/company/golden-dawn-
engineering/

We look forward to hearing from you!

Contents

1 Unconditional Image Generation with Gaussian Diffusion　　　**6**
　　Python Code Snippet . . . .　7
　　Key Implementation Details: . . . .　13

2 Conditional Image Generation through Class Labels　　　**15**
　　Python Code Snippet . . . .　16
　　Key Implementation Details: . . . .　23

3 Text-to-Image Diffusion for Artwork and Scene Generation　　　**25**
　　Python Code Snippet . . . .　25
　　Key Implementation Details: . . . .　36

4 Image Inpainting and Outpainting with Diffusion　　　**38**
　　Python Code Snippet . . . .　38
　　Key Implementation Details: . . . .　47

5 Image Super-Resolution and Restoration　　　**49**
　　Python Code Snippet . . . .　49
　　Key Implementation Details: . . . .　58

6 Image-to-Image Translation with Diffusion　　　**60**
　　Python Code Snippet . . . .　60
　　Key Implementation Details: . . . .　69

7 3D Shape Generation with Diffusion Models　　　**70**
　　Python Code Snippet . . . .　70
　　Key Implementation Details: . . . .　78

8   3D Shape Reconstruction from Partial Observations 80
 Python Code Snippet 80
 Key Implementation Details: 88

9   Audio Denoising and Enhancement with Diffusion 90
 Python Code Snippet 91
 Key Implementation Details: 100

10 Speech Enhancement and Dereverberation   101
 Python Code Snippet 101
 Key Implementation Details: 111

11 Audio Generation for Music Composition and Effects   113
 Python Code Snippet 113
 Key Implementation Details: 122

12 Text Generation and Refinement with Diffusion   123
 Python Code Snippet 123
 Key Implementation Details: 132

13 Sketch-to-Image Synthesis with Diffusion   134
 Python Code Snippet 134
 Key Implementation Details: 143

14 Face Editing and Restoration via Diffusion   145
 Python Code Snippet 145
 Key Implementation Details: 154

15 Style Transfer in Diffusion Models   155
 Python Code Snippet 155
 Key Implementation Details: 165

16 Colorization of Grayscale Images   167
 Python Code Snippet 167
 Key Implementation Details: 177

17 Data Augmentation for Classification and Detection178
 Python Code Snippet 178
 Key Implementation Details: 187

18 Anomaly Detection in Visual Inspection   **188**
     Python Code Snippet 188
     Key Implementation Details: 197

19 Motion Planning in Robotics with Diffusion   **198**
     Python Code Snippet 198
     Key Implementation Details: 205

20 Navigation Path Generation for Autonomous Systems   **207**
     Python Code Snippet 207
     Key Implementation Details: 215

21 Protein Structure Sampling and Folding   **217**
     Python Code Snippet 217
     Key Implementation Details: 224

22 Chemical Molecule Generation for Drug Discovery **226**
     Python Code Snippet 226
     Key Implementation Details: 235

23 Therapeutic Protein and Ligand Co-Design   **236**
     Python Code Snippet 236
     Key Implementation Details: 245

24 Partial Differential Equation Solvers with Diffusion **247**
     Python Code Snippet 247
     Key Implementation Details: 254

25 Climate Data Modeling and Forecasting   **256**
     Python Code Snippet 256
     Key Implementation Details: 264

26 Financial Time Series Forecasting and Simulation **266**
     Python Code Snippet 266
     Key Implementation Details: 274

27 Generating Synthetic Tabular Data for Privacy and Analysis   **276**
     Python Code Snippet 276
     Key Implementation Details: 283

28 Domain Adaptation in Vision with Diffusion   285
   Python Code Snippet 285
   Key Implementation Details: 294

29 Adversarial Example Generation for Robustness   296
   Python Code Snippet 296
   Key Implementation Details: 306

30 Reflection and Haze Removal in Photographs   308
   Python Code Snippet 308
   Key Implementation Details: 317

31 Neural Rendering and View Synthesis   319
   Python Code Snippet 320
   Key Implementation Details: 328

32 Generative Design for Mechanical and Architectural Parts   330
   Python Code Snippet 330
   Key Implementation Details: 338

33 Multimodal Generation with Diffusion for Audio-Visual Synthesis   340
   Python Code Snippet 341
   Key Implementation Details: 348

Chapter 1

Unconditional Image Generation with Gaussian Diffusion

This chapter focuses on generating images from pure noise using a foundational Gaussian Diffusion process. Common use cases include generating artistic visuals, synthetic training data, and exploratory image designs. First, we define a forward procedure to add Gaussian noise to training images, gradually increasing noise over fixed time steps. Next, we explain the reverse diffusion process, where a UNet-based neural network learns to iteratively remove the noise. Construction begins by choosing a variance schedule, typically linear or cosine, that dictates how much noise to add at each step. The core training objective is to predict the noise at each step and minimize the difference (often with an L2 loss) between the predicted and actual noise. Implementation steps include: (1) loading and normalizing an image dataset, (2) setting up an increasing noise schedule, (3) constructing a UNet with skip connections at varying scales, (4) training with mini-batches to learn the reverse denoising path, and (5) sampling new images by reversing the diffusion from random noise. Finally, an innovative trick is introduced that scales model outputs with a guidance parameter to achieve enhanced control over image quality and diversity.

Python Code Snippet

```python
import os
import random
import math
import torch
import torch.nn as nn
from torch.utils.data import DataLoader
import torchvision
import torchvision.transforms as transforms
import torch.optim as optim
import matplotlib.pyplot as plt


# ----------------------------------------------------------------
# 1) Set random seed for reproducibility
# ----------------------------------------------------------------
def set_seed(seed=42):
    random.seed(seed)
    torch.manual_seed(seed)
    if torch.cuda.is_available():
        torch.cuda.manual_seed_all(seed)


# ----------------------------------------------------------------
# 2) Create a simple U-Net for image denoising
# ----------------------------------------------------------------
class DoubleConv(nn.Module):
    '''
    A helper module that performs two convolutions (each followed by
    ↪  ReLU)
    to reduce block boilerplate in the U-Net.
    '''

    def __init__(self, in_channels, out_channels):
        super(DoubleConv, self).__init__()
        self.conv = nn.Sequential(
            nn.Conv2d(in_channels, out_channels, 3, padding=1),
            nn.ReLU(inplace=True),
            nn.Conv2d(out_channels, out_channels, 3, padding=1),
            nn.ReLU(inplace=True)
        )

    def forward(self, x):
        return self.conv(x)

class UNet(nn.Module):
    '''
    A simplified U-Net architecture with down-sampling (encoder)
    and up-sampling (decoder) blocks, plus skip connections.
    '''

    def __init__(self, in_channels=1, out_channels=1,
    ↪  base_channels=64):
        super(UNet, self).__init__()
```

```python
        # Down-sampling (encoder)
        self.down1 = DoubleConv(in_channels, base_channels)
        self.down2 = DoubleConv(base_channels, base_channels*2)
        self.down3 = DoubleConv(base_channels*2, base_channels*4)

        self.pool = nn.MaxPool2d(2)

        # Bottleneck
        self.bottleneck = DoubleConv(base_channels*4,
        ↪   base_channels*8)

        # Up-sampling (decoder)
        self.up1 = nn.ConvTranspose2d(base_channels*8,
        ↪   base_channels*4, kernel_size=2, stride=2)
        self.conv_up1 = DoubleConv(base_channels*8, base_channels*4)

        self.up2 = nn.ConvTranspose2d(base_channels*4,
        ↪   base_channels*2, kernel_size=2, stride=2)
        self.conv_up2 = DoubleConv(base_channels*4, base_channels*2)

        self.up3 = nn.ConvTranspose2d(base_channels*2,
        ↪   base_channels, kernel_size=2, stride=2)
        self.conv_up3 = DoubleConv(base_channels*2, base_channels)

        # Final output
        self.final_conv = nn.Conv2d(base_channels, out_channels,
        ↪   kernel_size=1)

    def forward(self, x):
        # Encoder
        x1 = self.down1(x)
        x2 = self.pool(x1)

        x2 = self.down2(x2)
        x3 = self.pool(x2)

        x3 = self.down3(x3)
        x4 = self.pool(x3)

        # Bottleneck
        b = self.bottleneck(x4)

        # Decoder
        x = self.up1(b)
        x = torch.cat([x, x3], dim=1)   # skip connection
        x = self.conv_up1(x)

        x = self.up2(x)
        x = torch.cat([x, x2], dim=1)
        x = self.conv_up2(x)

        x = self.up3(x)
        x = torch.cat([x, x1], dim=1)
```

```
        x = self.conv_up3(x)

        # Final
        out = self.final_conv(x)
        return out


# ----------------------------------------------------------------
# 3) Define diffusion schedule and forward process
# ----------------------------------------------------------------
def make_beta_schedule(schedule_name, n_timestep, start=1e-4,
↪   end=2e-2):
    '''
    Creates a beta schedule for the diffusion process.
    We use a linear schedule as a straightforward example.
    '''
    if schedule_name == "linear":
        return torch.linspace(start, end, n_timestep)
    else:
        raise NotImplementedError("Only 'linear' schedule is
        ↪   implemented here.")


class Diffusion:
    '''
    A class that encapsulates:
    1) The forward noising process: q(x_t | x_0)
    2) The reverse denoising process: p(x_{t-1} | x_t)
    3) Utility for training and sampling.
    '''

    def __init__(self, n_steps=1000, beta_schedule='linear'):
        self.n_steps = n_steps
        self.betas = make_beta_schedule(beta_schedule, n_steps)
        self.alphas = 1.0 - self.betas
        self.alpha_cumprod = torch.cumprod(self.alphas, dim=0)
        self.alpha_cumprod_prev = torch.cat([torch.tensor([1.0]),
        ↪   self.alpha_cumprod[:-1]], dim=0)

        # Posterior variance term for p(x_{t-1} | x_t, x_0)
        self.posterior_variance = self.betas * (1.0 -
        ↪   self.alpha_cumprod_prev) / (1.0 - self.alpha_cumprod)

    def q_sample(self, x_start, t, noise=None):
        '''
        Forward diffusion: Adds noise to x_start at step t.
        x_t = sqrt(alpha_cumprod[t]) * x_start + sqrt(1 -
        ↪   alpha_cumprod[t]) * noise
        '''
        if noise is None:
            noise = torch.randn_like(x_start)
        sqrt_alpha_cumprod_t =
        ↪   self.alpha_cumprod[t].sqrt().unsqueeze(-1).
        unsqueeze(-1).unsqueeze(-1)
        sqrt_one_minus_alpha_cumprod_t = (1 -
        ↪   self.alpha_cumprod[t]).sqrt().unsqueeze(-1).
```

```python
            unsqueeze(-1).unsqueeze(-1)
        return sqrt_alpha_cumprod_t * x_start +
        ↪    sqrt_one_minus_alpha_cumprod_t * noise

    def predict_noise(self, model, x_t, t):
        '''
        Use the UNet model to predict the noise added at step t.
        '''
        return model(x_t)

    def p_sample(self, model, x_t, t, guidance_scale=1.0):
        '''
        One reverse diffusion step: p(x_{t-1} | x_t).
        The model predicts the noise e_t, and we compute the mean of
        ↪    p(x_{t-1} | x_t, x_0).
        We also demonstrate a "guidance_scale" that scales the
        ↪    predicted noise for more or less variation.
        '''
        betas_t = self.betas[t]
        alpha_t = self.alphas[t]
        alpha_cumprod_t = self.alpha_cumprod[t]
        alpha_cumprod_prev_t = self.alpha_cumprod_prev[t]

        # We do not have a classifier here, so "guidance_scale"
        # is a simplistic scaling of the noise estimate for
        ↪    demonstration.
        e_t = model(x_t) * guidance_scale

        # The model assumes x_0 ~ x_t - sqrt(1-alpha_t)* e_t /
        ↪    sqrt(alpha_t)
        # so we reconstruct x_0:
        sqrt_recip_alpha_t = (1.0 / alpha_t).sqrt()
        x_0_hat = (x_t - (1.0 - alpha_t).sqrt() * e_t) *
        ↪    sqrt_recip_alpha_t

        # We now compute the mean of the posterior q(x_{t-1} | x_t,
        ↪    x_0_hat)
        coef1 = ( (alpha_cumprod_prev_t).sqrt() * betas_t ) / (1.0 -
        ↪    alpha_cumprod_t)
        coef2 = ( (1.0 - alpha_cumprod_prev_t) * alpha_t.sqrt() ) /
        ↪    (1.0 - alpha_cumprod_t)

        mean = coef1 * x_0_hat + coef2 * x_t

        # Posterior variance
        posterior_var = self.posterior_variance[t]
        if t > 0:
            noise = torch.randn_like(x_t)
        else:
            noise = torch.zeros_like(x_t)

        x_prev = mean + noise * posterior_var.sqrt()
        return x_prev
```

```python
    def p_sample_loop(self, model, shape, device,
    ↪  guidance_scale=1.0):
        '''
        Repeatedly apply p_sample to go from x_T ~ N(0,I) to x_0.
        '''
        x_t = torch.randn(shape, device=device)
        for i in reversed(range(self.n_steps)):
            x_t = self.p_sample(model, x_t, i,
            ↪  guidance_scale=guidance_scale)
        return x_t

# --------------------------------------------------------------
# 4) Training and sampling routines
# --------------------------------------------------------------
def train_one_epoch(model, diffusion, optimizer, dataloader,
↪  device):
    '''
    A single training epoch for the diffusion model.
    We sample a random t, forward diffuse the image, and predict the
    ↪  noise.
    '''
    model.train()
    loss_sum = 0
    for images, _ in dataloader:
        images = images.to(device)

        # For each batch, sample a random time step
        t = torch.randint(0, diffusion.n_steps, (images.size(0),),
        ↪  device=device).long()

        # Create random noise
        noise = torch.randn_like(images)

        # Forward diffuse the real image at step t
        x_t = diffusion.q_sample(images, t, noise=noise)

        # Predict the noise with the model
        noise_pred = diffusion.predict_noise(model, x_t, t)

        # L2 loss to match the real noise
        loss = torch.nn.functional.mse_loss(noise_pred, noise)

        optimizer.zero_grad()
        loss.backward()
        optimizer.step()

        loss_sum += loss.item()

    return loss_sum / len(dataloader)

def evaluate_model(model, diffusion, dataloader, device):
    '''
```

```python
    A quick evaluation that reports average L2 error on a test set.
    '''
    model.eval()
    loss_sum = 0
    with torch.no_grad():
        for images, _ in dataloader:
            images = images.to(device)
            t = torch.randint(0, diffusion.n_steps,
            ↪  (images.size(0),), device=device).long()
            noise = torch.randn_like(images)
            x_t = diffusion.q_sample(images, t, noise=noise)
            noise_pred = diffusion.predict_noise(model, x_t, t)
            loss = torch.nn.functional.mse_loss(noise_pred, noise)
            loss_sum += loss.item()
    return loss_sum / len(dataloader)


def sample_and_save(model, diffusion, device, epoch,
↪  guidance_scale=1.0):
    '''
    Samples a batch of images from the diffusion model and saves a
    ↪  grid for inspection.
    '''
    model.eval()
    with torch.no_grad():
        sample_batch_size = 16
        # shape: B x C x H x W
        generated = diffusion.p_sample_loop(model,
        ↪  (sample_batch_size, 1, 28, 28), device, guidance_scale)
        # Normalize to [0,1] and plot
        generated = (generated.clamp(-1.0, 1.0) + 1) * 0.5  # from
        ↪  [-1,1] to [0,1]

        grid = torchvision.utils.make_grid(generated, nrow=4)
        os.makedirs("results", exist_ok=True)
        plt.figure(figsize=(6,6))
        plt.axis("off")
        plt.imshow(grid.permute(1, 2, 0).cpu().numpy())

        ↪  plt.savefig(f"results/epoch_{epoch}_gs_{guidance_scale}.png")
        plt.close()


# ------------------------------------------------------------
# 5) Main script: load data, initialize model, and train
# ------------------------------------------------------------
def main():
    set_seed(42)
    device = torch.device('cuda' if torch.cuda.is_available() else
    ↪  'cpu')

    # Load MNIST (as an example for unconditional image generation)
    transform = transforms.Compose([
        transforms.ToTensor(),
        # Rescale images from [0,1] to [-1,1]
```

12

```
        transforms.Normalize((0.5,), (0.5,))
    ])
    train_dataset = torchvision.datasets.MNIST(root='data',
    ↪   train=True, download=True, transform=transform)
    test_dataset = torchvision.datasets.MNIST(root='data',
    ↪   train=False, download=True, transform=transform)

    train_loader = DataLoader(train_dataset, batch_size=64,
    ↪   shuffle=True)
    test_loader = DataLoader(test_dataset, batch_size=64,
    ↪   shuffle=False)

    # Create UNet
    model = UNet(in_channels=1, out_channels=1,
    ↪   base_channels=64).to(device)

    # Diffusion process with 200 time steps and linear schedule
    diffusion = Diffusion(n_steps=200, beta_schedule='linear')

    # Optimizer
    optimizer = optim.Adam(model.parameters(), lr=1e-4)

    # Train for a few epochs
    epochs = 5
    for epoch in range(epochs):
        train_loss = train_one_epoch(model, diffusion, optimizer,
        ↪   train_loader, device)
        val_loss = evaluate_model(model, diffusion, test_loader,
        ↪   device)
        print(f"Epoch [{epoch+1}/{epochs}] - Train Loss:
        ↪   {train_loss:.4f}, Val Loss: {val_loss:.4f}")

        # Generate samples at the end of each epoch
        sample_and_save(model, diffusion, device, epoch,
        ↪   guidance_scale=1.0)
        # Optionally try a higher guidance scale:
        sample_and_save(model, diffusion, device, epoch,
        ↪   guidance_scale=2.0)

    print("Training complete! Check the 'results' folder for
    ↪   generated samples.")

if __name__ == "__main__":
    main()
```

Key Implementation Details:

- **Forward Diffusion:** We implement `q_sample` to corrupt
  each input image with noise, controlled by a linear beta schedule. At step t, the fraction of noise added is governed by

13

`betas[t]` and the cumulative products of `alphas`.

- **Reverse Diffusion (Sampling):** The function `p_sample_loop` applies the denoising model step by step, starting from random noise. Each call to `p_sample` uses the learned noise prediction and the diffusion equations to produce a cleaner image.

- **UNet Architecture:** The `UNet` in this snippet features an encoder-decoder structure with skip connections. Convolutional downsampling captures broad context, and transposed convolutions restore spatial resolution.

- **Training Objective:** We directly predict and compare the added noise via a mean-squared error (MSE) loss between the network's prediction and the actual Gaussian noise.

- **Guidance Parameter:** A `guidance_scale` (e.g., 2.0 vs. 1.0) can be used to scale the model's predicted noise. Although this snippet showcases a simplistic approach, it demonstrates how adding a multiplier can adjust the balance between fidelity and diversity in the final images.

- **End-to-End Pipeline:** The `main` function brings everything together—loading MNIST data, defining the diffusion schedule, training the network for multiple epochs, and periodically sampling images that are saved to disk for evaluation.

Chapter 2

Conditional Image Generation through Class Labels

This chapter expands image generation by conditioning diffusion models on class labels. Common use cases include generating class-specific images for data augmentation or artistic expression tied to object categories. We begin by adapting the training process: each sample is paired with a one-hot or embedding vector for the designated class. The forward noising process remains the same, but the network now learns to predict noise in a manner consistent with the provided label. To build this system, we embed labels and inject them into the UNet, typically through concatenation or cross-attention. Implementation steps include: (1) preparing a labeled dataset, (2) constructing a label embedding pipeline, (3) modifying the UNet to accept label embeddings at multiple scales, (4) training with a loss function that accounts for both image and label consistency, and (5) sampling images by providing a target label during reverse diffusion. Finally, we explore a novel approach that uses classifier guidance, multiplying score estimates by class likelihood factors to improve quality and label fidelity.

Python Code Snippet

```python
import os
import random
import math
import torch
import torch.nn as nn
from torch.utils.data import DataLoader
import torchvision
import torchvision.transforms as transforms
import torch.optim as optim
import matplotlib.pyplot as plt
import torch.nn.functional as F


# ----------------------------------------------------------------
# 1) Set random seed for reproducibility
# ----------------------------------------------------------------
def set_seed(seed=42):
    random.seed(seed)
    torch.manual_seed(seed)
    if torch.cuda.is_available():
        torch.cuda.manual_seed_all(seed)


# ----------------------------------------------------------------
# 2) A DoubleConv helper for the UNet building blocks
# ----------------------------------------------------------------
class DoubleConv(nn.Module):
    '''
    A helper module that performs two convolutions (each followed by
    ↪  ReLU)
    to reduce block boilerplate in the UNet.
    '''

    def __init__(self, in_channels, out_channels):
        super(DoubleConv, self).__init__()
        self.conv = nn.Sequential(
            nn.Conv2d(in_channels, out_channels, 3, padding=1),
            nn.ReLU(inplace=True),
            nn.Conv2d(out_channels, out_channels, 3, padding=1),
            nn.ReLU(inplace=True)
        )

    def forward(self, x):
        return self.conv(x)


# ----------------------------------------------------------------
# 3) Conditional UNet architecture
# ----------------------------------------------------------------
class ConditionalUNet(nn.Module):
    '''
    A simplified UNet architecture that accepts a label (class)
    and injects its embedding into the input at the first layer.
    '''
```

```python
    def __init__(self, in_channels=1, out_channels=1,
↪    num_classes=10,
                 base_channels=64, label_emb_dim=16, img_size=28):
        super(ConditionalUNet, self).__init__()

        # Label embedding
        self.label_emb = nn.Embedding(num_classes, label_emb_dim)

        # The first layer will see (in_channels + label_emb_dim)
        ↪    channels,
        # because we concatenate the label embedding.
        self.down1 = DoubleConv(in_channels + label_emb_dim,
        ↪    base_channels)
        self.pool = nn.MaxPool2d(2)

        self.down2 = DoubleConv(base_channels, base_channels*2)
        self.down3 = DoubleConv(base_channels*2, base_channels*4)

        # Bottleneck
        self.bottleneck = DoubleConv(base_channels*4,
        ↪    base_channels*8)

        # Up-sampling (decoder)
        self.up1 = nn.ConvTranspose2d(base_channels*8,
        ↪    base_channels*4,
                                      kernel_size=2, stride=2)
        self.conv_up1 = DoubleConv(base_channels*8, base_channels*4)

        self.up2 = nn.ConvTranspose2d(base_channels*4,
        ↪    base_channels*2,
                                      kernel_size=2, stride=2)
        self.conv_up2 = DoubleConv(base_channels*4, base_channels*2)

        self.up3 = nn.ConvTranspose2d(base_channels*2,
        ↪    base_channels,
                                      kernel_size=2, stride=2)
        self.conv_up3 = DoubleConv(base_channels*2, base_channels)

        # Final output
        self.final_conv = nn.Conv2d(base_channels, out_channels,
        ↪    kernel_size=1)

        self.img_size = img_size

    def forward(self, x, labels):
        '''
        x is the input image, labels is a tensor of class indices
        ↪    (B).
        '''
        # Embed the labels: shape => (B, label_emb_dim)
        label_embedding = self.label_emb(labels)  # (B,
        ↪    label_emb_dim)
```

17

```python
        # Reshape and expand to match the image spatial dimensions
        # for direct channel-wise concatenation: (B, label_emb_dim,
        ↪   H, W)
        label_embedding = label_embedding.unsqueeze(2).unsqueeze(3)
        label_embedding = label_embedding.repeat(1, 1, x.shape[2],
        ↪   x.shape[3])

        # Concatenate along channel dimension
        x = torch.cat([x, label_embedding], dim=1)

        # Downsample path
        x1 = self.down1(x)
        x2 = self.pool(x1)

        x2 = self.down2(x2)
        x3 = self.pool(x2)

        x3 = self.down3(x3)
        x4 = self.pool(x3)

        # Bottleneck
        b = self.bottleneck(x4)

        # Up-sample path
        x = self.up1(b)
        x = torch.cat([x, x3], dim=1)    # skip connection
        x = self.conv_up1(x)

        x = self.up2(x)
        x = torch.cat([x, x2], dim=1)
        x = self.conv_up2(x)

        x = self.up3(x)
        x = torch.cat([x, x1], dim=1)
        x = self.conv_up3(x)

        out = self.final_conv(x)
        return out


# -------------------------------------------------------------
# 4) Beta schedule and Diffusion class
# -------------------------------------------------------------
def make_beta_schedule(schedule_name, n_timestep, start=1e-4,
↪   end=2e-2):
    '''
    Creates a beta schedule for the diffusion process.
    Here we implement a simple linear schedule.
    '''
    if schedule_name == "linear":
        return torch.linspace(start, end, n_timestep)
    else:
        raise NotImplementedError("Only 'linear' schedule is
        ↪   implemented here.")
```

18

```
class Diffusion:
    '''
    Encapsulates the forward noising process (q) and reverse
    ↪ sampling process (p).
    Now includes label conditioning in the model calls.
    '''

    def __init__(self, n_steps=1000, beta_schedule='linear'):
        self.n_steps = n_steps
        self.betas = make_beta_schedule(beta_schedule, n_steps)
        self.alphas = 1.0 - self.betas
        self.alpha_cumprod = torch.cumprod(self.alphas, dim=0)
        self.alpha_cumprod_prev = torch.cat(
            [torch.tensor([1.0]), self.alpha_cumprod[:-1]], dim=0
        )

        # For posterior q(x_{t-1}|x_t, x_0)
        self.posterior_variance = self.betas * \
            (1.0 - self.alpha_cumprod_prev) / (1.0 -
            ↪ self.alpha_cumprod)

    def q_sample(self, x_start, t, noise=None):
        '''
        x_t = sqrt(alpha_cumprod[t]) * x_start + sqrt(1 -
        ↪ alpha_cumprod[t]) * noise
        '''
        if noise is None:
            noise = torch.randn_like(x_start)
        sqrt_alpha_cumprod_t =
        ↪ self.alpha_cumprod[t].sqrt().unsqueeze(-1).
        unsqueeze(-1).unsqueeze(-1)
        sqrt_one_minus_alpha_cumprod_t = (1 -
        ↪ self.alpha_cumprod[t]).sqrt().unsqueeze(-1).
        unsqueeze(-1).unsqueeze(-1)
        return sqrt_alpha_cumprod_t * x_start +
        ↪ sqrt_one_minus_alpha_cumprod_t * noise

    def predict_noise(self, model, x_t, t, labels):
        '''
        Model predicts the noise added at step t, conditioning on
        ↪ class labels.
        '''
        return model(x_t, labels)

    def p_sample(self, model, x_t, t, labels, guidance_scale=1.0):
        '''
        One reverse diffusion step: p(x_{t-1} | x_t).
        We incorporate label conditioning and a naive guidance scale
        that simply scales the predicted noise.
        '''
        betas_t = self.betas[t]
        alpha_t = self.alphas[t]
        alpha_cumprod_t = self.alpha_cumprod[t]
```

```python
        alpha_cumprod_prev_t = self.alpha_cumprod_prev[t]

        # Predict noise with label conditioning
        e_t = model(x_t, labels) * guidance_scale

        sqrt_recip_alpha_t = (1.0 / alpha_t).sqrt()
        # Approximate x_0
        x_0_hat = (x_t - (1.0 - alpha_t).sqrt() * e_t) *
        ↪ sqrt_recip_alpha_t

        coef1 = ((alpha_cumprod_prev_t).sqrt() * betas_t) / (1.0 -
        ↪ alpha_cumprod_t)
        coef2 = ((1.0 - alpha_cumprod_prev_t) * alpha_t.sqrt()) /
        ↪ (1.0 - alpha_cumprod_t)

        mean = coef1 * x_0_hat + coef2 * x_t

        posterior_var = self.posterior_variance[t]
        if t > 0:
            noise = torch.randn_like(x_t)
        else:
            noise = torch.zeros_like(x_t)

        x_prev = mean + noise * posterior_var.sqrt()
        return x_prev

    def p_sample_loop(self, model, shape, device, labels,
    ↪ guidance_scale=1.0):
        '''
        Repeatedly apply p_sample, from x_T -> x_0, given the label.
        '''
        x_t = torch.randn(shape, device=device)
        for i in reversed(range(self.n_steps)):
            x_t = self.p_sample(model, x_t, i, labels,
            ↪ guidance_scale=guidance_scale)
        return x_t


# ----------------------------------------------------------------
# 5) Training routine
# ----------------------------------------------------------------
def train_one_epoch(model, diffusion, optimizer, dataloader,
↪ device):
    '''
    Each iteration, pick a random t, apply the forward diffusion,
    and train the model to predict the added noise with label
    ↪ conditioning.
    '''
    model.train()
    loss_sum = 0
    for images, labels in dataloader:
        images = images.to(device)
        labels = labels.to(device)
```

```python
        # Random t in [0, n_steps)
        t = torch.randint(
            0, diffusion.n_steps, (images.size(0),), device=device
        ).long()

        noise = torch.randn_like(images)

        # Forward diffusion
        x_t = diffusion.q_sample(images, t, noise=noise)

        # Predict noise given labels
        noise_pred = diffusion.predict_noise(model, x_t, t, labels)

        # MSE loss
        loss = F.mse_loss(noise_pred, noise)

        optimizer.zero_grad()
        loss.backward()
        optimizer.step()

        loss_sum += loss.item()

    return loss_sum / len(dataloader)

def evaluate_model(model, diffusion, dataloader, device):
    '''
    Simple evaluation loop: measure the average MSE between
    predicted noise and true noise on a validation set.
    '''
    model.eval()
    loss_sum = 0
    with torch.no_grad():
        for images, labels in dataloader:
            images = images.to(device)
            labels = labels.to(device)
            t = torch.randint(0, diffusion.n_steps,
            ↪ (images.size(0),), device=device).long()
            noise = torch.randn_like(images)
            x_t = diffusion.q_sample(images, t, noise=noise)
            noise_pred = diffusion.predict_noise(model, x_t, t,
            ↪ labels)
            loss = F.mse_loss(noise_pred, noise)
            loss_sum += loss.item()
    return loss_sum / len(dataloader)


# ---------------------------------------------------------------
# 6) Sampling utility (label-conditioned)
# ---------------------------------------------------------------
def sample_and_save(model, diffusion, device, epoch, label,
↪ guidance_scale=1.0):
    '''
    Generates a batch of images for a single label and saves a grid.
    label is an integer class label (e.g., 0..9 for MNIST).
```

21

```python
    '''
    model.eval()
    with torch.no_grad():
        sample_batch_size = 16
        shape = (sample_batch_size, 1, 28, 28)

        # Repeat the same label for the entire batch
        labels = torch.tensor([label]*sample_batch_size,
        ↪  device=device)

        # Generate from pure noise
        generated = diffusion.p_sample_loop(model, shape, device,
        ↪  labels, guidance_scale)

        # Scale from [-1,1] to [0,1]
        generated = (generated.clamp(-1.0, 1.0) + 1) * 0.5

        grid = torchvision.utils.make_grid(generated, nrow=4)
        os.makedirs("results_conditional", exist_ok=True)
        plt.figure(figsize=(6,6))
        plt.axis("off")
        plt.imshow(grid.permute(1, 2, 0).cpu().numpy())
        plt.title(f"Label = {label}, Guidance Scale =
        ↪  {guidance_scale}")
        plt.savefig(f"results_conditional/
        epoch_{epoch}_label_{label}_gs_{guidance_scale}.png")
        plt.close()

# --------------------------------------------------------------
# 7) Main execution
# --------------------------------------------------------------
def main():
    set_seed(42)
    device = torch.device("cuda" if torch.cuda.is_available() else
    ↪  "cpu")

    # MNIST has 10 classes, perfect for label-conditioning
    transform = transforms.Compose([
        transforms.ToTensor(),
        transforms.Normalize((0.5,), (0.5,))
    ])

    train_dataset = torchvision.datasets.MNIST(
        root='data', train=True, download=True, transform=transform
    )
    test_dataset = torchvision.datasets.MNIST(
        root='data', train=False, download=True, transform=transform
    )

    train_loader = DataLoader(train_dataset, batch_size=64,
    ↪  shuffle=True)
    test_loader = DataLoader(test_dataset, batch_size=64,
    ↪  shuffle=False)
```

22

```python
# Initialize the conditional U-Net
model = ConditionalUNet(
    in_channels=1,
    out_channels=1,
    num_classes=10,
    base_channels=64,
    label_emb_dim=16,
    img_size=28
).to(device)

# Define the diffusion process (fewer steps to speed up
↪   training)
diffusion = Diffusion(n_steps=200, beta_schedule='linear')

# Optimizer
optimizer = optim.Adam(model.parameters(), lr=1e-4)

# Train
epochs = 5
for epoch in range(epochs):
    train_loss = train_one_epoch(model, diffusion, optimizer,
    ↪   train_loader, device)
    val_loss = evaluate_model(model, diffusion, test_loader,
    ↪   device)
    print(f"Epoch [{epoch+1}/{epochs}] - Train Loss:
    ↪   {train_loss:.4f}, Val Loss: {val_loss:.4f}")

    # Sample images for a few specific labels to check
    ↪   performance
    sample_and_save(model, diffusion, device, epoch, label=0,
    ↪   guidance_scale=1.0)
    sample_and_save(model, diffusion, device, epoch, label=7,
    ↪   guidance_scale=1.0)
    # Try a higher guidance scale for variety
    sample_and_save(model, diffusion, device, epoch, label=7,
    ↪   guidance_scale=2.0)

    print("Training complete! Check the 'results_conditional' folder
    ↪   for generated samples.")

if __name__ == "__main__":
    main()
```

Key Implementation Details:

- **Forward Diffusion:** Implemented in `q_sample`, where each input image is gradually corrupted by Gaussian noise according to a linear beta schedule.

23

- **Reverse Diffusion (Sampling):** The function `p_sample_loop` iteratively applies the reverse step (via `p_sample`), using the model's noise predictions and label embeddings to reconstruct class-consistent images from random noise.

- **Conditional UNet Architecture:** The `ConditionalUNet` class constructs a label embedding that is concatenated as extra channels. This allows the network to learn label-dependent denoising.

- **Training Objective:** We predict the noise added at each time step via a mean-squared error loss between `noise_pred` and the actual noise, ensuring label-conditioned reconstructions.

- **Guidance Parameter:** A naive `guidance_scale` is demonstrated by scaling the predicted noise, serving as a stand-in for more sophisticated classifier or classifier-free guidance approaches.

- **End-to-End Pipeline:** The `main` function loads MNIST, trains the conditional diffusion model, and periodically samples labeled images for visual inspection, saving them to disk.

Chapter 3

Text-to-Image Diffusion for Artwork and Scene Generation

Here, we integrate natural language prompts as the conditioning for diffusion-based image generation. Common use cases include generating compelling artwork and concept designs guided by textual descriptions. The chapter describes how to tokenize text prompts into embeddings using a pretrained language model. These embeddings feed into the diffusion network, typically via cross-attention layers inserted at multiple resolutions. Implementation steps involve: (1) training a text encoder to convert prompts into vector representations, (2) creating a collaboration between the text embeddings and noise-injected latent representations in the UNet, (3) applying the standard diffusion forward and reverse processes, and (4) optimizing with a noise prediction loss that incorporates text context. The result is an image that aligns with the prompt semantics. Finally, we discuss an innovative approach where large language models generate refined prompts or expansions dynamically, boosting visual quality and thematic coherence.

Python Code Snippet

```
import os
import random
import math
```

```python
import torch
import torch.nn as nn
from torch.utils.data import Dataset, DataLoader
import torchvision
import torchvision.transforms as transforms
import torch.optim as optim
import matplotlib.pyplot as plt

# --------------------------------------------------------------
# 1) Set random seed for reproducibility
# --------------------------------------------------------------
def set_seed(seed=42):
    random.seed(seed)
    torch.manual_seed(seed)
    if torch.cuda.is_available():
        torch.cuda.manual_seed_all(seed)

# --------------------------------------------------------------
# 2) Simple text tokenizer and encoder (demo only)
# --------------------------------------------------------------
class DummyTextTokenizer:
    '''
    A naive tokenizer that splits text by spaces and assigns random
    ↪   IDs
    (for demonstration purposes). In practice, use a pretrained
    ↪   tokenizer.
    '''
    def __init__(self, vocab_size=1000, max_length=10):
        self.vocab_size = vocab_size
        self.max_length = max_length

    def __call__(self, text):
        tokens = text.strip().split()
        # Truncate or pad tokens
        tokens = tokens[:self.max_length]
        # Map tokens to random IDs
        token_ids = []
        for _ in tokens:
            token_ids.append(random.randint(1, self.vocab_size-1))
        # Pad
        while len(token_ids) < self.max_length:
            token_ids.append(0)
        return torch.tensor(token_ids, dtype=torch.long)


class SimpleTextEncoder(nn.Module):
    '''
    A toy text encoder that embeds token IDs and extracts a single
    ↪   vector
    for conditioning. Real-world systems might use
    ↪   transformert-based encoders.
    '''
```

```python
    def __init__(self, vocab_size=1000, embedding_dim=128,
    ↪   max_length=10):
        super(SimpleTextEncoder, self).__init__()
        self.embedding = nn.Embedding(vocab_size, embedding_dim)
        self.fc = nn.Linear(embedding_dim, embedding_dim)
        self.max_length = max_length

    def forward(self, token_ids):
        '''
        token_ids: B x max_length
        returns: B x embedding_dim
        '''
        # shape: (B, max_length, embedding_dim)
        embedded = self.embedding(token_ids)
        # Mean pooling over tokens
        mean_emb = embedded.mean(dim=1)
        # Additional projection
        out = self.fc(mean_emb)   # shape: (B, embedding_dim)
        return out

# ---------------------------------------------------------------
# 3) Cross Attention block (simplified)
# ---------------------------------------------------------------
class CrossAttentionBlock(nn.Module):
    '''
    A minimal multi-head cross-attention mechanism that merges text
    ↪   embeddings
    into image feature maps. In practice, you'd apply more
    ↪   sophisticated
    cross-attention. This block is just a demonstration.
    '''
    def __init__(self, dim, text_dim, num_heads=4):
        super(CrossAttentionBlock, self).__init__()
        self.num_heads = num_heads
        self.query_proj = nn.Linear(dim, dim)
        self.key_proj = nn.Linear(text_dim, dim)
        self.value_proj = nn.Linear(text_dim, dim)
        self.out_proj = nn.Linear(dim, dim)

    def forward(self, x, text_emb):
        '''
        x: B x C x H x W (feature map)
        text_emb: B x text_dim (text encoder output)

        We'll treat the feature map as a set of tokens (flattened),
        and apply cross-attention to the text_emb (treated as 1
        ↪   token).
        This is extremely simplified: in real usage, you'd pass
        ↪   multiple
        tokens from the text model.
        '''
        B, C, H, W = x.shape
```

```python
x_reshaped = x.view(B, C, -1).permute(0, 2, 1)  # B x (H*W)
↪    x C
# Query
queries = self.query_proj(x_reshaped)  # B x (H*W) x dim

# We'll expand text_emb to match (H*W) tokens for attention
text_emb = text_emb.unsqueeze(1)  # B x 1 x text_dim
keys = self.key_proj(text_emb)       # B x 1 x dim
values = self.value_proj(text_emb)  # B x 1 x dim

# Split heads
def split_heads(tensor, num_heads):
    B_, T_, D_ = tensor.shape
    assert D_ % num_heads == 0
    head_dim = D_ // num_heads
    tensor = tensor.view(B_, T_, num_heads, head_dim)
    return tensor.permute(0, 2, 1, 3)  # B_, num_heads, T_,
    ↪    head_dim

Q = split_heads(queries, self.num_heads)  # B, heads, (H*W),
↪    dim_head
K = split_heads(keys, self.num_heads)     # B, heads, 1,
↪    dim_head
V = split_heads(values, self.num_heads)   # B, heads, 1,
↪    dim_head

# Attention scores = Q*K^T
attn_scores = torch.matmul(Q, K.transpose(-1, -2))  # B,
↪    heads, (H*W), 1
attn_scores = attn_scores / math.sqrt(K.shape[-1])
attn_weights = torch.softmax(attn_scores, dim=-2)    # B,
↪    heads, (H*W), 1

# Weighted sum of values
out = attn_weights * V  # B, heads, (H*W), dim_head
out = out.sum(dim=-2)     # sum over (H*W)? This is not
↪    standard, but demonstrates idea
# Alternatively, you'd keep the shape and do a more typical
↪    approach.

# Merge heads
out = out.permute(0, 2, 1)  # B, dim_head, heads
out = out.reshape(B, 1, -1)  # B, 1, dim

out = self.out_proj(out)     # B, 1, dim
# Broadcast back to each spatial location (extremely
↪    simplified)
out_expanded = out.repeat(1, H*W, 1)  # B, (H*W), dim
# Reshape back to feature map
out_expanded = out_expanded.permute(0, 2, 1).view(B, C, H,
↪    W)

# Merge with original
```

```python
            x = x + out_expanded
            return x


# ---------------------------------------------------------------
# 4) Conditioned U-Net with cross-attention
# ---------------------------------------------------------------
class DoubleConv(nn.Module):
    '''
    A helper module that performs two convolutions (each followed by
    ↪ ReLU).
    '''

    def __init__(self, in_channels, out_channels):
        super(DoubleConv, self).__init__()
        self.conv = nn.Sequential(
            nn.Conv2d(in_channels, out_channels, 3, padding=1),
            nn.ReLU(inplace=True),
            nn.Conv2d(out_channels, out_channels, 3, padding=1),
            nn.ReLU(inplace=True)
        )

    def forward(self, x):
        return self.conv(x)

class ConditionedUNet(nn.Module):
    '''
    A simplified UNet architecture that inserts cross-attention
    ↪ blocks
    at multiple scales to incorporate text embeddings.
    '''

    def __init__(self, in_channels=1, out_channels=1,
    ↪ base_channels=64, text_emb_dim=128):
        super(ConditionedUNet, self).__init__()

        # Down-sampling
        self.down1 = DoubleConv(in_channels, base_channels)
        self.ca1 = CrossAttentionBlock(base_channels, text_emb_dim)
        self.down2 = DoubleConv(base_channels, base_channels*2)
        self.ca2 = CrossAttentionBlock(base_channels*2,
        ↪ text_emb_dim)

        self.pool = nn.MaxPool2d(2)

        # Bottleneck
        self.bottleneck = DoubleConv(base_channels*2,
        ↪ base_channels*4)
        self.ca_bottleneck = CrossAttentionBlock(base_channels*4,
        ↪ text_emb_dim)

        # Up-sampling
        self.up1 = nn.ConvTranspose2d(base_channels*4,
        ↪ base_channels*2, kernel_size=2, stride=2)
        self.conv_up1 = DoubleConv(base_channels*4, base_channels*2)
```

29

```python
        self.ca_up1 = CrossAttentionBlock(base_channels*2,
        ↪   text_emb_dim)

        self.up2 = nn.ConvTranspose2d(base_channels*2,
        ↪   base_channels, kernel_size=2, stride=2)
        self.conv_up2 = DoubleConv(base_channels*2, base_channels)
        self.ca_up2 = CrossAttentionBlock(base_channels,
        ↪   text_emb_dim)

        # Final
        self.final_conv = nn.Conv2d(base_channels, out_channels,
        ↪   kernel_size=1)

    def forward(self, x, text_emb):
        # Encoder
        x1 = self.down1(x)
        x1 = self.ca1(x1, text_emb)

        x2 = self.pool(x1)
        x2 = self.down2(x2)
        x2 = self.ca2(x2, text_emb)

        x3 = self.pool(x2)

        # Bottleneck
        b = self.bottleneck(x3)
        b = self.ca_bottleneck(b, text_emb)

        # Decoder
        x = self.up1(b)
        x = torch.cat([x, x2], dim=1)
        x = self.conv_up1(x)
        x = self.ca_up1(x, text_emb)

        x = self.up2(x)
        x = torch.cat([x, x1], dim=1)
        x = self.conv_up2(x)
        x = self.ca_up2(x, text_emb)

        out = self.final_conv(x)
        return out


# ----------------------------------------------------------------
# 5) Diffusion schedule and processes
# ----------------------------------------------------------------
def make_beta_schedule(schedule_name, n_timestep, start=1e-4,
↪   end=2e-2):
    '''
    Creates a beta schedule for the diffusion process.
    We use a linear schedule as a straightforward example.
    '''
    if schedule_name == "linear":
        return torch.linspace(start, end, n_timestep)
```

```
        else:
            raise NotImplementedError("Only 'linear' schedule is
            ↪  implemented here.")

class Diffusion:
    '''
    1) Forward noising: q(x_t | x_0)
    2) Reverse denoising: p(x_{t-1} | x_t)
    3) Utilities for training and sampling.
    '''

    def __init__(self, n_steps=1000, beta_schedule='linear'):
        self.n_steps = n_steps
        self.betas = make_beta_schedule(beta_schedule, n_steps)
        self.alphas = 1.0 - self.betas
        self.alpha_cumprod = torch.cumprod(self.alphas, dim=0)
        self.alpha_cumprod_prev = torch.cat(
            [torch.tensor([1.0]), self.alpha_cumprod[:-1]], dim=0
        )

        # Posterior variance term for p(x_{t-1}|x_t,x_0)
        self.posterior_variance = self.betas * (1.0 -
        ↪  self.alpha_cumprod_prev) / (1.0 - self.alpha_cumprod)

    def q_sample(self, x_start, t, noise=None):
        '''
        x_t = sqrt(alpha_cumprod[t]) * x_start +
        ↪  sqrt(1-alpha_cumprod[t]) * noise
        '''
        if noise is None:
            noise = torch.randn_like(x_start)
        sqrt_alpha_cumprod_t =
        ↪  self.alpha_cumprod[t].sqrt().unsqueeze(-1).
        unsqueeze(-1).unsqueeze(-1)
        sqrt_one_minus_alpha_cumprod_t = (1. -
        ↪  self.alpha_cumprod[t]).sqrt().unsqueeze(-1).
        unsqueeze(-1).unsqueeze(-1)
        return sqrt_alpha_cumprod_t * x_start +
        ↪  sqrt_one_minus_alpha_cumprod_t * noise

    def predict_noise(self, model, x_t, t, text_emb):
        '''
        Use the conditioned UNet model to predict the noise at step
        ↪  t.
        '''
        return model(x_t, text_emb)

    def p_sample(self, model, x_t, t, text_emb, guidance_scale=1.0):
        '''
        Single reverse diffusion step: p(x_{t-1} | x_t).
        The model predicts the noise (e_t), and we compute the mean
        ↪  of p(x_{t-1} | x_t, x_0).
        '''
        betas_t = self.betas[t]
```

```python
        alpha_t = self.alphas[t]
        alpha_cumprod_t = self.alpha_cumprod[t]
        alpha_cumprod_prev_t = self.alpha_cumprod_prev[t]

        # Model's noise estimate
        e_t = model(x_t, text_emb) * guidance_scale

        sqrt_recip_alpha_t = (1.0 / alpha_t).sqrt()
        # Reconstruct x_0
        x_0_hat = (x_t - (1.0 - alpha_t).sqrt() * e_t) * \
        ↪  sqrt_recip_alpha_t

        # Coefficients for q(x_{t-1}|x_t, x_0_hat)
        coef1 = ( (alpha_cumprod_prev_t).sqrt() * betas_t ) / (1.0 -
        ↪  alpha_cumprod_t)
        coef2 = ( (1.0 - alpha_cumprod_prev_t) * alpha_t.sqrt() ) /
        ↪  (1.0 - alpha_cumprod_t)

        mean = coef1 * x_0_hat + coef2 * x_t
        posterior_var = self.posterior_variance[t]

        if t > 0:
            noise = torch.randn_like(x_t)
        else:
            noise = torch.zeros_like(x_t)

        x_prev = mean + noise * posterior_var.sqrt()
        return x_prev

    def p_sample_loop(self, model, shape, device, text_emb,
    ↪  guidance_scale=1.0):
        '''
        Iteratively call p_sample going from x_T ~ N(0,I) to x_0.
        '''
        x_t = torch.randn(shape, device=device)
        for i in reversed(range(self.n_steps)):
            x_t = self.p_sample(model, x_t, i, text_emb,
            ↪  guidance_scale)
        return x_t


# ------------------------------------------------------------
# 6) A sample dataset that pairs random text with MNIST images
# ------------------------------------------------------------
class TextImageDataset(Dataset):
    '''
    For demonstration, we'll load MNIST images and pair them with
    ↪  dummy prompts
    like "digit zero", "digit one", etc.
    '''
    def __init__(self, image_dataset, tokenizer, digit_labels):
        self.image_dataset = image_dataset
        self.tokenizer = tokenizer
        self.digit_labels = digit_labels
```

32

```python
    def __len__(self):
        return len(self.image_dataset)

    def __getitem__(self, idx):
        img, label = self.image_dataset[idx]
        # Convert label to text prompt
        prompt_text = f"digit {self.digit_labels[label]}"
        token_ids = self.tokenizer(prompt_text)
        return img, token_ids


# ------------------------------------------------------------------
# 7) Training and evaluation
# ------------------------------------------------------------------
def train_one_epoch(model, diffusion, optimizer, dataloader,
    text_encoder, device):
    model.train()
    loss_sum = 0
    for images, token_ids in dataloader:
        images = images.to(device)
        token_ids = token_ids.to(device)

        # Encode text
        text_emb = text_encoder(token_ids)

        # Sample random time step
        t = torch.randint(0, diffusion.n_steps, (images.size(0),),
            device=device).long()

        noise = torch.randn_like(images)
        x_t = diffusion.q_sample(images, t, noise=noise)

        # Predict noise given x_t and text embedding
        noise_pred = diffusion.predict_noise(model, x_t, t,
            text_emb)

        # L2 loss
        loss = nn.MSELoss()(noise_pred, noise)

        optimizer.zero_grad()
        loss.backward()
        optimizer.step()

        loss_sum += loss.item()
    return loss_sum / len(dataloader)

def evaluate_model(model, diffusion, dataloader, text_encoder,
    device):
    model.eval()
    loss_sum = 0
    with torch.no_grad():
        for images, token_ids in dataloader:
            images = images.to(device)
```

```python
            token_ids = token_ids.to(device)
            text_emb = text_encoder(token_ids)
            t = torch.randint(0, diffusion.n_steps,
            ↪  (images.size(0),), device=device).long()
            noise = torch.randn_like(images)
            x_t = diffusion.q_sample(images, t, noise=noise)
            noise_pred = diffusion.predict_noise(model, x_t, t,
            ↪  text_emb)
            loss = nn.MSELoss()(noise_pred, noise)
            loss_sum += loss.item()
    return loss_sum / len(dataloader)


def sample_and_save(model, diffusion, text_encoder, prompts, device,
↪  epoch, guidance_scale=1.0):
    '''
    Sample images given a list of prompts and save them in a grid.
    '''
    model.eval()
    with torch.no_grad():
        text_tokens = []
        for prompt in prompts:
            token_ids = text_encoder.tokenizer(prompt).to(device)
            text_tokens.append(token_ids.unsqueeze(0))
        # Concatenate for batch
        text_tokens = torch.cat(text_tokens, dim=0)   # B x
        ↪  max_length

        text_embs = text_encoder(text_tokens)          # B x emb_dim

        # shape: (batch_size, 1, H, W)
        generated = diffusion.p_sample_loop(
            model, (len(prompts), 1, 28, 28), device,
            ↪  text_emb=text_embs,
            guidance_scale=guidance_scale
        )

        # Convert from [-1,1] to [0,1]
        generated = (generated.clamp(-1.0, 1.0) + 1) * 0.5

        grid = torchvision.utils.make_grid(generated,
        ↪  nrow=len(prompts))
        os.makedirs("results_text2img", exist_ok=True)
        plt.figure(figsize=(len(prompts)*2, 2))
        plt.axis("off")
        plt.imshow(grid.permute(1, 2, 0).cpu().numpy())
        plt.title(f"Guidance Scale = {guidance_scale}")
        plt.savefig(f"results_text2img/
        epoch_{epoch}_gs_{guidance_scale}.png")
        plt.close()


# ---------------------------------------------------------------
# 8) Main script
# ---------------------------------------------------------------
```

34

```python
def main():
    set_seed(42)
    device = torch.device("cuda" if torch.cuda.is_available() else
    ↪    "cpu")

    # Prepare MNIST
    transform = transforms.Compose([
        transforms.ToTensor(),
        transforms.Normalize((0.5,), (0.5,))
    ])
    train_mnist = torchvision.datasets.MNIST(root='data',
    ↪    train=True, download=True, transform=transform)
    test_mnist  = torchvision.datasets.MNIST(root='data',
    ↪    train=False, download=True, transform=transform)

    # Tokenizer and label to text
    tokenizer = DummyTextTokenizer(vocab_size=1000, max_length=5)
    digit_labels = ["zero","one","two","three","four","five",
    "six","seven","eight","nine"]

    # Create text-image datasets
    train_dataset = TextImageDataset(train_mnist, tokenizer,
    ↪    digit_labels)
    test_dataset = TextImageDataset(test_mnist,  tokenizer,
    ↪    digit_labels)

    train_loader = DataLoader(train_dataset, batch_size=32,
    ↪    shuffle=True)
    test_loader  = DataLoader(test_dataset,  batch_size=32,
    ↪    shuffle=False)

    # Text encoder
    text_encoder = SimpleTextEncoder(vocab_size=1000,
    ↪    embedding_dim=128, max_length=5).to(device)

    # Conditioned UNet
    model = ConditionedUNet(in_channels=1, out_channels=1,
    ↪    base_channels=64, text_emb_dim=128).to(device)

    # Diffusion process
    diffusion = Diffusion(n_steps=200, beta_schedule='linear')

    # Optimizer
    optimizer = optim.Adam(list(model.parameters()) +
    ↪    list(text_encoder.parameters()), lr=1e-4)

    epochs = 3
    for epoch in range(epochs):
        train_loss = train_one_epoch(model, diffusion, optimizer,
        ↪    train_loader, text_encoder, device)
        val_loss = evaluate_model(model, diffusion, test_loader,
        ↪    text_encoder, device)
```

```
    print(f"Epoch [{epoch+1}/{epochs}] - Train Loss:
    ↪  {train_loss:.4f}, Val Loss: {val_loss:.4f}")

    # Sample images for a few text prompts
    prompts = ["digit zero", "digit one", "digit seven"]
    sample_and_save(model, diffusion, text_encoder, prompts,
    ↪  device, epoch, guidance_scale=1.0)
    sample_and_save(model, diffusion, text_encoder, prompts,
    ↪  device, epoch, guidance_scale=2.0)

    print("Training complete! Check the 'results_text2img' folder
    ↪  for generated samples.")
if __name__ == "__main__":
    main()
```

Key Implementation Details:

- **Text Conditioning:** We introduce a naive text tokenizer (DummyTextTokenizer) and a basic embedding network (SimpleTextEncoder). Real-world systems typically rely on sophisticated pretrained encoders.

- **Cross-Attention:** The CrossAttentionBlock demonstrates a minimal multi-head cross-attention idea, allowing the text embedding to inform the image feature maps. It is placed at multiple scales within the ConditionedUNet.

- **Forward Diffusion:** The Diffusion class implements q_sample, which injects noise into images governed by a linear beta schedule. The outputs are intermediate noisy versions of the input.

- **Reverse Diffusion:** During sampling (p_sample_loop), the model predicts and removes noise step by step, starting from random Gaussian noise in latent space.

- **Training Objective:** We compute the L2 loss between the model's predicted noise and the actual Gaussian noise added in each training step. This approach aligns with the typical diffusion training scheme.

- **Guidance Scale:** A guidance_scale can amplify the text conditioning effect, balancing between following the text prompt and image diversity.

- **End-to-End Pipeline:** The `main` function loads the MNIST dataset, constructs text-image pairs, initializes the conditioned UNet and diffusion model, trains them, and saves sample generations at each epoch for observation.

Chapter 4

Image Inpainting and Outpainting with Diffusion

Diffusion inpainting replaces missing or corrupted regions of an image, while outpainting extends the borders beyond the original canvas. Common applications include photo restoration, object removal, and background expansion. The construction modifies the standard diffusion pipeline by conditioning on a partially masked input. We start with an image that has a known mask indicating missing pixels. During training, noise is added to the entire image, but the model learns to invert noise selectively while respecting the original context. Key steps include: (1) applying a mask to zero out missing regions, (2) injecting the masked image and noise level into the UNet, (3) training the model to predict the noise specifically where information is missing, and (4) sampling with the reverse diffusion to fill in or extend the image. As an innovative extension, we incorporate structure or edge maps to guide the filling process, improving coherence for large missing areas.

Python Code Snippet

```
import os
import math
import random
import torch
```

```python
import torch.nn as nn
import torch.optim as optim
import torchvision
import torchvision.transforms as transforms
from torch.utils.data import DataLoader
import matplotlib.pyplot as plt


# --------------------------------------------------------------
# 1) Utility: Set random seed for reproducibility
# --------------------------------------------------------------
def set_seed(seed=42):
    random.seed(seed)
    torch.manual_seed(seed)
    if torch.cuda.is_available():
        torch.cuda.manual_seed_all(seed)


# --------------------------------------------------------------
# 2) Create a simple U-Net, modified to accept an additional mask
# ↪   channel
# --------------------------------------------------------------
class DoubleConv(nn.Module):
    """
    A helper module that performs two convolutions (each followed by
    ↪   ReLU)
    to reduce repetitive code in the U-Net.
    """
    def __init__(self, in_channels, out_channels):
        super(DoubleConv, self).__init__()
        self.conv = nn.Sequential(
            nn.Conv2d(in_channels, out_channels, kernel_size=3,
            ↪   padding=1),
            nn.ReLU(inplace=True),
            nn.Conv2d(out_channels, out_channels, kernel_size=3,
            ↪   padding=1),
            nn.ReLU(inplace=True)
        )

    def forward(self, x):
        return self.conv(x)


class UNet(nn.Module):
    """
    A simplified U-Net architecture with down-sampling (encoder) and
    up-sampling (decoder) blocks, plus skip connections.

    For inpainting, we include the mask as an additional channel for
    ↪   input:
    Input shape: (B, 2, H, W) => (grayscale image + mask)
    Output: predicted noise for the full image shape: (B, 1, H, W)
    """
    def __init__(self, in_channels=2, out_channels=1,
    ↪   base_channels=64):
        super(UNet, self).__init__()
```

```python
        # Downsampling (encoder)
        self.down1 = DoubleConv(in_channels, base_channels)
        self.down2 = DoubleConv(base_channels, base_channels*2)
        self.down3 = DoubleConv(base_channels*2, base_channels*4)

        self.pool = nn.MaxPool2d(2)

        # Bottleneck
        self.bottleneck = DoubleConv(base_channels*4,
        ↪   base_channels*8)

        # Upsampling (decoder)
        self.up1 = nn.ConvTranspose2d(base_channels*8,
        ↪   base_channels*4, kernel_size=2, stride=2)
        self.conv_up1 = DoubleConv(base_channels*8, base_channels*4)

        self.up2 = nn.ConvTranspose2d(base_channels*4,
        ↪   base_channels*2, kernel_size=2, stride=2)
        self.conv_up2 = DoubleConv(base_channels*4, base_channels*2)

        self.up3 = nn.ConvTranspose2d(base_channels*2,
        ↪   base_channels, kernel_size=2, stride=2)
        self.conv_up3 = DoubleConv(base_channels*2, base_channels)

        # Final output
        self.final_conv = nn.Conv2d(base_channels, out_channels,
        ↪   kernel_size=1)

    def forward(self, x):
        # Encoder
        x1 = self.down1(x)
        x2 = self.pool(x1)

        x2 = self.down2(x2)
        x3 = self.pool(x2)

        x3 = self.down3(x3)
        x4 = self.pool(x3)

        # Bottleneck
        b = self.bottleneck(x4)

        # Decoder
        x = self.up1(b)
        x = torch.cat([x, x3], dim=1)   # skip connection
        x = self.conv_up1(x)

        x = self.up2(x)
        x = torch.cat([x, x2], dim=1)
        x = self.conv_up2(x)

        x = self.up3(x)
```

```python
        x = torch.cat([x, x1], dim=1)
        x = self.conv_up3(x)

        # Final
        out = self.final_conv(x)
        return out


# ----------------------------------------------------------------
# 3) Create a random mask generator
# ----------------------------------------------------------------
def generate_random_mask(img_shape, max_mask_size=10):
    """
    Generates a random square mask for an image, zeroing out a
    ↪  region.
    'max_mask_size' controls the maximum dimension of the square to
    ↪  remove.
    Return:
       mask (B, 1, H, W) with 1 for known region, 0 for missing
       ↪  region
    """
    B, C, H, W = img_shape
    mask = torch.ones((B, 1, H, W), dtype=torch.float32)
    for i in range(B):
        mask_size = random.randint(5, max_mask_size)
        top = random.randint(0, H - mask_size)
        left = random.randint(0, W - mask_size)
        mask[i, 0, top:top+mask_size, left:left+mask_size] = 0.0
    return mask


# ----------------------------------------------------------------
# 4) Define a linear beta schedule for forward diffusion
# ----------------------------------------------------------------
def make_beta_schedule(n_timestep, start=1e-4, end=2e-2):
    """
    Creates a linear beta schedule for the diffusion steps.
    """
    return torch.linspace(start, end, n_timestep)


# ----------------------------------------------------------------
# 5) The Diffusion class: forward noising and reverse sampling
# ----------------------------------------------------------------
class Diffusion:
    """
    Diffusion class that contains:
    1) Forward process q(x_t | x_0)
    2) Reverse process p(x_{t-1} | x_t)
    3) Methods for training and sampling
    """
    def __init__(self, n_steps=1000):
        self.n_steps = n_steps
        self.betas = make_beta_schedule(n_steps)  # linear
        self.alphas = 1.0 - self.betas
        self.alpha_cumprod = torch.cumprod(self.alphas, dim=0)
```

```python
        self.alpha_cumprod_prev = torch.cat([torch.tensor([1.0]),
        ↪    self.alpha_cumprod[:-1]], dim=0)

        # Posterior variance term for p(x_{t-1} | x_t, x_0)
        self.posterior_variance = self.betas * (1.0 -
        ↪    self.alpha_cumprod_prev) / (1.0 - self.alpha_cumprod)

    def q_sample(self, x_start, t, noise):
        """
        Forward diffusion: x_t = sqrt(alpha_cumprod[t]) * x_start
                               + sqrt(1 - alpha_cumprod[t]) * noise
        """
        sqrt_alpha_cumprod_t =
        ↪    self.alpha_cumprod[t].sqrt().unsqueeze(-1).
        unsqueeze(-1).unsqueeze(-1)
        sqrt_one_minus_alpha_cumprod_t = (1 -
        ↪    self.alpha_cumprod[t]).sqrt().unsqueeze(-1).
        unsqueeze(-1).unsqueeze(-1)
        return sqrt_alpha_cumprod_t * x_start +
        ↪    sqrt_one_minus_alpha_cumprod_t * noise

    def predict_noise(self, model, x_t_masked, t):
        """
        The UNet model predicts the noise based on the masked image
        and the noised input. We feed x_t_masked as the model input.
        """
        return model(x_t_masked)

    def p_sample(self, model, x_t, mask, t):
        """
        One step of reverse diffusion: p(x_{t-1} | x_t).
        We first predict the noise, then compute x_{t-1}.
        We also re-apply the mask so that known regions remain
        ↪    untouched
        (outpainting/inpainting scenario).
        """
        betas_t = self.betas[t]
        alpha_t = self.alphas[t]
        alpha_cumprod_t = self.alpha_cumprod[t]
        alpha_cumprod_prev_t = self.alpha_cumprod_prev[t]
        posterior_var_t = self.posterior_variance[t]

        # Predict the noise
        # Combine x_t and mask for the model input
        x_t_with_mask = torch.cat([x_t * mask, mask], dim=1)
        noise_pred = self.predict_noise(model, x_t_with_mask, t)

        # Estimate x_0
        sqrt_recip_alpha_t = (1.0 / alpha_t).sqrt()
        x_0_hat = (x_t - (1.0 - alpha_t).sqrt() * noise_pred) *
        ↪    sqrt_recip_alpha_t

        # Posterior mean of q(x_{t-1} | x_t, x_0_hat)
```

```
        coef1 = (alpha_cumprod_prev_t.sqrt() * betas_t) / (1.0 -
        ↪   alpha_cumprod_t)
        coef2 = ((1.0 - alpha_cumprod_prev_t) * alpha_t.sqrt()) /
        ↪   (1.0 - alpha_cumprod_t)

        mean = coef1 * x_0_hat + coef2 * x_t
        if t > 0:
            z = torch.randn_like(x_t)
        else:
            z = torch.zeros_like(x_t)

        x_prev = mean + z * posterior_var_t.sqrt()

        # For inpainting: known regions stay from x_t
        # For outpainting: we also keep existing content in mask==1
        # but x_prev is used for masked areas.
        x_prev = mask * x_t + (1.0 - mask) * x_prev
        return x_prev

    def p_sample_loop(self, model, x_init, mask, device):
        """
        Iteratively apply p_sample to get from x_T to x_0.
        x_init is the noised sample at T (often standard Gaussian).
        """
        x_t = x_init
        for step in reversed(range(self.n_steps)):
            x_t = self.p_sample(model, x_t, mask, step)
        return x_t


# ----------------------------------------------------------------
# 6) Training loop
# ----------------------------------------------------------------
def train_one_epoch(model, diffusion, dataloader, optimizer,
↪   device):
    """
    One epoch of training for diffusion inpainting: we randomize a
    ↪   mask,
    forward diffuse the full image, then feed the masked noisy image
    to the model to predict the noise.
    """
    model.train()
    total_loss = 0.0
    for batch_idx, (images, _) in enumerate(dataloader):
        images = images.to(device)
        B, C, H, W = images.shape

        # Generate a random mask (1=known, 0=missing)
        mask = generate_random_mask((B, C, H, W)).to(device)

        # Sample random t
        t = torch.randint(0, diffusion.n_steps, (B,),
        ↪   device=device).long()
```

```python
        # Noise for forward diffusion
        noise = torch.randn_like(images)

        # x_t = q_sample
        x_t = diffusion.q_sample(images, t, noise)

        # Combine x_t and mask as input to the model
        x_t_masked = x_t * mask   # keep known region from x_t
        net_input = torch.cat([x_t_masked, mask], dim=1)

        # Predict noise
        noise_pred = model(net_input)

        # MSE loss
        loss = nn.functional.mse_loss(noise_pred, noise)

        optimizer.zero_grad()
        loss.backward()
        optimizer.step()

        total_loss += loss.item()

    return total_loss / len(dataloader)

def evaluate_model(model, diffusion, dataloader, device):
    """
    Quick evaluation: compute average MSE on a validation set.
    """
    model.eval()
    total_loss = 0.0
    with torch.no_grad():
        for images, _ in dataloader:
            images = images.to(device)
            B, C, H, W = images.shape

            # Random mask
            mask = generate_random_mask((B, C, H, W)).to(device)

            t = torch.randint(0, diffusion.n_steps, (B,),
            ↪   device=device).long()
            noise = torch.randn_like(images)
            x_t = diffusion.q_sample(images, t, noise)

            x_t_masked = x_t * mask
            net_input = torch.cat([x_t_masked, mask], dim=1)
            noise_pred = model(net_input)

            loss = nn.functional.mse_loss(noise_pred, noise)
            total_loss += loss.item()
    return total_loss / len(dataloader)

# ----------------------------------------------------------------
# 7) Sampling function for inpainting or outpainting
```

```
# ----------------------------------------------------------------
def inpaint_sample_and_save(model, diffusion, dataloader, device,
↪   epoch, results_dir="results"):
    """
    Takes one batch from the dataloader, masks it,
    forward diffuses it to x_T, then reverse samples back
    to x_0 using the diffusion process.
    """
    model.eval()
    os.makedirs(results_dir, exist_ok=True)

    with torch.no_grad():
        images, _ = next(iter(dataloader))
        images = images.to(device)
        B, C, H, W = images.shape

        # Create random mask
        mask = generate_random_mask((B, C, H, W)).to(device)

        # Forward diffusion to x_T
        x_t = torch.randn_like(images)  # x_T ~ N(0,1), an
        ↪   alternative is q_sample repeatedly
        # For demonstration here, we can start from pure Gaussian or
        ↪   do partial q_sample:
        # We'll do partial q_sample steps just as an example:
        # but simpler is to define x_t = N(0,1).

        # We'll do a partial approach to remain consistent with the
        ↪   data distribution:
        # let's do 50% of the total steps as forward
        half_steps = diffusion.n_steps // 2
        for step in range(half_steps):
            t_batch = torch.tensor([step]*B, device=device).long()
            noise_rand = torch.randn_like(images)
            x_t = diffusion.q_sample(images, t_batch, noise_rand)

        # Now use p_sample_loop from the halfway noised image
        # but we actually have to define a new routine or we can
        ↪   trick the system to do it.
        # We'll do a simpler approach: we define x_init from the
        ↪   above x_t.
        # Then p_sample_loop will do the rest of the steps from
        ↪   half_steps down to 0.

        # A simpler approach is to define x_init as random if we
        ↪   want outpainting-like scenario:
        x_init = x_t.clone()

        # We'll do the reverse steps by overriding the total steps,
        # but let's keep it simpler: we just proceed from n_steps-1
        ↪   down:
        # We'll do a small hack to illustrate:
```

45

```python
    x_in = x_init
    for step in reversed(range(half_steps, diffusion.n_steps)):
        x_in = diffusion.p_sample(model, x_in, mask, step)

    # x_in is now x_0 ideally
    reconstructed = x_in

    # Reintroduce the known region from the original just to
    ↪  highlight the difference
    # In practice, the code above constrains known regions at
    ↪  each step.
    # So let's visualize:

    # Convert to [0,1] range
    original = (images.clamp(-1,1)+1)*0.5
    rec = (reconstructed.clamp(-1,1)+1)*0.5

    # Create a grid for comparison
    # 1: Original
    # 2: Masked input
    # 3: Reconstructed
    masked_input = x_init * mask
    masked_vis = (masked_input.clamp(-1,1) + 1)*0.5

    combined = torch.cat([original[:8], masked_vis[:8],
    ↪  rec[:8]], dim=0)
    grid = torchvision.utils.make_grid(combined, nrow=8,
    ↪  padding=2)

    plt.figure(figsize=(20,6))
    plt.axis('off')
    plt.imshow(grid.permute(1,2,0).cpu().numpy())
    plt.title(f"Inpainting/Outpainting at epoch {epoch}")
    save_path = os.path.join(results_dir,
    ↪  f"inpaint_outpaint_epoch_{epoch}.png")
    plt.savefig(save_path)
    plt.close()


# ------------------------------------------------------------
# 8) Main function: train and visualize results
# ------------------------------------------------------------
def main():
    set_seed(42)
    device = torch.device("cuda" if torch.cuda.is_available() else
    ↪  "cpu")

    # Load MNIST as a demonstration dataset (grayscale, 1 channel)
    transform = transforms.Compose([
        transforms.ToTensor(),
        # Rescale from [0,1] to [-1,1] for convenience
        transforms.Normalize((0.5,), (0.5,))
    ])
```

46

```
train_dataset = torchvision.datasets.MNIST(root='data',
↪    train=True, download=True, transform=transform)
test_dataset = torchvision.datasets.MNIST(root='data',
↪    train=False, download=True, transform=transform)

train_dataloader = DataLoader(train_dataset, batch_size=64,
↪    shuffle=True)
test_dataloader = DataLoader(test_dataset, batch_size=64,
↪    shuffle=False)

# Initialize UNet: 2 input channels (image + mask), 1 output
↪    channel (noise)
model = UNet(in_channels=2, out_channels=1,
↪    base_channels=64).to(device)

# Diffusion with 200 steps
diffusion = Diffusion(n_steps=200)

# Optimizer
optimizer = optim.Adam(model.parameters(), lr=1e-4)

# Train
epochs = 5
for epoch in range(epochs):
    train_loss = train_one_epoch(model, diffusion,
↪        train_dataloader, optimizer, device)
    val_loss = evaluate_model(model, diffusion, test_dataloader,
↪        device)
    print(f"Epoch [{epoch+1}/{epochs}] | Train Loss:
↪        {train_loss:.4f} | Val Loss: {val_loss:.4f}")

    # Perform inpainting/outpainting on a sample batch
    inpaint_sample_and_save(model, diffusion, test_dataloader,
↪        device, epoch)

print("Training and sampling complete! Check the 'results'
↪    folder for images.")

if __name__ == "__main__":
    main()
```

Key Implementation Details:

- **Mask Input:** We feed the masked noisy image concatenated with the binary mask as two input channels to UNet. This conditioning guides the network on which regions it must fill.

- **Forward Diffusion (q_sample):** We apply standard Gaussian noise to the entire image. During inpainting, the model pays special attention to masked areas, as indicated by the mask channel.

- **Reverse Diffusion (`p_sample_loop`):** We iteratively reverse the diffusion, clamping known regions to their original values so that the network only modifies masked areas.

- **Training Objective:** We compute an MSE loss between the network's predicted noise and the actual noise. This indirect supervision teaches the model to restore missing regions.

- **Inpainting/Outpainting Demo:** The `inpaint_sample_and_save` function shows how to half-noise an image (or optionally start from pure noise) and reconstruct the missing parts via the reverse diffusion process.

Chapter 5

Image Super-Resolution and Restoration

This chapter investigates how diffusion models can upsample low-resolution images to higher resolutions, or restore degraded images. Common use cases include enhancing archival photos, improving compressed footage, and generating high-res details in design. We adapt the diffusion process to treat low-resolution inputs as partial conditions, integrating them into the UNet at each denoising step. Implementation steps encompass: (1) preparing paired datasets of low-resolution and high-resolution images, (2) injecting the low-resolution image into the diffusion network by concatenating feature maps, (3) applying a noise schedule that progressively corrupts the high-resolution target images, (4) defining a noise-prediction loss sensitive to the upsampling condition, and (5) reversing the process to yield a super-res image. A novel twist is multi-scale conditioning, where intermediate super-resolution images at successive scales build an even more refined final output.

Python Code Snippet

```python
import os
import math
import random
import torch
```

```python
import torch.nn as nn
import torch.optim as optim
from torch.utils.data import Dataset, DataLoader
from torchvision import datasets, transforms, utils
import matplotlib.pyplot as plt
import numpy as np

#
↪  -------------------------------------------------------------------
# 1) Utility: set random seed for reproducibility
#
↪  -------------------------------------------------------------------
def set_seed(seed=42):
    random.seed(seed)
    np.random.seed(seed)
    torch.manual_seed(seed)
    if torch.cuda.is_available():
        torch.cuda.manual_seed_all(seed)


#
↪  -------------------------------------------------------------------
# 2) Custom dataset for Super-Resolution: pairs (HR, LR)
#     We will use CIFAR-10 for illustration, resizing it to smaller
↪  LR
#     and returning both LR and HR images.
#
↪  -------------------------------------------------------------------
class SuperResolutionDataset(Dataset):
    """
    A dataset that yields pairs (lr_image, hr_image), both as
    ↪  tensors.
    """
    def __init__(self, root, train=True, transform=None,
    ↪  lr_transform=None, download=True):
        super().__init__()
        self.hr_data = datasets.CIFAR10(
            root=root,
            train=train,
            transform=transform,
            download=download
        )
        self.lr_transform = lr_transform

    def __len__(self):
        return len(self.hr_data)

    def __getitem__(self, idx):
        hr_img, _ = self.hr_data[idx]   # high-res image
        if self.lr_transform:
            lr_img = self.lr_transform(hr_img)   # downsample to low
            ↪  resolution
        else:
            lr_img = hr_img
```

```
        return lr_img, hr_img

#
↪    --------------------------------------------------------------------
# 3) Conditioning UNet for Super-Resolution
#    This UNet will accept concatenated LR and noised HR as input.
#
↪    --------------------------------------------------------------------
class DoubleConv(nn.Module):
    """
    Basic block: two convolutions + ReLU.
    """
    def __init__(self, in_channels, out_channels):
        super(DoubleConv, self).__init__()
        self.conv = nn.Sequential(
            nn.Conv2d(in_channels, out_channels, 3, padding=1),
            nn.ReLU(inplace=True),
            nn.Conv2d(out_channels, out_channels, 3, padding=1),
            nn.ReLU(inplace=True)
        )

    def forward(self, x):
        return self.conv(x)

class ConditionedUNet(nn.Module):
    """
    A UNet that accepts (lr_img, x_t) as a single tensor [B, C_in,
    ↪   H, W].
    For color images: lr_img has 3 channels, x_t has 3 channels =>
    ↪   total 6 input channels.
    Output: 3 channels of predicted noise.
    """
    def __init__(self, base_channels=64):
        super(ConditionedUNet, self).__init__()

        # We have 6 input channels (LR=3, noised-HR=3), output 3
        ↪   noise channels
        self.in_channels = 6
        self.out_channels = 3

        # ----------------------
        # Encoder (Downsample)
        # ----------------------
        self.down1 = DoubleConv(self.in_channels, base_channels)
        self.pool1 = nn.MaxPool2d(2)
        self.down2 = DoubleConv(base_channels, base_channels * 2)
        self.pool2 = nn.MaxPool2d(2)
        self.down3 = DoubleConv(base_channels * 2, base_channels *
        ↪   4)
        self.pool3 = nn.MaxPool2d(2)

        # Bottleneck
```

```python
        self.bottleneck = DoubleConv(base_channels * 4,
        ↪   base_channels * 8)

        # --------------------
        # Decoder (Upsample)
        # --------------------
        self.up1 = nn.ConvTranspose2d(base_channels * 8,
        ↪   base_channels * 4, kernel_size=2, stride=2)
        self.conv_up1 = DoubleConv(base_channels * 8, base_channels
        ↪   * 4)

        self.up2 = nn.ConvTranspose2d(base_channels * 4,
        ↪   base_channels * 2, kernel_size=2, stride=2)
        self.conv_up2 = DoubleConv(base_channels * 4, base_channels
        ↪   * 2)

        self.up3 = nn.ConvTranspose2d(base_channels * 2,
        ↪   base_channels, kernel_size=2, stride=2)
        self.conv_up3 = DoubleConv(base_channels * 2, base_channels)

        # Final output
        self.final_conv = nn.Conv2d(base_channels,
        ↪   self.out_channels, kernel_size=1)

    def forward(self, lr_hr_concat):
        """
        lr_hr_concat: shape [B, 6, H, W]
          - channels 0..2: LR image
          - channels 3..5: noised HR image (x_t)
        """
        # --------------------
        # Encoder pass
        # --------------------
        x1 = self.down1(lr_hr_concat)
        x2 = self.pool1(x1)

        x2 = self.down2(x2)
        x3 = self.pool2(x2)

        x3 = self.down3(x3)
        x4 = self.pool3(x3)

        # Bottleneck
        b = self.bottleneck(x4)

        # --------------------
        # Decoder pass
        # --------------------
        d1 = self.up1(b)
        d1 = torch.cat([d1, x3], dim=1)
        d1 = self.conv_up1(d1)

        d2 = self.up2(d1)
```

```python
        d2 = torch.cat([d2, x2], dim=1)
        d2 = self.conv_up2(d2)

        d3 = self.up3(d2)
        d3 = torch.cat([d3, x1], dim=1)
        d3 = self.conv_up3(d3)

        out = self.final_conv(d3)
        return out


# ---------------------------------------------------------------------
# 4) Diffusion schedule and forward process for HR images
#    We'll treat LR images as a conditioning to guide
#    super-resolution.
# ---------------------------------------------------------------------
def make_beta_schedule(schedule_name, n_timestep, start=1e-4,
    end=2e-2):
    """
    Creates a beta schedule for the diffusion process.
    We'll stick to 'linear' for clarity.
    """
    if schedule_name == "linear":
        return torch.linspace(start, end, n_timestep)
    else:
        raise NotImplementedError("Only 'linear' schedule is
            implemented.")


class DiffusionSR:
    """
    Encapsulates forward noising q(x_t|x_0) and reverse sampling
        p(x_{t-1}|x_t).
    """
    def __init__(self, n_steps=200, beta_schedule='linear',
        device='cpu'):
        self.device = device
        self.n_steps = n_steps
        self.betas = make_beta_schedule(beta_schedule,
            n_steps).to(device)
        self.alphas = 1.0 - self.betas
        self.alpha_cumprod = torch.cumprod(self.alphas, dim=0)
        self.alpha_cumprod_prev = torch.cat([torch.tensor([1.0],
            device=device), self.alpha_cumprod[:-1]], dim=0)

        # Posterior variance: var of p(x_{t-1}|x_t,x_0)
        self.posterior_variance = self.betas * (1.0 -
            self.alpha_cumprod_prev) / (1.0 - self.alpha_cumprod)

    def q_sample(self, x_start, t, noise=None):
        """
        Diffuse the HR image x_start at step t, returning x_t.
```

```
    x_t = sqrt(alpha_cumprod[t])*x_start +
    ↪  sqrt(1-alpha_cumprod[t])*noise
    """

    if noise is None:
        noise = torch.randn_like(x_start)
    sqrt_alpha_cumprod_t =
    ↪  self.alpha_cumprod[t].sqrt().view(-1,1,1,1)
    sqrt_one_minus_alpha_cumprod_t = (1.0 -
    ↪  self.alpha_cumprod[t]).sqrt().view(-1,1,1,1)

    return sqrt_alpha_cumprod_t * x_start +
    ↪  sqrt_one_minus_alpha_cumprod_t * noise

def predict_noise(self, model, lr_image, x_t, t):
    """
    Model predicts noise. We concatenate LR image with x_t along
    ↪  channels.
    """
    # Expand t to match batch dimension
    while len(t.shape) < len(x_t.shape):
        t = t.unsqueeze(-1)
    # We'll ignore t in the forward pass here, but it could be
    ↪  used for positional encoding if desired.
    # Concatenate LR and x_t
    inp = torch.cat([lr_image, x_t], dim=1)
    noise_pred = model(inp)
    return noise_pred

def p_sample(self, model, lr_image, x_t, t):
    """
    One reverse step. Returns x_{t-1}.
    p(x_{t-1}|x_t) with model's predicted noise e_t.
    """
    betas_t = self.betas[t].view(-1,1,1,1)
    alpha_t = self.alphas[t].view(-1,1,1,1)
    alpha_cumprod_t = self.alpha_cumprod[t].view(-1,1,1,1)
    alpha_cumprod_prev_t =
    ↪  self.alpha_cumprod_prev[t].view(-1,1,1,1)

    e_t = self.predict_noise(model, lr_image, x_t, t)

    # x_0 hat
    sqrt_recip_alpha_t = (1.0 / alpha_t).sqrt()
    x_0_hat = (x_t - (1.0 - alpha_t).sqrt() * e_t) *
    ↪  sqrt_recip_alpha_t

    # Compute mean of q(x_{t-1}|x_t, x_0_hat)
    coef1 = (alpha_cumprod_prev_t.sqrt() * betas_t) / (1.0 -
    ↪  alpha_cumprod_t)
    coef2 = ((1.0 - alpha_cumprod_prev_t) * alpha_t.sqrt()) /
    ↪  (1.0 - alpha_cumprod_t)
    mean = coef1 * x_0_hat + coef2 * x_t
```

```python
        # sample noise
        var = self.posterior_variance[t].view(-1,1,1,1)
        if t[0] > 0:  # multiple samples in a batch share the same t
            noise = torch.randn_like(x_t)
        else:
            noise = torch.zeros_like(x_t)
        x_prev = mean + noise * var.sqrt()
        return x_prev

    def p_sample_loop(self, model, lr_image, shape):
        """
        Repeatedly apply p_sample from T-1 down to 0, starting from
        ↪    x_T ~ N(0,I).
        lr_image: [B, 3, H, W], shape: (B, 3, H, W) for the final
        ↪    sample
        """
        batch_size = shape[0]
        x_t = torch.randn(shape, device=self.device)
        for i in reversed(range(self.n_steps)):
            # create a batch of timesteps
            t_batch = torch.full((batch_size,), i,
            ↪    device=self.device, dtype=torch.long)
            x_t = self.p_sample(model, lr_image, x_t, t_batch)
        return x_t

#
↪    -------------------------------------------------------------------
# 5) Training and evaluation
#
↪    -------------------------------------------------------------------
def train_one_epoch(model, diffusion, optimizer, dataloader,
↪    device):
    """
    Train for one epoch:
    1) Sample random t
    2) Forward diffuse x_0 -> x_t
    3) Predict noise
    4) MSE loss with real noise
    """
    model.train()
    total_loss = 0
    for lr_img, hr_img in dataloader:
        lr_img = lr_img.to(device)  # [B, 3, H, W]
        hr_img = hr_img.to(device)  # [B, 3, H, W]

        # Sample a random time step
        t = torch.randint(0, diffusion.n_steps, (lr_img.size(0),),
        ↪    device=device).long()

        # Random noise
        noise = torch.randn_like(hr_img)

        x_t = diffusion.q_sample(hr_img, t, noise=noise)
```

55

```python
        noise_pred = diffusion.predict_noise(model, lr_img, x_t, t)

        loss = nn.functional.mse_loss(noise_pred, noise)

        optimizer.zero_grad()
        loss.backward()
        optimizer.step()

        total_loss += loss.item()

    return total_loss / len(dataloader)


def evaluate_model(model, diffusion, dataloader, device):
    """
    Evaluate by reporting average MSE against the true noise.
    """
    model.eval()
    total_loss = 0
    with torch.no_grad():
        for lr_img, hr_img in dataloader:
            lr_img = lr_img.to(device)
            hr_img = hr_img.to(device)
            t = torch.randint(0, diffusion.n_steps,
            ↪  (lr_img.size(0),), device=device).long()
            noise = torch.randn_like(hr_img)
            x_t = diffusion.q_sample(hr_img, t, noise=noise)
            noise_pred = diffusion.predict_noise(model, lr_img, x_t,
            ↪  t)
            loss = nn.functional.mse_loss(noise_pred, noise)
            total_loss += loss.item()
    return total_loss / len(dataloader)


def sample_and_save(model, diffusion, lr_img, epoch,
↪  outdir="results"):
    """
    Given an LR image, sample a super-res output from random noise
    ↪  and save the result.
    """
    model.eval()
    with torch.no_grad():
        # lr_img shape: [B, 3, H, W]
        # We'll assume B=1 just for demonstration of saving an image
        if lr_img.size(0) > 1:
            lr_img = lr_img[:1]  # take first, for demonstration
        batch_size, _, hr_h, hr_w = lr_img.shape

        # Generate super-res by reverse diffusion
        sr_out = diffusion.p_sample_loop(model, lr_img, (batch_size,
        ↪  3, hr_h, hr_w))

        # Convert to [0,1] range
        sr_out = (sr_out.clamp(-1.0, 1.0) + 1) * 0.5
        lr_vis = (lr_img.clamp(-1.0, 1.0) + 1) * 0.5
```

```python
    # Save a side-by-side comparison
    comparison = torch.cat([lr_vis, sr_out], dim=3)   #
    ↪   horizontally
    os.makedirs(outdir, exist_ok=True)
    grid = utils.make_grid(comparison, nrow=1)

    plt.figure(figsize=(8,4))
    plt.axis("off")
    plt.imshow(grid.permute(1, 2, 0).cpu().numpy())
    plt.savefig(os.path.join(outdir,
    ↪   f"epoch_{epoch}_superres.png"))
    plt.close()

#
↪   --------------------------------------------------------------------
# 6) Main function: run the entire pipeline
#
↪   --------------------------------------------------------------------
def main():
    set_seed(42)
    device = torch.device("cuda" if torch.cuda.is_available() else
    ↪   "cpu")
    print("Using device:", device)

    # Transforms for HR images
    hr_transform = transforms.Compose([
        transforms.ToTensor(),
        transforms.Normalize((0.5, 0.5, 0.5), (0.5, 0.5, 0.5)) # to
        ↪   [-1,1]
    ])

    # Transforms for LR images (downsample x4)
    lr_transform = transforms.Compose([
        transforms.ToPILImage(),
        transforms.Resize((8, 8)),      # from 32x32 down to 8x8
        transforms.ToTensor(),
        transforms.Normalize((0.5, 0.5, 0.5), (0.5, 0.5, 0.5))
    ])

    # Create training and test datasets
    train_dataset = SuperResolutionDataset(
        root="data",
        train=True,
        transform=hr_transform,
        lr_transform=lr_transform,
        download=True
    )
    test_dataset = SuperResolutionDataset(
        root="data",
        train=False,
        transform=hr_transform,
        lr_transform=lr_transform,
```

57

```
        download=True
    )

    # Dataloaders
    train_loader = DataLoader(train_dataset, batch_size=16,
    ↪   shuffle=True, num_workers=2)
    test_loader = DataLoader(test_dataset, batch_size=16,
    ↪   shuffle=False, num_workers=2)

    # Initialize model & diffusion
    model = ConditionedUNet(base_channels=64).to(device)
    diffusion = DiffusionSR(n_steps=200, beta_schedule='linear',
    ↪   device=device)

    # Optimizer
    optimizer = optim.Adam(model.parameters(), lr=1e-4)

    # Training loop
    epochs = 3
    for epoch in range(epochs):
        train_loss = train_one_epoch(model, diffusion, optimizer,
        ↪   train_loader, device)
        val_loss = evaluate_model(model, diffusion, test_loader,
        ↪   device)
        print(f"Epoch [{epoch+1}/{epochs}], Train Loss:
        ↪   {train_loss:.4f}, Val Loss: {val_loss:.4f}")

        # Try sampling from random LR from test set
        lr_img, _ = next(iter(test_loader))
        lr_img = lr_img.to(device)

        sample_and_save(model, diffusion, lr_img, epoch,
        ↪   outdir="results")

    print("Training complete! Check the 'results' folder for sample
    ↪   outputs.")

if __name__ == "__main__":
    main()
```

Key Implementation Details:

- **Conditioning on LR Input:** We implement `ConditionedUNet`
  which concatenates low-resolution and noised high-resolution
  images over the channel dimension to guide super-resolution.

- **Forward Diffusion:** The function `q_sample` introduces noise
  to the original high-resolution image at a random diffusion
  step t, creating `x_t`.

- **Reverse Diffusion (Sampling):** The method `p_sample_loop` iteratively applies `p_sample` to remove noise, guided by the LR condition, until a super-res image is reconstructed.

- **Network Architecture:** The code uses a UNet-like encoder-decoder with skip connections, adapted to accept 6 input channels (3 for LR, 3 for noised-HR).

- **Noise-Prediction Loss:** We compare predicted noise with the actual noise via MSE. Minimizing this trains the model to accurately remove noise at each diffusion step.

- **Multi-Scale Extension:** While this code focuses on single-scale usage, a multi-scale approach could incorporate intermediate super-resolution outputs, refining detail at each scale.

- **Practical Pipeline:** The `main` function demonstrates an end-to-end flow: loading CIFAR-10, creating LR-HR pairs, training the diffusion model, and sampling super-res outputs saved to disk.

Chapter 6

Image-to-Image Translation with Diffusion

In this chapter, diffusion serves to transform one image domain into another, such as converting sketches to paintings or day to night scenes. A popular use is domain adaptation for style transfer or complex artistic transformations. The diffusion network incorporates both a source image and desired target style or domain label. To construct the model, we: (1) define a forward process that adds noise to target-domain images, (2) feed the source image through an encoder module or simply concatenate it as a conditioning map, (3) train the UNet to denoise while aligning the output to the target domain features, and (4) sample by injecting a source image at each reverse diffusion step while scaling domain-specific guidance. Innovatively, we can apply a multi-branch UNet that dedicates separate pathways to distinct style features, enabling more nuanced transformations without retraining from scratch for each style.

Python Code Snippet

```
import os
import random
import math
import torch
import torch.nn as nn
```

```python
from torch.utils.data import Dataset, DataLoader
import torchvision.transforms as transforms
import torchvision.utils as vutils
import torch.optim as optim
import numpy as np
from PIL import Image
import matplotlib.pyplot as plt


# ----------------------------------------------------------------
# 1) Utilities: set seed, etc.
# ----------------------------------------------------------------
def set_seed(seed=42):
    random.seed(seed)
    np.random.seed(seed)
    torch.manual_seed(seed)
    if torch.cuda.is_available():
        torch.cuda.manual_seed_all(seed)


# ----------------------------------------------------------------
# 2) Custom Dataset for Domain Pairs (source, target)
# ----------------------------------------------------------------
class DomainPairDataset(Dataset):
    """
    A minimal example dataset that expects pairs of images:
    source: images from domain A (e.g., sketches)
    target: images from domain B (e.g., paintings)

    Assumes two folders, 'source' and 'target', with corresponding
    filenames aligned.
    """
    def __init__(self, source_dir, target_dir, transform=None):
        super(DomainPairDataset, self).__init__()
        self.source_dir = source_dir
        self.target_dir = target_dir
        self.source_files = sorted(os.listdir(source_dir))
        self.target_files = sorted(os.listdir(target_dir))
        self.transform = transform

        # Simple check: ensure same length
        assert len(self.source_files) == len(self.target_files), \
            "Mismatch in number of source and target images!"

    def __len__(self):
        return len(self.source_files)

    def __getitem__(self, idx):
        # Load source image
        source_path = os.path.join(self.source_dir,
        ↪ self.source_files[idx])
        source_img = Image.open(source_path).convert("RGB")

        # Load target image
```

```python
        target_path = os.path.join(self.target_dir,
        ↪   self.target_files[idx])
        target_img = Image.open(target_path).convert("RGB")

        if self.transform is not None:
            source_img = self.transform(source_img)
            target_img = self.transform(target_img)

        return (source_img, target_img)


# ------------------------------------------------------------
# 3) A Conditioning U-Net for Domain Adaptation
#    We simply concatenate the source image and the noisy target
#    as the input.
# ------------------------------------------------------------
class DoubleConv(nn.Module):
    """
    Reusable double-convolution block with ReLU activations.
    """
    def __init__(self, in_channels, out_channels):
        super(DoubleConv, self).__init__()
        self.conv = nn.Sequential(
            nn.Conv2d(in_channels, out_channels, kernel_size=3,
            ↪   padding=1),
            nn.ReLU(inplace=True),
            nn.Conv2d(out_channels, out_channels, kernel_size=3,
            ↪   padding=1),
            nn.ReLU(inplace=True)
        )

    def forward(self, x):
        return self.conv(x)


class UNetConditioned(nn.Module):
    """
    A U-Net variant where we accept two images (source + noisy
    ↪   target)
    as input channels. For RGB, that's 3 channels for source, 3 for
    ↪   target,
    total in_channels = 6. The output is an RGB-like noise
    ↪   prediction (3 channels).
    """
    def __init__(self, in_channels=6, out_channels=3,
    ↪   base_channels=64):
        super(UNetConditioned, self).__init__()

        # Down-sampling
        self.down1 = DoubleConv(in_channels, base_channels)
        self.pool1 = nn.MaxPool2d(2)

        self.down2 = DoubleConv(base_channels, base_channels*2)
        self.pool2 = nn.MaxPool2d(2)
```

62

```python
        self.down3 = DoubleConv(base_channels*2, base_channels*4)
        self.pool3 = nn.MaxPool2d(2)

        # Bottleneck
        self.bottleneck = DoubleConv(base_channels*4,
        ↪  base_channels*8)

        # Up-sampling
        self.up1 = nn.ConvTranspose2d(base_channels*8,
        ↪  base_channels*4, kernel_size=2, stride=2)
        self.conv_up1 = DoubleConv(base_channels*8, base_channels*4)

        self.up2 = nn.ConvTranspose2d(base_channels*4,
        ↪  base_channels*2, kernel_size=2, stride=2)
        self.conv_up2 = DoubleConv(base_channels*4, base_channels*2)

        self.up3 = nn.ConvTranspose2d(base_channels*2,
        ↪  base_channels, kernel_size=2, stride=2)
        self.conv_up3 = DoubleConv(base_channels*2, base_channels)

        # Final output
        self.final_conv = nn.Conv2d(base_channels, out_channels,
        ↪  kernel_size=1)

    def forward(self, x):
        # x has shape (batch_size, 6, H, W) => (source + noisy
        ↪  target)

        # Encoder
        d1 = self.down1(x)      # -> (base_channels, H, W)
        p1 = self.pool1(d1)     # -> half resolution

        d2 = self.down2(p1)     # -> (base_channels*2, H/2, W/2)
        p2 = self.pool2(d2)     # -> quarter resolution

        d3 = self.down3(p2)     # -> (base_channels*4, H/4, W/4)
        p3 = self.pool3(d3)     # -> eighth resolution

        # Bottleneck
        b = self.bottleneck(p3)

        # Decoder
        up_1 = self.up1(b)
        cat1 = torch.cat([up_1, d3], dim=1)
        up_1c = self.conv_up1(cat1)

        up_2 = self.up2(up_1c)
        cat2 = torch.cat([up_2, d2], dim=1)
        up_2c = self.conv_up2(cat2)

        up_3 = self.up3(up_2c)
        cat3 = torch.cat([up_3, d1], dim=1)
        up_3c = self.conv_up3(cat3)
```

63

```python
        # Final
        out = self.final_conv(up_3c)
        return out

# ---------------------------------------------------------------
# 4) Diffusion Schedule and Core Routines
# ---------------------------------------------------------------
def make_beta_schedule(schedule_name, n_timestep, start=1e-4,
↪   end=2e-2):
    """
    Creates a linear beta schedule for demonstration.
    """
    if schedule_name == "linear":
        return torch.linspace(start, end, n_timestep)
    else:
        raise NotImplementedError("Only 'linear' schedule is
        ↪   implemented here.")

class Diffusion:
    """
    Encapsulates the forward (q) and reverse (p) processes for
    ↪   image-to-image diffusion:
    1) q(x_t | x_0) for forward noising.
    2) p(x_{t-1} | x_t, x_src) for reverse denoising, conditioned on
    ↪   the source image x_src.
        (We insert x_src by concatenation with x_t when calling the
        ↪   model.)
    """
    def __init__(self, n_steps=200, beta_schedule='linear'):
        self.n_steps = n_steps
        self.betas = make_beta_schedule(beta_schedule, n_steps)
        self.alphas = 1.0 - self.betas
        self.alpha_cumprod = torch.cumprod(self.alphas, dim=0)
        self.alpha_cumprod_prev = torch.cat([torch.tensor([1.0]),
        ↪   self.alpha_cumprod[:-1]], dim=0)

        # Posterior variance for p(x_{t-1} | x_t, x_0)
        self.posterior_variance = self.betas * (1.0 -
        ↪   self.alpha_cumprod_prev) / (1.0 - self.alpha_cumprod)

    def q_sample(self, x_start, t, noise=None):
        """
        Forward diffusion: x_t = sqrt(alpha_cumprod[t]) * x_start +
        ↪   sqrt(1-alpha_cumprod[t]) * noise
        """
        if noise is None:
            noise = torch.randn_like(x_start)
        sqrt_alpha_cumprod_t =
        ↪   self.alpha_cumprod[t].sqrt().view(-1,1,1,1)
        sqrt_one_minus_alpha_cumprod_t = (1 -
        ↪   self.alpha_cumprod[t]).sqrt().view(-1,1,1,1)
```

64

```python
        return sqrt_alpha_cumprod_t * x_start +
        ↪    sqrt_one_minus_alpha_cumprod_t * noise

    def predict_noise(self, model, x_t, x_src, t):
        """
        Predict the noise using the model, which concatenates x_src
        ↪    and x_t.
        """
        # x_src, x_t each has shape (B, C, H, W)
        # Concatenate along channel dim => (B, 6, H, W) for RGB
        combined = torch.cat([x_src, x_t], dim=1)
        noise_pred = model(combined)
        return noise_pred

    def p_sample(self, model, x_t, x_src, t, guidance_scale=1.0):
        """
        One reverse step: x_{t-1} ~ N(mean, variance),
        where mean depends on model's noise prediction + posterior
        ↪    coefficients.
        """
        betas_t = self.betas[t]
        alpha_t = self.alphas[t]
        alpha_cumprod_t = self.alpha_cumprod[t]
        alpha_cumprod_prev_t = self.alpha_cumprod_prev[t]
        # Predict noise
        noise_pred = self.predict_noise(model, x_t, x_src, t)
        noise_pred = noise_pred * guidance_scale

        # Reconstruct x_0 estimate
        sqrt_recip_alpha_t = (1.0 / alpha_t).sqrt()
        x_0_hat = (x_t - (1.0 - alpha_t).sqrt() * noise_pred) *
        ↪    sqrt_recip_alpha_t

        # Compute the mean of q(x_{t-1} | x_t, x_0)
        coef1 = (alpha_cumprod_prev_t.sqrt() * betas_t) / (1.0 -
        ↪    alpha_cumprod_t)
        coef2 = ((1.0 - alpha_cumprod_prev_t) * alpha_t.sqrt()) /
        ↪    (1.0 - alpha_cumprod_t)
        mean = coef1 * x_0_hat + coef2 * x_t

        # Posterior variance
        posterior_var = self.posterior_variance[t]

        if t > 0:
            noise = torch.randn_like(x_t)
        else:
            noise = torch.zeros_like(x_t)

        x_prev = mean + noise * posterior_var.sqrt()
        return x_prev

    def p_sample_loop(self, model, x_src, shape, device,
    ↪    guidance_scale=1.0):
```

```python
        """
        Start from x_T (Gaussian noise) and iteratively sample
        ↪  backward.
        x_src remains the same at each step.
        """
        b, c, h, w = shape
        x_t = torch.randn((b, c, h, w), device=device)
        for i in reversed(range(self.n_steps)):
            # replicate the t index for batch dimension
            t_tensor = torch.tensor([i]*b, device=device).long()
            x_t = self.p_sample(model, x_t, x_src, t_tensor,
            ↪  guidance_scale=guidance_scale)
        return x_t


# ---------------------------------------------------------------
# 5) Training and validation routines
# ---------------------------------------------------------------
def train_one_epoch(model, diffusion, optimizer, dataloader,
↪  device):
    model.train()
    total_loss = 0.0
    for batch_idx, (source, target) in enumerate(dataloader):
        source = source.to(device)  # (B, 3, H, W)
        target = target.to(device)  # (B, 3, H, W)

        # random t
        t = torch.randint(0, diffusion.n_steps, (source.size(0),),
        ↪  device=device).long()

        # random noise
        noise = torch.randn_like(target)

        # forward diffuse the target
        x_t = diffusion.q_sample(target, t, noise=noise)

        # predict noise
        noise_pred = diffusion.predict_noise(model, x_t, source, t)

        # L2 loss between actual noise and predicted noise
        loss = nn.MSELoss()(noise_pred, noise)

        optimizer.zero_grad()
        loss.backward()
        optimizer.step()

        total_loss += loss.item()

    avg_loss = total_loss / len(dataloader)
    return avg_loss

def evaluate_model(model, diffusion, dataloader, device):
    model.eval()
    total_loss = 0.0
```

```python
    with torch.no_grad():
        for batch_idx, (source, target) in enumerate(dataloader):
            source = source.to(device)
            target = target.to(device)
            t = torch.randint(0, diffusion.n_steps,
            ↪ (source.size(0),), device=device).long()
            noise = torch.randn_like(target)

            x_t = diffusion.q_sample(target, t, noise=noise)
            noise_pred = diffusion.predict_noise(model, x_t, source,
            ↪ t)
            loss = nn.MSELoss()(noise_pred, noise)
            total_loss += loss.item()

    return total_loss / len(dataloader)

def sample_images(model, diffusion, source_batch, device, epoch,
↪ guidance_scale=1.0):
    """
    Given a batch of source images, sample the translated images
    from random noise in the target domain.
    """
    model.eval()
    with torch.no_grad():
        # shape is (B, 3, H, W)
        # We'll generate the same batch size for the target domain
        shape = source_batch.shape
        # perform the sampler
        generated = diffusion.p_sample_loop(model, source_batch,
        ↪ shape, device, guidance_scale)
        # clamp and scale to [0,1]
        generated = (generated.clamp(-1.0, 1.0) + 1.0) * 0.5

        # convert to grid
        grid = vutils.make_grid(generated, nrow=4)
        os.makedirs("results_domain", exist_ok=True)
        plt.figure(figsize=(8,8))
        plt.axis("off")
        plt.title(f"Epoch {epoch} - GS {guidance_scale}")
        plt.imshow(np.transpose(grid.cpu().numpy(), (1,2,0)))
        plt.savefig(f"results_domain/
        epoch_{epoch}_gs_{guidance_scale}.png")
        plt.close()

# ---------------------------------------------------------------
# 6) Main function: putting it all together
# ---------------------------------------------------------------
def main():
    set_seed(42)
    device = torch.device("cuda" if torch.cuda.is_available() else
    ↪ "cpu")

    # Example transforms for 64x64 training
```

67

```python
common_transforms = transforms.Compose([
    transforms.Resize((64,64)),
    transforms.ToTensor(),
    transforms.Normalize((0.5,0.5,0.5), (0.5,0.5,0.5))
])

# Example directories (you would replace these with your actual
↪   data)
source_dir = "path_to_sketches_or_domainA"
target_dir = "path_to_paintings_or_domainB"

# Create dataset and loader
dataset = DomainPairDataset(source_dir, target_dir,
↪   transform=common_transforms)
dataloader = DataLoader(dataset, batch_size=4, shuffle=True)

# Initialize conditional UNet (6 in channels for (source + noisy
↪   target), 3 out channels for predicted noise)
model = UNetConditioned(in_channels=6, out_channels=3,
↪   base_channels=64).to(device)

# Diffusion for 100 steps, linear schedule
diffusion = Diffusion(n_steps=100, beta_schedule='linear')

optimizer = optim.Adam(model.parameters(), lr=1e-4)

# Basic training loop
epochs = 5
for epoch in range(epochs):
    train_loss = train_one_epoch(model, diffusion, optimizer,
    ↪   dataloader, device)
    val_loss = evaluate_model(model, diffusion, dataloader,
    ↪   device)
    print(f"[Epoch {epoch+1}/{epochs}] Train Loss:
    ↪   {train_loss:.4f}, Val Loss: {val_loss:.4f}")

    # Sample using the first batch of source images
    # For demonstration, fetch one batch from dataloader
    source_batch, _ = next(iter(dataloader))
    source_batch = source_batch.to(device)
    sample_images(model, diffusion, source_batch, device, epoch,
    ↪   guidance_scale=1.0)
    sample_images(model, diffusion, source_batch, device, epoch,
    ↪   guidance_scale=2.0)

print("Training complete. Check 'results_domain' folder for
↪   samples.")

if __name__ == "__main__":
    main()
```

Key Implementation Details:

- **Forward Diffusion:** We implement `q_sample` to corrupt the target-domain image with noise, mixing it according to the linear `beta` schedule.

- **Reverse Diffusion (Sampling):** The function `p_sample_loop` iterates backward through time steps, using the model to predict noise in a conditioned manner by concatenating the source image with the noisy target at each step.

- **Conditioned U-Net:** The `UNetConditioned` takes in source + noisy target as a single tensor (in_channels = 6 for RGB) and outputs a 3-channel noise estimate. This concatenation is a simple version of domain conditioning.

- **Training Objective:** We compute an MSE loss between the predicted noise and the sampled noise. By matching noise, the model learns how to align the target domain image with the source domain's structure or style.

- **Guidance Parameter:** `guidance_scale` multiplies the predicted noise, offering a rough way to control style intensity or variability in the final translated image.

- **Data Handling:** Our `DomainPairDataset` obtains corresponding source-target image pairs. This framework supports transformations and can be adapted to tasks like sketch-to-painting or day-to-night translation.

- **End-to-End Pipeline:** The `main` function sets up data, model, diffusion schedule, and runs both training and sampling. After each epoch, a few sample translations are saved to visualize progress.

Chapter 7

3D Shape Generation with Diffusion Models

Diffusion approaches can also generate 3D objects by treating voxel grids, point clouds, or mesh representations as structured data. Common use cases include rapid prototyping of product designs and creating novel shapes for gaming or simulation. The model construction starts by defining a 3D data representation—voxel grids are the simplest, but can be memory-intensive. We then apply a diffusion process by perturbing 3D data with noise, systematically corrupting voxel intensities or point locations. The UNet-like network is adapted to 3D convolutions or a specialized architecture for point-based operations. Training entails minimizing the difference between predicted and actual noise at each diffusion step. For sampling, the reverse diffusion recovers a coherent 3D object from random initialization. A novel direction explored here is hierarchical shape representation, where a coarse diffusion network sets the global structure, and a finer diffusion network refines local details.

Python Code Snippet

```python
import os
import random
import math
import torch
import torch.nn as nn
import torch.optim as optim
from torch.utils.data import Dataset, DataLoader
```

```python
import numpy as np
import matplotlib.pyplot as plt

# ----------------------------------------------------------------
# 1) Set random seed for reproducibility
# ----------------------------------------------------------------
def set_seed(seed=42):
    random.seed(seed)
    np.random.seed(seed)
    torch.manual_seed(seed)
    if torch.cuda.is_available():
        torch.cuda.manual_seed_all(seed)

# ----------------------------------------------------------------
# 2) A simple Dataset generating synthetic 3D voxel shapes
# ----------------------------------------------------------------
class RandomVoxelDataset(Dataset):
    '''
    A dataset that returns random voxel grids of simple 3D shapes,
    e.g., spheres or cubes, for demonstration purposes.
    Each voxel grid is a tensor of shape [1, size, size, size].
    '''
    def __init__(self, length=2000, size=32):
        super().__init__()
        self.length = length
        self.size = size

    def __len__(self):
        return self.length

    def __getitem__(self, idx):
        # Randomly decide if we create a sphere or a cube:
        shape_type = random.choice(['sphere', 'cube'])
        voxel = np.zeros((self.size, self.size, self.size),
        ↪   dtype=np.float32)

        if shape_type == 'sphere':
            # Random center and radius
            cx, cy, cz = [random.randint(8, self.size-8) for _ in
            ↪   range(3)]
            r = random.randint(4, 8)
            for x in range(self.size):
                for y in range(self.size):
                    for z in range(self.size):
                        if (x - cx)**2 + (y - cy)**2 + (z - cz)**2 <
                        ↪   r*r:
                            voxel[x, y, z] = 1.0
        else:  # 'cube'
            # Random corner coords
            x1, x2 = sorted([random.randint(0, self.size-1) for _ in
            ↪   range(2)])
            y1, y2 = sorted([random.randint(0, self.size-1) for _ in
            ↪   range(2)])
```

```python
            z1, z2 = sorted([random.randint(0, self.size-1) for _ in
            ↪  range(2)])
            voxel[x1:x2, y1:y2, z1:z2] = 1.0

        # Normalize to [-1,1]
        voxel = 2.0 * voxel - 1.0
        voxel_tensor = torch.from_numpy(voxel).unsqueeze(0)  #
        ↪  shape: [1, size, size, size]

        return voxel_tensor, 0  # dummy label


# --------------------------------------------------------------
# 3) Create a 3D U-Net-like architecture
# --------------------------------------------------------------
class DoubleConv3D(nn.Module):
    '''
    A helper module that performs two 3D convolutions (each with
    ↪  ReLU)
    to reduce repeated boilerplate in the 3D U-Net.
    '''
    def __init__(self, in_channels, out_channels):
        super(DoubleConv3D, self).__init__()
        self.conv = nn.Sequential(
            nn.Conv3d(in_channels, out_channels, 3, padding=1),
            nn.ReLU(inplace=True),
            nn.Conv3d(out_channels, out_channels, 3, padding=1),
            nn.ReLU(inplace=True)
        )

    def forward(self, x):
        return self.conv(x)


class UNet3D(nn.Module):
    '''
    A simplified 3D U-Net architecture with down-up sampling blocks
    ↪  (using 3D convolutions)
    and skip connections.
    '''
    def __init__(self, in_channels=1, out_channels=1,
    ↪  base_channels=16):
        super(UNet3D, self).__init__()

        # Down-sampling
        self.down1 = DoubleConv3D(in_channels, base_channels)
        self.pool1 = nn.MaxPool3d(2)

        self.down2 = DoubleConv3D(base_channels, base_channels*2)
        self.pool2 = nn.MaxPool3d(2)

        self.down3 = DoubleConv3D(base_channels*2, base_channels*4)
        self.pool3 = nn.MaxPool3d(2)

        # Bottleneck
```

```python
        self.bottleneck = DoubleConv3D(base_channels*4,
        ↪  base_channels*8)

        # Up-sampling
        self.up3 = nn.ConvTranspose3d(base_channels*8,
        ↪  base_channels*4, 2, stride=2)
        self.conv_up3 = DoubleConv3D(base_channels*8,
        ↪  base_channels*4)

        self.up2 = nn.ConvTranspose3d(base_channels*4,
        ↪  base_channels*2, 2, stride=2)
        self.conv_up2 = DoubleConv3D(base_channels*4,
        ↪  base_channels*2)

        self.up1 = nn.ConvTranspose3d(base_channels*2,
        ↪  base_channels, 2, stride=2)
        self.conv_up1 = DoubleConv3D(base_channels*2, base_channels)

        # Final output
        self.final_conv = nn.Conv3d(base_channels, out_channels,
        ↪  kernel_size=1)

    def forward(self, x):
        # Encoder
        x1 = self.down1(x)      # [B, base, D, H, W]
        x1p = self.pool1(x1)    # downsample

        x2 = self.down2(x1p)    # [B, 2*base, D/2, H/2, W/2]
        x2p = self.pool2(x2)

        x3 = self.down3(x2p)    # [B, 4*base, D/4, H/4, W/4]
        x3p = self.pool3(x3)

        # Bottleneck
        b = self.bottleneck(x3p)  # [B, 8*base, D/8, H/8, W/8]

        # Decoder
        x = self.up3(b)           # upsample
        x = torch.cat([x, x3], dim=1)
        x = self.conv_up3(x)

        x = self.up2(x)
        x = torch.cat([x, x2], dim=1)
        x = self.conv_up2(x)

        x = self.up1(x)
        x = torch.cat([x, x1], dim=1)
        x = self.conv_up1(x)

        out = self.final_conv(x)
        return out

# -----------------------------------------------------------------
```

```python
# 4) Define diffusion schedule & forward/reverse processes
# -------------------------------------------------------------
def make_beta_schedule(schedule_name, n_timestep, start=1e-4,
↪   end=2e-2):
    '''
    Creates a beta schedule for the diffusion process.
    We'll use a linear schedule as an example.
    '''

    if schedule_name == "linear":
        return torch.linspace(start, end, n_timestep)
    else:
        raise NotImplementedError("Only 'linear' schedule is
        ↪   supported in this snippet.")


class Diffusion3D:
    '''
    A 3D diffusion class for:
     - forward noising: q(x_t | x_0)
     - reverse denoising: p(x_{t-1} | x_t)
     - utilities for training and sampling
    '''
    def __init__(self, n_steps=200, beta_schedule='linear'):
        self.n_steps = n_steps
        self.betas = make_beta_schedule(beta_schedule, n_steps)   #
        ↪   [n_steps]
        self.alphas = 1.0 - self.betas
        self.alpha_cumprod = torch.cumprod(self.alphas, dim=0)    #
        ↪   [n_steps]
        self.alpha_cumprod_prev = torch.cat(
            [torch.tensor([1.0]), self.alpha_cumprod[:-1]], dim=0
        )

        # Posterior variance for p(x_{t-1} | x_t, x_0)
        self.posterior_variance = (
            self.betas
            * (1.0 - self.alpha_cumprod_prev)
            / (1.0 - self.alpha_cumprod)
        )

    def q_sample(self, x_start, t, noise=None):
        '''
        Forward diffusion: x_t = sqrt(alpha_cumprod[t]) * x_0 +
        ↪   sqrt(1 - alpha_cumprod[t]) * noise
        '''
        if noise is None:
            noise = torch.randn_like(x_start)
        # Expand to match shape: (batch_size, 1, 1, 1, 1)
        sqrt_alpha_cumprod_t = self.alpha_cumprod[t].sqrt().view(-1,
        ↪   1, 1, 1, 1)
        sqrt_one_minus_alpha_t = (1 -
        ↪   self.alpha_cumprod[t]).sqrt().view(-1, 1, 1, 1, 1)
        return sqrt_alpha_cumprod_t * x_start +
        ↪   sqrt_one_minus_alpha_t * noise
```

74

```python
def predict_noise(self, model, x_t, t):
    '''
    The UNet3D model predicts the noise from a noisy voxel grid.
    '''
    return model(x_t)

def p_sample(self, model, x_t, t, guidance_scale=1.0):
    '''
    One step of reverse diffusion: p(x_{t-1} | x_t).
    We compute an estimate of x_0, then the mean of the
    ↪ posterior, plus noise.
    '''
    beta_t = self.betas[t]
    alpha_t = self.alphas[t]
    alpha_cumprod_t = self.alpha_cumprod[t]
    alpha_cumprod_prev_t = self.alpha_cumprod_prev[t]

    # Model's predicted noise
    e_t = model(x_t) * guidance_scale

    # Estimate x_0
    sqrt_recip_alpha_t = (1.0 / alpha_t).sqrt()
    x_0_hat = (x_t - (1.0 - alpha_t).sqrt() * e_t) *
    ↪ sqrt_recip_alpha_t

    # Posterior mean coefficients
    coef1 = ( (alpha_cumprod_prev_t).sqrt() * beta_t ) / (1.0 -
    ↪ alpha_cumprod_t)
    coef2 = ( (1.0 - alpha_cumprod_prev_t) * alpha_t.sqrt() ) /
    ↪ (1.0 - alpha_cumprod_t)

    mean = coef1 * x_0_hat + coef2 * x_t

    # Posterior variance
    posterior_var = self.posterior_variance[t]
    if t > 0:
        noise = torch.randn_like(x_t)
    else:
        noise = torch.zeros_like(x_t)

    x_prev = mean + noise * posterior_var.sqrt()
    return x_prev

def p_sample_loop(self, model, shape, device,
↪ guidance_scale=1.0):
    '''
    Iteratively apply reverse diffusion from x_T ~ N(0,I) to
    ↪ x_0.
    shape is (batch_size, channels, D, H, W).
    '''
    x = torch.randn(shape, device=device)
    for i in reversed(range(self.n_steps)):
```

```python
            x = self.p_sample(model, x, i, guidance_scale)
        return x

# -------------------------------------------------------------
# 5) Training and evaluation routines
# -------------------------------------------------------------
def train_one_epoch(model, diffusion, optimizer, dataloader,
↪ device):
    model.train()
    epoch_loss = 0.0
    for batch in dataloader:
        x_0, _ = batch
        x_0 = x_0.to(device)   # shape: [B, 1, D, H, W]

        # Random step t for each sample
        t = torch.randint(0, diffusion.n_steps, (x_0.size(0),),
        ↪ device=device).long()

        # Create random noise
        noise = torch.randn_like(x_0)

        # Forward diffuse x_0 at step t
        x_t = diffusion.q_sample(x_0, t, noise=noise)

        # Predict the noise
        noise_pred = diffusion.predict_noise(model, x_t, t)

        # MSE loss
        loss = nn.functional.mse_loss(noise_pred, noise)

        optimizer.zero_grad()
        loss.backward()
        optimizer.step()

        epoch_loss += loss.item()

    return epoch_loss / len(dataloader)

def evaluate_model(model, diffusion, dataloader, device):
    model.eval()
    epoch_loss = 0.0
    with torch.no_grad():
        for batch in dataloader:
            x_0, _ = batch
            x_0 = x_0.to(device)
            t = torch.randint(0, diffusion.n_steps, (x_0.size(0),),
            ↪ device=device).long()
            noise = torch.randn_like(x_0)
            x_t = diffusion.q_sample(x_0, t, noise=noise)
            noise_pred = diffusion.predict_noise(model, x_t, t)
            loss = nn.functional.mse_loss(noise_pred, noise)
            epoch_loss += loss.item()
    return epoch_loss / len(dataloader)
```

```
# ------------------------------------------------------------
# 6) Visualization of a 3D voxel by plotting filled locations
# ------------------------------------------------------------
def visualize_voxel(voxel, threshold=0.0, save_path="voxel.png"):
    '''
    Simple 3D scatter plot of voxel > threshold.
    voxel is a 3D numpy array with shape [D, H, W].
    '''
    coords = np.argwhere(voxel > threshold)
    if coords.size == 0:
        # no points
        coords = np.array([[0,0,0]])
    fig = plt.figure(figsize=(5,5))
    ax = fig.add_subplot(projection='3d')
    xs, ys, zs = coords[:,0], coords[:,1], coords[:,2]
    ax.scatter(xs, ys, zs, s=1, c='red')
    ax.set_xlim([0, voxel.shape[0]])
    ax.set_ylim([0, voxel.shape[1]])
    ax.set_zlim([0, voxel.shape[2]])
    ax.invert_zaxis()
    ax.set_xlabel('X')
    ax.set_ylabel('Y')
    ax.set_zlabel('Z')
    plt.savefig(save_path)
    plt.close()

def sample_and_visualize(model, diffusion, device, epoch,
↪   guidance_scale=1.0):
    '''
    Samples new 3D shapes and saves a scatter plot for inspection.
    '''
    model.eval()
    with torch.no_grad():
        # shape: [1, 1, 32, 32, 32]
        x_gen = diffusion.p_sample_loop(model, (1, 1, 32, 32, 32),
        ↪   device, guidance_scale)
        # from [-1,1] to [0,1]
        x_gen = (x_gen.clamp(-1.0, 1.0) + 1) * 0.5
        # Visualize
        voxel_np = x_gen.squeeze(0).squeeze(0).cpu().numpy()
        visualize_voxel(voxel_np, threshold=0.5,
        ↪   save_path=f"epoch_{epoch}_gs_{guidance_scale}.png")

# ------------------------------------------------------------
# 7) Main script
# ------------------------------------------------------------
def main():
    set_seed(42)
    device = torch.device('cuda' if torch.cuda.is_available() else
    ↪   'cpu')

    # Create train/test dataset of random shapes
```

77

```
    train_dataset = RandomVoxelDataset(length=400, size=32)
    test_dataset = RandomVoxelDataset(length=100, size=32)

    train_loader = DataLoader(train_dataset, batch_size=4,
    ↪  shuffle=True)
    test_loader = DataLoader(test_dataset, batch_size=4,
    ↪  shuffle=False)

    # Define model, diffusion, and optimizer
    model = UNet3D(in_channels=1, out_channels=1,
    ↪  base_channels=16).to(device)
    diffusion = Diffusion3D(n_steps=100, beta_schedule='linear')
    optimizer = optim.Adam(model.parameters(), lr=1e-4)

    epochs = 2
    for epoch in range(epochs):
        train_loss = train_one_epoch(model, diffusion, optimizer,
        ↪  train_loader, device)
        val_loss = evaluate_model(model, diffusion, test_loader,
        ↪  device)
        print(f"Epoch [{epoch+1}/{epochs}] - Train Loss:
        ↪  {train_loss:.4f}, Val Loss: {val_loss:.4f}")

        # Sample a few shapes
        sample_and_visualize(model, diffusion, device, epoch,
        ↪  guidance_scale=1.0)
        sample_and_visualize(model, diffusion, device, epoch,
        ↪  guidance_scale=2.0)

    print("Training complete! Check the saved PNG files for shape
    ↪  visualizations.")

if __name__ == "__main__":
    main()
```

Key Implementation Details:

- **Forward Diffusion:** We use `q_sample` to add Gaussian noise to the initial 3D voxel grid (x_0) at a random time step t. The linear `beta_schedule` controls how much noise is added across timesteps.

- **Reverse Diffusion (Sampling):** In `p_sample_loop`, we start from random Gaussian noise in a 3D grid and iteratively apply `p_sample` to remove noise using the trained `UNet3D`, eventually obtaining a coherent 3D shape.

- **3D U-Net:** The `UNet3D` class adapts the 2D U-Net concept to 3D by using `Conv3d`, `MaxPool3d`, and `ConvTranspose3d`. Skip connections help preserve spatial details across layers.

- **Training Objective:** We directly predict the noise at each diffusion step and optimize an MSE loss between the model's prediction and the real noise, driving the model to learn the denoising process.

- **Guidance Scale:** A `guidance_scale` factor can be applied to the predicted noise at each reverse step, adjusting the trade-off between sampling diversity and shape fidelity.

- **Data Generation Loop:** The `RandomVoxelDataset` synthesizes basic shapes (spheres and cubes) to illustrate how the diffusion model can learn 3D structures from examples.

- **End-to-End Pipeline:** The `main` function initializes the dataset, trains the model over multiple epochs, and saves sampled 3D voxel visualizations that demonstrate the generative capabilities of the diffusion process.

Chapter 8

3D Shape Reconstruction from Partial Observations

This chapter focuses on reconstructing complete 3D shapes from partial scans or incomplete point clouds, commonly needed in robotics and VR. The diffusion pipeline is modified to accept partial geometry as a condition. During training, a partial mask is applied to the 3D representation, and noise is added to the missing regions. The network learns to fill in these missing parts while denoising the overall shape. Implementation steps include: (1) collecting datasets of complete 3D objects along with simulated partial scans, (2) adding noise across the entire 3D volume, (3) encoding partial observations as a mask or conditioning vector, (4) training the diffusion UNet to predict the noise in areas of missing geometry, and (5) sampling reconstructed shapes by reversing the process from noisy partial inputs. As an innovative technique, local shape priors are introduced for specific object classes to improve detail and accuracy in difficult reconstructions.

Python Code Snippet

```python
import os
import random
import math
import numpy as np
```

```python
import torch
import torch.nn as nn
from torch.utils.data import Dataset, DataLoader
import torch.optim as optim

# -------------------------------------------------------------
# 1) Set random seed for reproducibility
# -------------------------------------------------------------
def set_seed(seed=42):
    random.seed(seed)
    np.random.seed(seed)
    torch.manual_seed(seed)
    if torch.cuda.is_available():
        torch.cuda.manual_seed_all(seed)


# -------------------------------------------------------------
# 2) Create a simple 3D U-Net for volumetric denoising
# -------------------------------------------------------------
class DoubleConv3D(nn.Module):
    '''
    A helper module that performs two 3D convolutions (each followed
    ↪   by ReLU).
    '''
    def __init__(self, in_channels, out_channels):
        super(DoubleConv3D, self).__init__()
        self.conv = nn.Sequential(
            nn.Conv3d(in_channels, out_channels, kernel_size=3,
            ↪   padding=1),
            nn.ReLU(inplace=True),
            nn.Conv3d(out_channels, out_channels, kernel_size=3,
            ↪   padding=1),
            nn.ReLU(inplace=True)
        )

    def forward(self, x):
        return self.conv(x)

class UNet3D(nn.Module):
    '''
    A simplified 3D U-Net architecture with downsampling (encoder)
    and upsampling (decoder) blocks, plus skip connections.
    For this example, we treat partial volumes + noisy volumes as
    ↪   input (2 channels).
    The model predicts a single channel representing the noise in
    ↪   the ground truth shape.
    '''
    def __init__(self, in_channels=2, out_channels=1,
    ↪   base_channels=32):
        super(UNet3D, self).__init__()

        # Encoder (downsampling)
        self.down1 = DoubleConv3D(in_channels, base_channels)
        self.pool1 = nn.MaxPool3d(2)
```

```python
        self.down2 = DoubleConv3D(base_channels, base_channels*2)
        self.pool2 = nn.MaxPool3d(2)

        # Bottleneck
        self.bottleneck = DoubleConv3D(base_channels*2,
        ↪   base_channels*4)

        # Decoder (upsampling)
        self.up1 = nn.ConvTranspose3d(base_channels*4,
        ↪   base_channels*2, kernel_size=2, stride=2)
        self.conv_up1 = DoubleConv3D(base_channels*4,
        ↪   base_channels*2)

        self.up2 = nn.ConvTranspose3d(base_channels*2,
        ↪   base_channels, kernel_size=2, stride=2)
        self.conv_up2 = DoubleConv3D(base_channels*2, base_channels)

        # Final projection
        self.final_conv = nn.Conv3d(base_channels, out_channels,
        ↪   kernel_size=1)

    def forward(self, x):
        # x shape: (B, 2, D, H, W)
        x1 = self.down1(x)          # (B, base_channels, D, H, W)
        x2 = self.pool1(x1)         # (B, base_channels, D/2, H/2,
        ↪   W/2)

        x2 = self.down2(x2)         # (B, base_channels*2, ...)
        x3 = self.pool2(x2)         # (B, base_channels*2, D/4, H/4,
        ↪   W/4)

        b = self.bottleneck(x3)     # (B, base_channels*4, ...)

        x = self.up1(b)             # (B, base_channels*2, D/2, H/2,
        ↪   W/2)
        x = torch.cat([x, x2], dim=1)
        x = self.conv_up1(x)        # (B, base_channels*2, ...)

        x = self.up2(x)             # (B, base_channels, D, H, W)
        x = torch.cat([x, x1], dim=1)
        x = self.conv_up2(x)        # (B, base_channels, ...)

        out = self.final_conv(x)    # (B, out_channels, D, H, W)
        return out


# ----------------------------------------------------------------
# 3) Diffusion schedule and forward process for 3D shapes
# ----------------------------------------------------------------
def make_beta_schedule(schedule_name, n_timestep, start=1e-4,
↪   end=2e-2):
    '''
    Creates a beta schedule for the diffusion process.
    We use a linear schedule as a straightforward example.
```

82

```
    '''
    if schedule_name == "linear":
        return torch.linspace(start, end, n_timestep)
    else:
        raise NotImplementedError("Only 'linear' schedule is
        ↪   implemented here.")

class Diffusion3D:
    '''
    A class that encapsulates:
    1) The forward noising process: q(x_t | x_0)
    2) The reverse denoising process: p(x_{t-1} | x_t)
    3) Utility for training and sampling in 3D volumes.
    '''

    def __init__(self, n_steps=100, beta_schedule='linear'):
        self.n_steps = n_steps
        self.betas = make_beta_schedule(beta_schedule, n_steps)
        self.alphas = 1.0 - self.betas
        self.alpha_cumprod = torch.cumprod(self.alphas, dim=0)
        self.alpha_cumprod_prev = torch.cat(
            [torch.tensor([1.0]), self.alpha_cumprod[:-1]], dim=0
        )
        self.posterior_variance = self.betas * (1.0 -
        ↪   self.alpha_cumprod_prev) / \
                                  (1.0 - self.alpha_cumprod)

    def q_sample(self, x_start, t, noise=None):
        '''
        Forward diffusion: Adds noise to x_start at step t.
        x_t = sqrt(alpha_cumprod[t]) * x_start + sqrt(1 -
        ↪   alpha_cumprod[t]) * noise
        '''
        if noise is None:
            noise = torch.randn_like(x_start)
        shape = x_start.shape
        sqrt_alpha_cumprod_t =
        ↪   self.alpha_cumprod[t].sqrt().view(-1,1,1,1,1)
        sqrt_one_minus_alpha_cumprod_t = (1.0 -
        ↪   self.alpha_cumprod[t]).sqrt().view(-1,1,1,1,1)
        # We expand to match the batch dimension
        sqrt_alpha_cumprod_t = sqrt_alpha_cumprod_t.expand(shape[0],
        ↪   -1, shape[2], shape[3], shape[4])
        sqrt_one_minus_alpha_cumprod_t =
        ↪   sqrt_one_minus_alpha_cumprod_t.expand(
            shape[0], -1, shape[2], shape[3], shape[4]
        )

        return sqrt_alpha_cumprod_t * x_start +
        ↪   sqrt_one_minus_alpha_cumprod_t * noise

    def predict_noise(self, model, partial_data, x_t, device):
        '''
```

```
    The UNet model receives partial data + x_t as a 2-channel
    ⤷   input,
    and predicts the noise in the ground truth shape.
    '''
    inp = torch.cat([partial_data, x_t], dim=1).to(device)
    noise_pred = model(inp)
    return noise_pred

def p_sample(self, model, partial_data, x_t, t,
⤷ guidance_scale=1.0):
    '''
    One reverse diffusion step: p(x_{t-1} | x_t).
    The model predicts the noise e_t, and we compute the mean of
    ⤷   p(x_{t-1} | x_t, x_0).
    guidance_scale can alter the variance of the predicted
    ⤷   shape.
    '''
    betas_t = self.betas[t]
    alpha_t = self.alphas[t]
    alpha_cumprod_t = self.alpha_cumprod[t]
    alpha_cumprod_prev_t = self.alpha_cumprod_prev[t]

    e_t = self.predict_noise(model, partial_data, x_t,
    ⤷   x_t.device) * guidance_scale
    sqrt_recip_alpha_t = (1.0 / alpha_t).sqrt()
    x_0_hat = (x_t - (1.0 - alpha_t).sqrt() * e_t) *
    ⤷   sqrt_recip_alpha_t

    coef1 = (alpha_cumprod_prev_t.sqrt() * betas_t) / (1.0 -
    ⤷   alpha_cumprod_t)
    coef2 = ((1.0 - alpha_cumprod_prev_t) * alpha_t.sqrt()) /
    ⤷   (1.0 - alpha_cumprod_t)

    mean = coef1 * x_0_hat + coef2 * x_t
    posterior_var = self.posterior_variance[t]
    if t > 0:
        noise = torch.randn_like(x_t)
    else:
        noise = torch.zeros_like(x_t)

    x_prev = mean + noise * posterior_var.sqrt()
    return x_prev

def p_sample_loop(self, model, partial_data, shape, device,
⤷ guidance_scale=1.0):
    '''
    Repeatedly apply p_sample to go from x_T ~ N(0,I) to x_0.
    partial_data is kept constant as conditioning throughout.
    '''
    x_t = torch.randn(shape, device=device)
    for i in reversed(range(self.n_steps)):
        x_t = self.p_sample(model, partial_data, x_t, i,
        ⤷   guidance_scale=guidance_scale)
```

```
            return x_t

# -------------------------------------------------------------
# 4) Synthetic dataset for partial and complete 3D volumes
# -------------------------------------------------------------
class Partial3DShapesDataset(Dataset):
    '''
    A toy dataset that generates random 3D shapes (cubes or spheres)
    and simulates partial scans by zeroing out random sections.
    '''
    def __init__(self, length=1000, volume_size=32):
        super().__init__()
        self.length = length
        self.volume_size = volume_size

    def __len__(self):
        return self.length

    def __getitem__(self, idx):
        # Create an empty volume
        volume = np.zeros((self.volume_size, self.volume_size,
        ↪  self.volume_size), dtype=np.float32)

        # Random center, random radius or size
        shape_type = random.choice(["cube", "sphere"])
        if shape_type == "cube":
            size = random.randint(self.volume_size//8,
            ↪  self.volume_size//4)
            cx = random.randint(size, self.volume_size - size)
            cy = random.randint(size, self.volume_size - size)
            cz = random.randint(size, self.volume_size - size)
            volume[cx-size:cx+size, cy-size:cy+size,
            ↪  cz-size:cz+size] = 1.0
        else:
            radius = random.randint(self.volume_size//8,
            ↪  self.volume_size//4)
            cx = random.randint(radius, self.volume_size - radius)
            cy = random.randint(radius, self.volume_size - radius)
            cz = random.randint(radius, self.volume_size - radius)
            for x in range(cx-radius, cx+radius):
                for y in range(cy-radius, cy+radius):
                    for z in range(cz-radius, cz+radius):
                        if (x-cx)**2 + (y-cy)**2 + (z-cz)**2 <=
                        ↪  radius**2:
                            volume[x, y, z] = 1.0

        # Convert to torch tensor
        gt_3d = torch.from_numpy(volume).unsqueeze(0)  # shape: (1,
        ↪  D, H, W)

        # Create partial volume by zeroing out random planes
        partial_volume = gt_3d.clone()
```

```python
        # For example, randomly occlude some slices in depth
        ↪   dimension
        num_slices_to_remove = random.randint(1,
        ↪   self.volume_size//4)
        for _ in range(num_slices_to_remove):
            slice_idx = random.randint(0, self.volume_size-1)
            partial_volume[:, slice_idx, :, :] = 0.0

        return partial_volume, gt_3d


# --------------------------------------------------------------
# 5) Training and evaluation routines for 3D shape diffusion
# --------------------------------------------------------------
def train_one_epoch_3d(model, diffusion_3d, optimizer, dataloader,
↪   device):
    model.train()
    loss_sum = 0
    for partial_vol, gt_vol in dataloader:
        partial_vol = partial_vol.to(device)   # shape: (B, 1, D, H,
        ↪   W)
        gt_vol = gt_vol.to(device)             # shape: (B, 1, D, H,
        ↪   W)

        # For each batch, sample a random time step
        t = torch.randint(0, diffusion_3d.n_steps,
        ↪   (gt_vol.size(0),), device=device).long()

        # Create random noise
        noise = torch.randn_like(gt_vol)

        # Forward diffuse the real volume at step t
        x_t = diffusion_3d.q_sample(gt_vol, t, noise=noise)

        # Predict the noise with the model (conditioning on
        ↪   partial_vol)
        noise_pred = diffusion_3d.predict_noise(model, partial_vol,
        ↪   x_t, device)

        # L2 loss to match the real noise
        loss = nn.MSELoss()(noise_pred, noise)

        optimizer.zero_grad()
        loss.backward()
        optimizer.step()

        loss_sum += loss.item()

    return loss_sum / len(dataloader)

def evaluate_model_3d(model, diffusion_3d, dataloader, device):
    model.eval()
    loss_sum = 0
    with torch.no_grad():
```

```python
    for partial_vol, gt_vol in dataloader:
        partial_vol = partial_vol.to(device)
        gt_vol = gt_vol.to(device)
        t = torch.randint(0, diffusion_3d.n_steps,
        ↪    (gt_vol.size(0),), device=device).long()
        noise = torch.randn_like(gt_vol)
        x_t = diffusion_3d.q_sample(gt_vol, t, noise=noise)
        noise_pred = diffusion_3d.predict_noise(model,
        ↪    partial_vol, x_t, device)
        loss = nn.MSELoss()(noise_pred, noise)
        loss_sum += loss.item()
    return loss_sum / len(dataloader)

def sample_and_inspect_3d(model, diffusion_3d, partial_vol, device,
↪    guidance_scale=1.0):
    '''
    Given a single partial_vol, sample a reconstructed shape from
    ↪    random noise.
    We return the final predicted volume for inspection or further
    ↪    processing.
    '''
    model.eval()
    with torch.no_grad():
        shape = partial_vol.shape  # (B, 1, D, H, W)
        B, C, D, H, W = shape
        # We'll sample a single volume
        recon = diffusion_3d.p_sample_loop(
            model,
            partial_vol,
            shape=(B, C, D, H, W),
            device=device,
            guidance_scale=guidance_scale
        )
        return recon


# ----------------------------------------------------------------
# 6) Main script
# ----------------------------------------------------------------
def main():
    set_seed(42)
    device = torch.device('cuda' if torch.cuda.is_available() else
    ↪    'cpu')

    # Create a synthetic dataset with partial 3D shapes
    train_dataset = Partial3DShapesDataset(length=200,
    ↪    volume_size=32)
    test_dataset = Partial3DShapesDataset(length=50, volume_size=32)

    train_loader = DataLoader(train_dataset, batch_size=4,
    ↪    shuffle=True)
    test_loader = DataLoader(test_dataset, batch_size=4,
    ↪    shuffle=False)
```

```
# Create a 3D UNet
model_3d = UNet3D(in_channels=2, out_channels=1,
↪  base_channels=32).to(device)

# Diffusion process with 100 time steps
diffusion_3d = Diffusion3D(n_steps=100, beta_schedule='linear')

# Optimizer
optimizer = optim.Adam(model_3d.parameters(), lr=1e-4)

# Train for a few epochs
epochs = 5
for epoch in range(epochs):
    train_loss = train_one_epoch_3d(model_3d, diffusion_3d,
    ↪  optimizer, train_loader, device)
    val_loss = evaluate_model_3d(model_3d, diffusion_3d,
    ↪  test_loader, device)
    print(f"Epoch [{epoch+1}/{epochs}] - Train Loss:
    ↪  {train_loss:.4f}, Val Loss: {val_loss:.4f}")

# Try sampling on a few test volumes
partial_vol, gt_vol = next(iter(test_loader))
partial_vol, gt_vol = partial_vol[:1].to(device),
↪  gt_vol[:1].to(device)  # take one sample
reconstructed = sample_and_inspect_3d(model_3d, diffusion_3d,
↪  partial_vol, device, guidance_scale=1.0)

print("Reconstruction done. Shape of reconstructed volume:",
↪  reconstructed.shape)
# Optionally inspect slices from reconstructed or ground-truth
↪  volumes
# ...

print("Training and sampling complete!")

if __name__ == "__main__":
    main()
```

Key Implementation Details:

- **Forward Diffusion:** We implement `q_sample` to corrupt
  the ground truth volume by injecting noise according to a
  linear beta schedule across multiple timesteps.

- **Partial Geometry Conditioning:** The 3D `UNet3D` receives
  two channels as input—one for the partial volume and one
  for the noisy step volume. This enables the network to focus
  on filling missing regions.

- **Reverse Diffusion (Sampling):** The function `p_sample_loop` iteratively applies reverse steps to denoise from random initialization, guided by the known partial input.

- **3D UNet Architecture:** We adapt the 2D U-Net concept to 3D convolutions, pooling, and transposed convolutions. This retains spatial context across depth, height, and width.

- **Training Objective:** We minimize MSE between the predicted noise and the actual noise used during forward diffusion. This directs the network to learn how to accurately remove noise while respecting partial geometry constraints.

- **Local Shape Priors:** In real scenarios, known object-class priors can refine local shapes more accurately, but even this toy dataset demonstrates how partial volumes are reconstructed via denoising.

Chapter 9

Audio Denoising and Enhancement with Diffusion

This chapter applies diffusion modeling to clean or enhance audio signals, removing noise and improving clarity. Common usage spans from speech restoration in low-quality recordings to music remastering. We first represent the audio as a spectrogram or waveform. The forward diffusion gradually adds Gaussian noise to the audio representation across time steps. A convolutional or recurrent neural network, akin to a UNet adapted to time-frequency domains, is then trained to invert the noise. Key construction steps are:

- converting audio to a time-frequency spectrum.

- defining a noise schedule with increasing variance.

- using a 2D or 1D UNet to learn the reverse diffusion.

- minimizing an MSE or spectral-based loss on predicted vs. injected noise.

- doing iterative sampling to restore noisy audio.

A novel extension is to incorporate a multi-band approach, where separate sub-networks handle different frequency bands for enhanced fidelity.

Python Code Snippet

```python
import os
import random
import math
import torch
import torch.nn as nn
import torch.optim as optim
from torch.utils.data import Dataset, DataLoader
import torchaudio
import torchaudio.transforms as T
import matplotlib
matplotlib.use('Agg')
import matplotlib.pyplot as plt


# ----------------------------------------------------------------
# 1) Set random seed for reproducibility
# ----------------------------------------------------------------
def set_seed(seed=42):
    random.seed(seed)
    torch.manual_seed(seed)
    if torch.cuda.is_available():
        torch.cuda.manual_seed_all(seed)


# ----------------------------------------------------------------
# 2) Create a dataset class for loading audio files
# ----------------------------------------------------------------
class AudioDataset(Dataset):
    '''
    A dataset for loading .wav files from a specified directory.
    Returns a Mel spectrogram for each audio file.
    '''
    def __init__(self, root_dir, sample_rate=16000, n_fft=1024,
    ↪ hop_length=256, n_mels=80):
        super(AudioDataset, self).__init__()
        self.root_dir = root_dir
        self.files = [f for f in os.listdir(root_dir) if
        ↪ f.endswith('.wav')]
        self.sample_rate = sample_rate

        # MelSpectrogram for forward transform
        self.mel_transform = T.MelSpectrogram(
            sample_rate=sample_rate,
            n_fft=n_fft,
            hop_length=hop_length,
            n_mels=n_mels
        )

        # We use a GriffinLim transform to invert spectrograms for
        ↪ sampling
        self.griffin_lim = T.GriffinLim(
            n_fft=n_fft,
```

```python
            hop_length=hop_length
        )

        # Simple amplitude-based normalization
        self.amplitude_to_db = T.AmplitudeToDB()

    def __len__(self):
        return len(self.files)

    def __getitem__(self, idx):
        file_path = os.path.join(self.root_dir, self.files[idx])
        waveform, sr = torchaudio.load(file_path)

        # Ensure mono by picking first channel if more channels
        ↪ exist
        if waveform.size(0) > 1:
            waveform = waveform[:1, :]

        # Resample if needed
        if sr != self.sample_rate:
            resample_tf = T.Resample(sr, self.sample_rate)
            waveform = resample_tf(waveform)
            sr = self.sample_rate

        # Convert to Mel spectrogram -> shape: [n_mels, time]
        mel_spec = self.mel_transform(waveform)
        # Optionally convert amplitude to decibels
        mel_spec_db = self.amplitude_to_db(mel_spec)
        # Add channel dimension: [1, n_mels, time]
        mel_db_tensor = mel_spec_db.unsqueeze(0)

        return mel_db_tensor, 0  # Dummy label

# ---------------------------------------------------------------
# 3) Define a simple 2D U-Net for spectrogram denoising
# ---------------------------------------------------------------
class DoubleConv(nn.Module):
    '''
    A module that performs two consecutive convolutions (each
    ↪ followed by ReLU).
    Used as the basic building block in the U-Net.
    '''
    def __init__(self, in_channels, out_channels):
        super(DoubleConv, self).__init__()
        self.conv = nn.Sequential(
            nn.Conv2d(in_channels, out_channels, kernel_size=3,
            ↪ padding=1),
            nn.ReLU(inplace=True),
            nn.Conv2d(out_channels, out_channels, kernel_size=3,
            ↪ padding=1),
            nn.ReLU(inplace=True)
        )
```

```python
    def forward(self, x):
        return self.conv(x)

class UNet(nn.Module):
    '''
    A simplified U-Net architecture with down-sampling (encoder) and
    ↪  up-sampling (decoder),
    designed here for 2D spectrogram-like data. Skip connections
    ↪  merge encoder and decoder features.
    '''
    def __init__(self, in_channels=1, out_channels=1,
    ↪  base_channels=32):
        super(UNet, self).__init__()

        # Encoder
        self.down1 = DoubleConv(in_channels, base_channels)
        self.pool1 = nn.MaxPool2d(kernel_size=2)

        self.down2 = DoubleConv(base_channels, base_channels*2)
        self.pool2 = nn.MaxPool2d(kernel_size=2)

        self.down3 = DoubleConv(base_channels*2, base_channels*4)
        self.pool3 = nn.MaxPool2d(kernel_size=2)

        # Bottleneck
        self.bottleneck = DoubleConv(base_channels*4,
        ↪  base_channels*8)

        # Decoder
        self.up1 = nn.ConvTranspose2d(base_channels*8,
        ↪  base_channels*4, kernel_size=2, stride=2)
        self.conv_up1 = DoubleConv(base_channels*8, base_channels*4)

        self.up2 = nn.ConvTranspose2d(base_channels*4,
        ↪  base_channels*2, kernel_size=2, stride=2)
        self.conv_up2 = DoubleConv(base_channels*4, base_channels*2)

        self.up3 = nn.ConvTranspose2d(base_channels*2,
        ↪  base_channels, kernel_size=2, stride=2)
        self.conv_up3 = DoubleConv(base_channels*2, base_channels)

        self.final_conv = nn.Conv2d(base_channels, out_channels,
        ↪  kernel_size=1)

    def forward(self, x):
        # Encoder
        x1 = self.down1(x)
        x2 = self.pool1(x1)

        x2 = self.down2(x2)
        x3 = self.pool2(x2)

        x3 = self.down3(x3)
```

```python
        x4 = self.pool3(x3)

        # Bottleneck
        b = self.bottleneck(x4)

        # Decoder
        x = self.up1(b)
        x = torch.cat([x, x3], dim=1)
        x = self.conv_up1(x)

        x = self.up2(x)
        x = torch.cat([x, x2], dim=1)
        x = self.conv_up2(x)

        x = self.up3(x)
        x = torch.cat([x, x1], dim=1)
        x = self.conv_up3(x)

        return self.final_conv(x)


# --------------------------------------------------------------
# 4) Diffusion schedule and forward process
# --------------------------------------------------------------
def make_beta_schedule(schedule_name, n_timestep, start=1e-4,
↪    end=2e-2):
    '''
    Generates a beta schedule for the diffusion process.
    We implement a simple linear schedule here.
    '''
    if schedule_name == "linear":
        return torch.linspace(start, end, n_timestep)
    else:
        raise NotImplementedError("Only 'linear' schedule is
        ↪    implemented.")


class Diffusion:
    '''
    This class wraps:
    1) The forward noising process: q(x_t | x_0)
    2) The reverse sampling process: p(x_{t-1} | x_t)
    3) Utilities for training and inference (sampling).
    '''

    def __init__(self, n_steps=200, beta_schedule='linear'):
        self.n_steps = n_steps
        self.betas = make_beta_schedule(beta_schedule, n_steps)   #
        ↪    shape [n_steps]
        self.alphas = 1.0 - self.betas
        self.alpha_cumprod = torch.cumprod(self.alphas, dim=0)   #
        ↪    cumprod of alphas
        self.alpha_cumprod_prev = torch.cat(
            [torch.tensor([1.0]), self.alpha_cumprod[:-1]], dim=0
        )
```

```python
        # For posterior q(x_{t-1} | x_t, x_0)
        self.posterior_variance = self.betas * (1.0 -
        ↪  self.alpha_cumprod_prev) / (1.0 - self.alpha_cumprod)

    def q_sample(self, x_start, t, noise=None):
        '''
        Forward diffusion: x_t = sqrt(alpha_cumprod[t]) * x_start +
        ↪  sqrt(1 - alpha_cumprod[t]) * noise
        '''
        if noise is None:
            noise = torch.randn_like(x_start)

        sqrt_alpha_cumprod_t =
        ↪  self.alpha_cumprod[t].sqrt().view(-1,1,1,1)
        sqrt_one_minus_alpha_cumprod_t = (1 -
        ↪  self.alpha_cumprod[t]).sqrt().view(-1,1,1,1)

        return sqrt_alpha_cumprod_t * x_start +
        ↪  sqrt_one_minus_alpha_cumprod_t * noise

    def predict_noise(self, model, x_t, t):
        '''
        Use the UNet model to predict the noise at timestep t.
        The model's forward pass is conditioned on x_t only
        ↪  (unconditional version).
        '''
        return model(x_t)

    def p_sample(self, model, x_t, t, guidance_scale=1.0):
        '''
        Single reverse diffusion step: p(x_{t-1} | x_t).
        The model predicts the noise e_t, which we then use to
        ↪  compute the mean of q(x_{t-1} | x_t, x_0).
        We incorporate a simple guidance scale on the predicted
        ↪  noise.
        '''
        betas_t = self.betas[t]
        alpha_t = self.alphas[t]
        alpha_cumprod_t = self.alpha_cumprod[t]
        alpha_cumprod_prev_t = self.alpha_cumprod_prev[t]

        # Model's noise prediction
        e_t = model(x_t) * guidance_scale

        # Approximate x_0:   x_0 ~ (x_t - sqrt(1-alpha_t)* e_t) /
        ↪  sqrt(alpha_t)
        sqrt_recip_alpha_t = (1.0 / alpha_t).sqrt()
        x_0_hat = (x_t - (1.0 - alpha_t).sqrt() * e_t) *
        ↪  sqrt_recip_alpha_t

        # Coefficients for the posterior mean
        coef1 = (alpha_cumprod_prev_t.sqrt() * betas_t) / (1.0 -
        ↪  alpha_cumprod_t)
```

```python
        coef2 = ((1.0 - alpha_cumprod_prev_t) * alpha_t.sqrt()) /
        ↪  (1.0 - alpha_cumprod_t)
        mean = coef1 * x_0_hat + coef2 * x_t

        # Posterior variance
        posterior_var = self.posterior_variance[t]
        if t > 0:
            noise = torch.randn_like(x_t)
        else:
            noise = torch.zeros_like(x_t)

        x_prev = mean + noise * posterior_var.sqrt()
        return x_prev

    def p_sample_loop(self, model, shape, device,
    ↪  guidance_scale=1.0):
        '''
        Iteratively apply p_sample from T to 1, starting from x_T ~
        ↪  N(0, I),
        to reconstruct a clean spectrogram x_0.
        '''
        x_t = torch.randn(shape, device=device)
        for i in reversed(range(self.n_steps)):
            x_t = self.p_sample(model, x_t, i,
            ↪  guidance_scale=guidance_scale)
        return x_t

# ---------------------------------------------------------------
# 5) Training and evaluation loops
# ---------------------------------------------------------------
def train_one_epoch(model, diffusion, optimizer, dataloader,
↪  device):
    model.train()
    epoch_loss = 0
    for mel_specs, _ in dataloader:
        mel_specs = mel_specs.to(device)  # shape: [B, 1, n_mels,
        ↪  time]

        # Sample a random time step for each example in the batch
        t = torch.randint(0, diffusion.n_steps,
        ↪  (mel_specs.size(0),), device=device).long()

        # Generate random noise
        noise = torch.randn_like(mel_specs)

        # Forward-diffuse the mel spectrogram
        x_t = diffusion.q_sample(mel_specs, t, noise=noise)

        # Predict the noise with the model
        noise_pred = diffusion.predict_noise(model, x_t, t)

        # MSE loss
        loss = nn.functional.mse_loss(noise_pred, noise)
```

96

```
        optimizer.zero_grad()
        loss.backward()
        optimizer.step()

        epoch_loss += loss.item()

    return epoch_loss / len(dataloader)

def evaluate_model(model, diffusion, dataloader, device):
    model.eval()
    val_loss = 0
    with torch.no_grad():
        for mel_specs, _ in dataloader:
            mel_specs = mel_specs.to(device)
            t = torch.randint(0, diffusion.n_steps,
              ↪  (mel_specs.size(0),), device=device).long()
            noise = torch.randn_like(mel_specs)
            x_t = diffusion.q_sample(mel_specs, t, noise=noise)
            noise_pred = diffusion.predict_noise(model, x_t, t)
            loss = nn.functional.mse_loss(noise_pred, noise)
            val_loss += loss.item()
    return val_loss / len(dataloader)


# ----------------------------------------------------------------
# 6) Sampling routine
#    - We demonstrate how to recover audio from the generated
↪    spectrogram
#      using the GriffinLim algorithm.
# ----------------------------------------------------------------
def sample_and_save(model, diffusion, device, epoch,
↪  sample_rate=16000, n_mels=80, name_prefix="sample",
↪  guidance_scale=1.0):
    model.eval()
    with torch.no_grad():
        # We'll generate a single random sample:
        batch_size = 1
        # In practice, you'd match the typical spectrogram
        ↪   dimensions from your data
        # shape: (B, 1, n_mels, T)
        # Let's pick T=128 frames for demonstration
        generated_spec = diffusion.p_sample_loop(
            model, (batch_size, 1, n_mels, 128), device,
            ↪   guidance_scale=guidance_scale
        )

        # "Undo" the amplitude-to-dB transform by exponentiating,
        # but recall we used AmplitudeToDB. We'll do a rough
        ↪   inversion here:
        # So if y_db = 10 * log10(y), then y = 10^(y_db/10)
        # We'll clamp for safety to avoid extremely large values
        generated_spec = generated_spec.squeeze(0).clamp(-100, 100)
```

```python
        generated_spec_lin = torch.pow(torch.tensor(10.0),
        ↪  generated_spec / 10.0)

        # Use GriffinLim to invert the mel spectrogram
        # We constructed mel specs with T.MelSpectrogram, but direct
        # GriffinLim on mel spectrogram is not a perfect reversion.
        # For demonstration, let's pretend we can invert from mel to
        ↪  wave directly:
        # In a real pipeline, you might store linear spectrogram or
        ↪  use
        # a specialized mel-inversion model (e.g., a vocoder).

        # We can still use a basic T.InverseMelScale + T.GriffinLim
        ↪  approach:
        inv_mel_scale = T.InverseMelScale(
            n_stft=512,  # n_fft/2
            n_mels=n_mels,
            sample_rate=sample_rate
        ).to(device)

        griffin_lim = T.GriffinLim(
            n_fft=1024,
            hop_length=256
        ).to(device)

        # Move the generated_spec_lin to device
        generated_spec_lin = generated_spec_lin.to(device)
        linear_spec = inv_mel_scale(generated_spec_lin)
        # shape: [frequency_bins, time_frames]

        # Now apply GriffinLim
        audio_waveform = griffin_lim(linear_spec.unsqueeze(0))
        # shape: [1, time_samples]

        # Save the audio to disk
        out_dir = "audio_results"
        os.makedirs(out_dir, exist_ok=True)
        file_name =
        ↪  f"{name_prefix}_epoch_{epoch}_gs_{guidance_scale}.wav"
        out_path = os.path.join(out_dir, file_name)

        # Detach to CPU, convert to float for saving
        audio_waveform = audio_waveform.detach().cpu()
        torchaudio.save(out_path, audio_waveform, sample_rate)
        print(f"Saved sample with guidance scale {guidance_scale} to
        ↪  {out_path}")

# ------------------------------------------------------------
# 7) Main script: load data, initialize model, and train
# ------------------------------------------------------------
def main():
    set_seed(42)
```

```python
device = torch.device("cuda" if torch.cuda.is_available() else
↳   "cpu")

# Paths to training and testing folders (each containing .wav
↳   files)
train_folder = "data/train"
test_folder = "data/test"

# Dataset and DataLoader
train_dataset = AudioDataset(train_folder)
test_dataset = AudioDataset(test_folder)

train_loader = DataLoader(train_dataset, batch_size=4,
↳   shuffle=True)
test_loader = DataLoader(test_dataset, batch_size=4,
↳   shuffle=False)

# Instantiate the UNet
model = UNet(in_channels=1, out_channels=1,
↳   base_channels=32).to(device)

# Diffusion process
diffusion = Diffusion(n_steps=200, beta_schedule='linear')

# Optimizer
optimizer = optim.Adam(model.parameters(), lr=1e-4)

# Training loop
epochs = 5
for epoch in range(epochs):
    train_loss = train_one_epoch(model, diffusion, optimizer,
    ↳   train_loader, device)
    val_loss = evaluate_model(model, diffusion, test_loader,
    ↳   device)

    print(f"Epoch [{epoch+1}/{epochs}]: Train Loss:
    ↳   {train_loss:.4f}, Val Loss: {val_loss:.4f}")

    # Sample and reconstruct audio to hear progress
    sample_and_save(model, diffusion, device, epoch,
    ↳   guidance_scale=1.0)
    sample_and_save(model, diffusion, device, epoch,
    ↳   guidance_scale=2.0)

print("Training complete! Check 'audio_results' folder for
↳   generated samples.")

if __name__ == "__main__":
    main()
```

Key Implementation Details:

- **Forward Diffusion:** The function `q_sample` gradually corrupts an audio spectrogram with noise, using a time-dependent variance defined by a linear `beta` schedule.

- **Reverse Diffusion (Sampling):** `p_sample_loop` iteratively denoises from random noise to reconstruct a clean mel spectrogram. Each step calls `p_sample`, which uses the model's noise prediction to compute the posterior distribution and draw the next sample.

- **UNet Architecture:** While originally popular for images, a 2D `UNet` can process mel spectrograms (frequency vs. time) by leveraging downsampling, upsampling, and skip connections to capture multi-scale context in the spectrogram.

- **Training Objective:** The mean-squared error (MSE) between the predicted noise and the actual Gaussian noise is minimized at each step, driving the model to accurately invert the diffusion process.

- **Spectrogram Inversion:** Because we use Mel spectrograms, the code demonstrates a minimal approach with `InverseMelScale` and `GriffinLim` to approximate waveform inversion. In practice, a more sophisticated vocoder may be used for higher fidelity.

- **Multi-Band Extension:** The code can be extended to split the spectrogram into multiple frequency bands, training specialized sub-networks for each band and merging their outputs for enhanced clarity and realism.

- **End-to-End Workflow:** The `main` function orchestrates data loading, training, validation, and sampling, providing a self-contained pipeline for audio denoising and restoration via diffusion.

Chapter 10

Speech Enhancement and Dereverberation

Here, diffusion methods are specialized for speech cleaning by targeting room reverberation, background chatter, or echo artifacts. Common use cases include real-time communication and studio audio production. The approach begins with a dataset of clean speech and artificially reverberated or noisy recordings. A forward process adds various forms of distortion to the clean signal, and the diffusion network learns to reverse it. Implementation involves: (1) representing audio via short-time Fourier transform or mel spectrogram, (2) injecting reverberation and random noise to replicate real-world conditions, (3) building a UNet that handles the time-frequency representation, (4) training with a loss function focusing on phase and magnitude consistency, and (5) iteratively reconstructing anechoic speech signals. The innovative element is a real-time inference technique that approximates the iterative reverse process with fewer steps, enabling near-instant speech enhancement.

Python Code Snippet

```
import os
import random
import math
import torch
import torchaudio
import torchaudio.functional as AF
```

```python
import torch.nn as nn
import torch.nn.functional as F
from torch.utils.data import Dataset, DataLoader
import torch.optim as optim


# ----------------------------------------------------------------
# 1) Set random seed for reproducibility
# ----------------------------------------------------------------
def set_seed(seed=42):
    random.seed(seed)
    torch.manual_seed(seed)
    if torch.cuda.is_available():
        torch.cuda.manual_seed_all(seed)


# ----------------------------------------------------------------
# 2) Dataset for speech, applying artificial distortion
# ----------------------------------------------------------------
class SpeechDataset(Dataset):
    '''
    Loads clean audio files and applies random reverb + noise.
    Then converts both clean and distorted waveforms to Mel
    ↪  spectrograms.
    '''
    def __init__(self, data_dir, sample_rate=16000, n_mels=64,
    ↪  max_audio_len=3.0):
        super().__init__()
        self.sample_rate = sample_rate
        self.max_audio_len = max_audio_len
        self.audio_paths = []
        for root, _, files in os.walk(data_dir):
            for f in files:
                if f.endswith('.wav'):
                    self.audio_paths.append(os.path.join(root, f))

        self.mel_transform = torchaudio.transforms.MelSpectrogram(
            sample_rate=sample_rate,
            n_mels=n_mels,
            n_fft=1024,
            hop_length=256,
            win_length=1024
        )

    def __len__(self):
        return len(self.audio_paths)

    def __getitem__(self, idx):
        path = self.audio_paths[idx]
        clean_waveform, sr = torchaudio.load(path)
        if sr != self.sample_rate:
            clean_waveform =
            ↪  torchaudio.functional.resample(clean_waveform, sr,
            ↪  self.sample_rate)
```

102

```python
        # Trim or pad to fixed length for consistency
        max_len_samples = int(self.max_audio_len * self.sample_rate)
        clean_waveform = self._trim_or_pad(clean_waveform,
        ↪    max_len_samples)

        # Distort with random reverb + noise
        distorted_waveform =
        ↪    self.simulate_distortion(clean_waveform)

        # Convert to mel spectrograms
        clean_spec = self._waveform_to_mel(clean_waveform)
        distorted_spec = self._waveform_to_mel(distorted_waveform)

        # Shape [n_mels, time] => Expand so final shape: [1, n_mels,
        ↪    time]
        return distorted_spec.unsqueeze(0), clean_spec.unsqueeze(0)

    def _trim_or_pad(self, waveform, max_len):
        length = waveform.shape[1]
        if length > max_len:
            waveform = waveform[:, :max_len]
        elif length < max_len:
            pad_amount = max_len - length
            waveform = F.pad(waveform, (0,pad_amount))
        return waveform

    def simulate_distortion(self, waveform):
        '''
        Applies a random reverb-like convolution and random noise.
        '''
        # Random impulse response (IR) for reverb
        ir = self._random_reverb_ir()
        # Apply IR (conv1d expects shape: [batch, channel, time])
        w = waveform.unsqueeze(0)   # [1, channel, time]
        ir_reshaped = ir.unsqueeze(0).unsqueeze(0)   # [1, 1,
        ↪    ir_length]
        reverbed = F.conv1d(w, ir_reshaped,
        ↪    padding=int(ir.shape[0]//2))
        reverbed = reverbed.squeeze(0)   # back to [channel, time]

        # Random noise
        snr_db = random.uniform(10, 30)   # random SNR between 10-30
        ↪    dB
        snr_linear = 10 ** (snr_db / 10)
        signal_power = reverbed.pow(2).mean()
        noise_power = signal_power / snr_linear
        noise = torch.sqrt(noise_power) * torch.randn_like(reverbed)

        # Mix
        distorted = reverbed + noise
        return distorted

    def _random_reverb_ir(self, max_length=256):
```

103

```python
        length = random.randint(max_length // 2, max_length)
        ir = torch.zeros(length)
        # Randomly place some spikes
        for i in range(length):
            if random.random() < 0.02:
                ir[i] = random.uniform(0.5, 1.0)
        # Normalize to avoid extreme gains
        if ir.abs().sum() > 0:
            ir = ir / ir.abs().sum()
        else:
            ir[0] = 1.0
        return ir

    def _waveform_to_mel(self, waveform):
        '''
        Returns a log-mel spectrogram.
        '''
        with torch.no_grad():
            spec = self.mel_transform(waveform)
            # Spec shape: [channel, n_mels, time], take channel 0
            spec = spec[0]
            # Log scale (avoid log(0))
            spec = torch.log(spec + 1e-8)
        return spec


# ----------------------------------------------------------------
# 3) U-Net for time-frequency denoising
# ----------------------------------------------------------------
class DoubleConv(nn.Module):
    '''
    A helper module that performs two convolutions (each followed by
    ↪    ReLU)
    to reduce boilerplate in the U-Net.
    '''
    def __init__(self, in_channels, out_channels):
        super(DoubleConv, self).__init__()
        self.conv = nn.Sequential(
            nn.Conv2d(in_channels, out_channels, kernel_size=3,
            ↪    padding=1),
            nn.ReLU(inplace=True),
            nn.Conv2d(out_channels, out_channels, kernel_size=3,
            ↪    padding=1),
            nn.ReLU(inplace=True)
        )

    def forward(self, x):
        return self.conv(x)

class SpeechUNet(nn.Module):
    '''
    A simplified U-Net architecture for time-frequency
    ↪    representation:
```

104

```
input shape: [B, in_channels=1, n_mels, time]
output shape: [B, out_channels=1, n_mels, time]
'''
def __init__(self, in_channels=1, out_channels=1,
↪  base_channels=64):
    super(SpeechUNet, self).__init__()

    # Down-sampling (encoder)
    self.down1 = DoubleConv(in_channels, base_channels)
    self.down2 = DoubleConv(base_channels, base_channels*2)
    self.down3 = DoubleConv(base_channels*2, base_channels*4)

    self.pool = nn.MaxPool2d(kernel_size=2)

    # Bottleneck
    self.bottleneck = DoubleConv(base_channels*4,
    ↪  base_channels*8)

    # Up-sampling (decoder)
    self.up1 = nn.ConvTranspose2d(base_channels*8,
    ↪  base_channels*4, kernel_size=2, stride=2)
    self.conv_up1 = DoubleConv(base_channels*8, base_channels*4)

    self.up2 = nn.ConvTranspose2d(base_channels*4,
    ↪  base_channels*2, kernel_size=2, stride=2)
    self.conv_up2 = DoubleConv(base_channels*4, base_channels*2)

    self.up3 = nn.ConvTranspose2d(base_channels*2,
    ↪  base_channels, kernel_size=2, stride=2)
    self.conv_up3 = DoubleConv(base_channels*2, base_channels)

    # Final output
    self.final_conv = nn.Conv2d(base_channels, out_channels,
    ↪  kernel_size=1)

def forward(self, x):
    # Encoder
    x1 = self.down1(x)
    x2 = self.pool(x1)

    x2 = self.down2(x2)
    x3 = self.pool(x2)

    x3 = self.down3(x3)
    x4 = self.pool(x3)

    # Bottleneck
    b = self.bottleneck(x4)

    # Decoder
    x = self.up1(b)
    x = torch.cat([x, x3], dim=1)
    x = self.conv_up1(x)
```

```python
        x = self.up2(x)
        x = torch.cat([x, x2], dim=1)
        x = self.conv_up2(x)

        x = self.up3(x)
        x = torch.cat([x, x1], dim=1)
        x = self.conv_up3(x)

        # Final
        out = self.final_conv(x)
        return out


# ----------------------------------------------------------------
# 4) Define diffusion schedule and forward process
# ----------------------------------------------------------------
def make_beta_schedule(schedule_name, n_timestep, start=1e-4,
↪   end=2e-2):
    '''
    Creates a beta schedule for the diffusion process.
    We use a linear schedule as a straightforward example.
    '''
    if schedule_name == "linear":
        return torch.linspace(start, end, n_timestep)
    else:
        raise NotImplementedError("Only 'linear' schedule is
        ↪   implemented here.")


class Diffusion:
    '''
    A class that encapsulates:
    1) The forward noising process: q(x_t | x_0)
    2) The reverse denoising process: p(x_{t-1} | x_t)
    3) Utility for training and sampling on spectrograms.
    '''
    def __init__(self, n_steps=200, beta_schedule='linear'):
        self.n_steps = n_steps
        self.betas = make_beta_schedule(beta_schedule, n_steps)
        self.alphas = 1.0 - self.betas
        self.alpha_cumprod = torch.cumprod(self.alphas, dim=0)
        self.alpha_cumprod_prev = torch.cat(
            [torch.tensor([1.0]), self.alpha_cumprod[:-1]],
            dim=0
        )
        # Posterior variance for p(x_{t-1}| x_t, x_0)
        self.posterior_variance = self.betas * (1.0 -
        ↪   self.alpha_cumprod_prev) / (1.0 - self.alpha_cumprod)

    def q_sample(self, x_start, t, noise=None):
        '''
        Forward diffusion: Adds noise to x_start at step t.
```

```python
x_t = sqrt(alpha_cumprod[t]) * x_start + sqrt(1 -
↪ alpha_cumprod[t]) * noise
'''

if noise is None:
    noise = torch.randn_like(x_start)
sqrt_alpha_cumprod_t =
↪ self.alpha_cumprod[t].sqrt().view(-1,1,1,1)
sqrt_one_minus_alpha_cumprod_t = (1 -
↪ self.alpha_cumprod[t]).sqrt().view(-1,1,1,1)

return sqrt_alpha_cumprod_t * x_start +
↪ sqrt_one_minus_alpha_cumprod_t * noise

def predict_noise(self, model, x_t, t):
    '''
    Use the SpeechUNet model to predict the noise added at step
    ↪ t.
    '''
    return model(x_t)

def p_sample(self, model, x_t, t, guidance_scale=1.0):
    '''
    One reverse diffusion step: p(x_{t-1} | x_t).
    Model predicts the noise e_t, then we compute the mean of
    ↪ p(x_{t-1} | x_t, x_0).
    '''
    betas_t = self.betas[t].view(-1,1,1,1)
    alpha_t = self.alphas[t].view(-1,1,1,1)
    alpha_cumprod_t = self.alpha_cumprod[t].view(-1,1,1,1)
    alpha_cumprod_prev_t =
    ↪ self.alpha_cumprod_prev[t].view(-1,1,1,1)

    e_t = model(x_t) * guidance_scale

    sqrt_recip_alpha_t = (1.0 / alpha_t).sqrt()
    # x_0 estimate
    x_0_hat = (x_t - (1.0 - alpha_t).sqrt() * e_t) *
    ↪ sqrt_recip_alpha_t

    coef1 = ((alpha_cumprod_prev_t).sqrt() * betas_t) / (1.0 -
    ↪ alpha_cumprod_t)
    coef2 = ((1.0 - alpha_cumprod_prev_t) * alpha_t.sqrt()) /
    ↪ (1.0 - alpha_cumprod_t)

    mean = coef1 * x_0_hat + coef2 * x_t

    posterior_var = self.posterior_variance[t].view(-1,1,1,1)
    if t > 0:
        noise = torch.randn_like(x_t)
    else:
        noise = torch.zeros_like(x_t)

    x_prev = mean + noise * posterior_var.sqrt()
```

```
        return x_prev

    def p_sample_loop(self, model, shape, device,
    ↪    guidance_scale=1.0):
        '''
        Repeatedly apply p_sample to go from x_T ~ N(0,I) to x_0
        ↪    (enhanced spectrogram).
        '''
        x_t = torch.randn(shape, device=device)
        for i in reversed(range(self.n_steps)):
            x_t = self.p_sample(model, x_t, i,
            ↪    guidance_scale=guidance_scale)
        return x_t


# --------------------------------------------------------------
# 5) Training and evaluation routines
# --------------------------------------------------------------
def train_one_epoch(model, diffusion, optimizer, dataloader,
↪    device):
    model.train()
    total_loss = 0
    for distorted_spec, clean_spec in dataloader:
        distorted_spec = distorted_spec.to(device)
        clean_spec = clean_spec.to(device)

        # Random timestep
        t = torch.randint(0, diffusion.n_steps,
        ↪    (distorted_spec.size(0),), device=device).long()

        # Random noise
        noise = torch.randn_like(distorted_spec)

        # Forward diffuse the target (clean_spec) at step t
        x_t = diffusion.q_sample(clean_spec, t, noise=noise)

        # Predict the noise
        noise_pred = diffusion.predict_noise(model, x_t, t)

        # L2 loss
        loss = F.mse_loss(noise_pred, noise)

        optimizer.zero_grad()
        loss.backward()
        optimizer.step()

        total_loss += loss.item()
    return total_loss / len(dataloader)

def evaluate_model(model, diffusion, dataloader, device):
    model.eval()
    total_loss = 0
    with torch.no_grad():
```

```python
    for distorted_spec, clean_spec in dataloader:
        distorted_spec = distorted_spec.to(device)
        clean_spec = clean_spec.to(device)

        t = torch.randint(0, diffusion.n_steps,
        ↪    (distorted_spec.size(0),), device=device).long()
        noise = torch.randn_like(clean_spec)
        x_t = diffusion.q_sample(clean_spec, t, noise=noise)
        noise_pred = diffusion.predict_noise(model, x_t, t)
        loss = F.mse_loss(noise_pred, noise)
        total_loss += loss.item()
    return total_loss / len(dataloader)


# ----------------------------------------------------------------
# 6) Sampling (enhancement) and saving results
# ----------------------------------------------------------------
def enhance_and_save(model, diffusion, device, mel_transform,
↪   output_dir, file_prefix,
                     sample_rate=16000, n_fft=1024, hop_length=256):
    '''
    Enhances random noise using the reverse diffusion process and
    reconstructs a waveform from the predicted log-mel spectrogram.
    '''
    model.eval()
    os.makedirs(output_dir, exist_ok=True)
    with torch.no_grad():
        # Suppose we generate a batch of random shapes
        batch_size = 4
        n_mels = mel_transform.n_mels
        # We do not know the time dimension ahead of time, pick a
        ↪   small random length
        random_time = 100
        shape = (batch_size, 1, n_mels, random_time)

        enhanced_spec = diffusion.p_sample_loop(model, shape,
        ↪   device, guidance_scale=1.0)
        # Convert from log-mel to magnitude
        enhanced_spec = torch.exp(enhanced_spec)  # remove the log
        # Use GriffinLim to recover waveforms from mel. This is a
        ↪   rough approach.

        # Here, we attempt a naive mapping: mel -> linear -> wave
        # A more accurate approach would need an inverse mel filter
        ↪   bank + Griffin-Lim.
        # We'll do a partial demonstration for brevity.

        # Reconstruct waveforms one by one
        for i in range(batch_size):
            mag_i = enhanced_spec[i, 0].cpu()  # shape [n_mels,
            ↪   time]
            # Construct approximate wave via a mel->linear
            ↪   approximation
```

109

```python
        # We'll use torchaudio.transforms.Resize and then
        ↪ GriffinLim on freq dimension
        # or just demonstrate direct GriffinLim on the 'mag_i'
        ↪ as if it's full STFT.
        # This is not perfect but shown as a conceptual example.

        # Expand freq dimension to a typical STFT size to match
        ↪ n_fft.
        # We'll just pad or interpolate to n_fft//2+1 freq bins
        ↪ for demonstration.
        target_freq_bins = n_fft // 2 + 1
        mel_bins = mag_i.shape[0]
        # Resize freq dimension
        mag_i = mag_i.unsqueeze(0).unsqueeze(0)   #
        ↪ [1,1,n_mels,time]
        resize = nn.Upsample(size=(target_freq_bins,
        ↪ mag_i.shape[-1]), mode='bilinear')
        mag_lin = resize(mag_i).squeeze(0).squeeze(0)   #
        ↪ [freq_bins, time]

        # Use GriffinLim
        wave_enh = AF.griffinlim(mag_lin,
                                 n_fft=n_fft,
                                 hop_length=hop_length,

                                 ↪ window=torch.hann_window(n_fft),
                                 power=1.0,
                                 n_iter=32)
        # Save to file
        out_path = os.path.join(output_dir,
        ↪ f"{file_prefix}_sample_{i}.wav")
        torchaudio.save(out_path, wave_enh.unsqueeze(0),
        ↪ sample_rate)


# ------------------------------------------------------------
# 7) Main script: load data, initialize model, and train
# ------------------------------------------------------------
def main():
    set_seed(42)
    device = torch.device('cuda' if torch.cuda.is_available() else
    ↪ 'cpu')

    # Create dataset and dataloader
    train_dataset = SpeechDataset(data_dir='data/clean',
    ↪ sample_rate=16000, n_mels=64)
    train_loader = DataLoader(train_dataset, batch_size=8,
    ↪ shuffle=True, num_workers=0)

    # For simplicity, reuse the same set for validation
    val_dataset = SpeechDataset(data_dir='data/clean',
    ↪ sample_rate=16000, n_mels=64)
```

```python
val_loader = DataLoader(val_dataset, batch_size=8,
↪   shuffle=False, num_workers=0)

# Initialize UNet
model = SpeechUNet(in_channels=1, out_channels=1,
↪   base_channels=32).to(device)

# Define diffusion
diffusion = Diffusion(n_steps=200, beta_schedule='linear')

# Optimizer
optimizer = optim.Adam(model.parameters(), lr=1e-4)

# Train
epochs = 3
for epoch in range(epochs):
    train_loss = train_one_epoch(model, diffusion, optimizer,
↪       train_loader, device)
    val_loss = evaluate_model(model, diffusion, val_loader,
↪       device)
    print(f"Epoch [{epoch+1}/{epochs}] - Train Loss:
↪       {train_loss:.4f}, Val Loss: {val_loss:.4f}")

# After training, run a quick enhancement example with random
↪   shapes
# We reuse MelSpectrogram from dataset:
sample_mel_transform = train_dataset.mel_transform
enhance_and_save(model, diffusion, device, sample_mel_transform,
                 output_dir="enhanced_results",
↪                file_prefix="epoch_final",
                 sample_rate=16000)
print("Speech enhancement complete. Check 'enhanced_results'
↪   folder for samples.")

if __name__ == "__main__":
    main()
```

Key Implementation Details:

- **Short-Time Fourier Transform Representation:** We convert speech waveforms to log-mel spectrograms. This lets the diffusion model operate in the time-frequency domain for enhanced phase/magnitude consistency.

- **Forward Diffusion (q_sample):** Noise is added gradually to the clean spectrogram at random diffusion steps. This simulates the corruption process the model must learn to invert.

- **Reverse Diffusion (p_sample_loop):** Iteratively removes

111

noise, generating an enhanced spectrogram. We demonstrate a guidance parameter that can scale the predicted noise for potential variation trade-offs.

- **Speech-Focused U-Net:** The `SpeechUNet` is adapted for spectrogram inputs (two spatial dimensions: frequency and time). Skip connections preserve fine structure useful for accurate denoising.

- **Training Objective:** We deploy a mean-squared error (MSE) loss between the predicted noise and the true noise injected into the clean spectrogram. This straightforward approach often yields good speech quality.

- **Real-Time Inference Approximation:** By reducing the total diffusion steps or applying smaller updates at each iteration, near-instant speech enhancement can be approximated without fully iterating over the entire diffusion chain.

Chapter 11

Audio Generation for Music Composition and Effects

Diffusion models can be harnessed for music generation, allowing the creation of tunes or audio textures from scratch. Common applications include AI-assisted composition, sound design, and effect generation. Construction starts by encoding raw waveforms or spectrogram tokens, then applying a noise schedule to these representations. A specialized architecture, often combining convolution and attention, is trained to recover the uncorrupted spectrogram. Implementation details: (1) gather a variety of music tracks, covering multiple genres, (2) convert them to a consistent spectral format, (3) define a forward noise process that corrupts the spectrogram frames, (4) train a diffusion network to predict the noise while capturing harmonic and melodic structures, and (5) use an inverse process to generate entirely new compositions. A novel approach includes controlling high-level musical structures (e.g., chord progressions or tempo) by conditioning the model on symbolic representations like MIDI data during the denoising steps.

Python Code Snippet

```python
import os
import random
import math
```

```python
import torch
import torch.nn as nn
import torchaudio
import torch.optim as optim
from torch.utils.data import Dataset, DataLoader
import matplotlib.pyplot as plt


# ---------------------------------------------------------------
# 1) Set random seed for reproducibility
# ---------------------------------------------------------------
def set_seed(seed=42):
    random.seed(seed)
    torch.manual_seed(seed)
    if torch.cuda.is_available():
        torch.cuda.manual_seed_all(seed)


# ---------------------------------------------------------------
# 2) Create a custom dataset for loading music/audio as spectrograms
# ---------------------------------------------------------------
class MusicDataset(Dataset):
    '''
    Loads audio files from a directory, converts them to a
    ↪  consistent spectrogram format.
    Expects .wav files in the specified directory.
    '''
    def __init__(self, audio_dir, transform=None, sample_rate=16000,
    ↪  n_fft=1024, hop_length=256):
        super(MusicDataset, self).__init__()
        self.audio_paths = [
            os.path.join(audio_dir, fname)
            for fname in os.listdir(audio_dir)
            if fname.endswith('.wav')
        ]
        self.transform = transform
        self.sample_rate = sample_rate
        self.n_fft = n_fft
        self.hop_length = hop_length

    def __len__(self):
        return len(self.audio_paths)

    def __getitem__(self, idx):
        audio_path = self.audio_paths[idx]
        waveform, sr = torchaudio.load(audio_path)

        # Resample if necessary
        if sr != self.sample_rate:
            resampler = torchaudio.transforms.Resample(sr,
            ↪  self.sample_rate)
            waveform = resampler(waveform)

        # Convert to mono if stereo
        if waveform.shape[0] > 1:
```

114

```python
        waveform = torch.mean(waveform, dim=0, keepdim=True)

        spectrogram = torchaudio.transforms.Spectrogram(
            n_fft=self.n_fft,
            hop_length=self.hop_length
        )(waveform)

        # Optionally transform (e.g., normalization) if provided
        if self.transform:
            spectrogram = self.transform(spectrogram)

        # We want shape: [channels=1, freq, time]
        # torchaudio spectrogram shape is [1, freq_bins,
        ↪    time_frames]
        return spectrogram


# ----------------------------------------------------------------
# 3) Define a basic 2D UNet-like model for spectrogram denoising
# ----------------------------------------------------------------
class DoubleConv(nn.Module):
    '''
    A helper module that performs two convolutions (each followed by
    ↪    ReLU)
    to reduce block boilerplate in the U-Net.
    '''
    def __init__(self, in_channels, out_channels):
        super(DoubleConv, self).__init__()
        self.conv = nn.Sequential(
            nn.Conv2d(in_channels, out_channels, kernel_size=3,
            ↪    padding=1),
            nn.ReLU(inplace=True),
            nn.Conv2d(out_channels, out_channels, kernel_size=3,
            ↪    padding=1),
            nn.ReLU(inplace=True)
        )

    def forward(self, x):
        return self.conv(x)

class UNet2D(nn.Module):
    '''
    A simplified 2D U-Net architecture with down-sampling (encoder)
    and up-sampling (decoder) blocks, plus skip connections.
    Adapts from image-based U-Net to handle spectrogram shape.
    '''
    def __init__(self, in_channels=1, out_channels=1,
    ↪    base_channels=32):
        super(UNet2D, self).__init__()

        # Encoder
        self.down1 = DoubleConv(in_channels, base_channels)
        self.pool1 = nn.MaxPool2d(kernel_size=2)
        self.down2 = DoubleConv(base_channels, base_channels*2)
```

```python
        self.pool2 = nn.MaxPool2d(kernel_size=2)

        # Bottleneck
        self.bottleneck = DoubleConv(base_channels*2,
        ↪  base_channels*4)

        # Decoder
        self.up1 = nn.ConvTranspose2d(base_channels*4,
        ↪  base_channels*2, kernel_size=2, stride=2)
        self.conv_up1 = DoubleConv(base_channels*4, base_channels*2)
        self.up2 = nn.ConvTranspose2d(base_channels*2,
        ↪  base_channels, kernel_size=2, stride=2)
        self.conv_up2 = DoubleConv(base_channels*2, base_channels)

        # Output
        self.final_conv = nn.Conv2d(base_channels, out_channels,
        ↪  kernel_size=1)

    def forward(self, x):
        # Downsample
        x1 = self.down1(x)
        x2 = self.pool1(x1)

        x3 = self.down2(x2)
        x4 = self.pool2(x3)

        # Bottleneck
        b = self.bottleneck(x4)

        # Upsample
        x = self.up1(b)
        x = torch.cat([x, x3], dim=1)
        x = self.conv_up1(x)

        x = self.up2(x)
        x = torch.cat([x, x1], dim=1)
        x = self.conv_up2(x)

        # Final
        out = self.final_conv(x)
        return out


# -----------------------------------------------------------
# 4) Define diffusion schedule and forward process
# -----------------------------------------------------------
def make_beta_schedule(schedule_name, n_timestep, start=1e-4,
↪  end=2e-2):
    '''
    Creates a beta schedule for the diffusion process.
    We use a linear schedule for demonstration.
    '''
    if schedule_name == "linear":
        return torch.linspace(start, end, n_timestep)
```

```
        else:
            raise NotImplementedError("Only 'linear' schedule is
            ↪  implemented here.")

class Diffusion:
    '''
    A class that encapsulates:
    1) The forward noising process: q(x_t | x_0)
    2) The reverse denoising process: p(x_{t-1} | x_t)
    3) Utility for training and sampling.
    '''
    def __init__(self, n_steps=200, beta_schedule='linear',
    ↪  device='cpu'):
        self.n_steps = n_steps
        self.betas = make_beta_schedule(beta_schedule,
        ↪  n_steps).to(device)
        self.alphas = 1.0 - self.betas
        self.alpha_cumprod = torch.cumprod(self.alphas, dim=0)
        self.alpha_cumprod_prev = torch.cat([
            torch.tensor([1.0], device=device),
            self.alpha_cumprod[:-1]
        ], dim=0)

        # Posterior variance term for p(x_{t-1} | x_t, x_0)
        self.posterior_variance = self.betas * (1.0 -
        ↪  self.alpha_cumprod_prev) / (1.0 - self.alpha_cumprod)

    def q_sample(self, x_start, t, noise=None):
        '''
        Forward diffusion: x_t = sqrt(alpha_cumprod[t]) * x_start
                            + sqrt(1 - alpha_cumprod[t]) * noise
        '''
        if noise is None:
            noise = torch.randn_like(x_start)

        shape_len = len(x_start.shape)
        # Prepare gather indices for the batch dimension
        alpha_cumprod_t = self.alpha_cumprod[t].view(-1,
        ↪  *([1]*(shape_len-1)))
        sqrt_alpha_cumprod_t = alpha_cumprod_t.sqrt()
        sqrt_one_minus_alpha_cumprod_t = (1 -
        ↪  alpha_cumprod_t).sqrt()

        return sqrt_alpha_cumprod_t * x_start +
        ↪  sqrt_one_minus_alpha_cumprod_t * noise

    def predict_noise(self, model, x_t, t):
        '''
        Use the 2D UNet model to predict the noise added at step t.
        Here, t is used as an index (handy for conditional
        ↪  architecture).
        For simplicity, we ignore t inside the model. More advanced
```

117

```
    architectures incorporate t explicitly (e.g. via positional
    ↪   encoding).
    '''
    return model(x_t)

def p_sample(self, model, x_t, t, guidance_scale=1.0):
    '''
    One reverse diffusion step: p(x_{t-1} | x_t).
    We compute the mean of p(x_{t-1} | x_t, x_0).
    We also demonstrate a "guidance_scale" that scales the
    ↪   predicted noise for demonstration.
    '''
    betas_t = self.betas[t]
    alpha_t = self.alphas[t]
    alpha_cumprod_t = self.alpha_cumprod[t]
    alpha_cumprod_prev_t = self.alpha_cumprod_prev[t]

    # Predict noise
    e_t = model(x_t) * guidance_scale

    sqrt_recip_alpha_t = (1.0 / alpha_t).sqrt()
    x_0_hat = (x_t - (1.0 - alpha_t).sqrt() * e_t) *
    ↪   sqrt_recip_alpha_t

    coef1 = (alpha_cumprod_prev_t.sqrt() * betas_t) / (1.0 -
    ↪   alpha_cumprod_t)
    coef2 = ((1.0 - alpha_cumprod_prev_t) * alpha_t.sqrt()) /
    ↪   (1.0 - alpha_cumprod_t)

    mean = coef1 * x_0_hat + coef2 * x_t
    posterior_var = self.posterior_variance[t]

    if t > 0:
        noise = torch.randn_like(x_t)
    else:
        noise = torch.zeros_like(x_t)

    x_prev = mean + noise * posterior_var.sqrt()
    return x_prev

def p_sample_loop(self, model, shape, guidance_scale=1.0):
    '''
    Repeatedly apply p_sample to go from x_T ~ N(0,I) to x_0.
    Starting from random noise in spectrogram domain.
    '''
    x_t = torch.randn(shape, device=model.device)
    for i in reversed(range(self.n_steps)):
        x_t = self.p_sample(model, x_t, i,
        ↪   guidance_scale=guidance_scale)
    return x_t

# ---------------------------------------------------------------
# 5) Training routines
```

```python
# -------------------------------------------------------------------
def train_one_epoch(model, diffusion, optimizer, dataloader,
↪  device):
    '''
    A single training epoch for the diffusion model on spectrogram
    ↪  data.
    We sample a random t, forward diffuse the spectrogram, and
    ↪  predict the noise.
    '''
    model.train()
    total_loss = 0
    for spectrogram in dataloader:
        spectrogram = spectrogram.to(device)

        # Each spectrogram is shape [1, freq, time] or [channels,
        ↪  freq, time].
        # We might need an extra batch dimension: B x 1 x freq x
        ↪  time
        spectrogram = spectrogram.float()

        # Random time step
        t = torch.randint(0, diffusion.n_steps,
        ↪  (spectrogram.size(0),), device=device).long()

        # Create random noise
        noise = torch.randn_like(spectrogram)

        # Forward diffuse
        x_t = diffusion.q_sample(spectrogram, t, noise=noise)

        # Predict the noise
        noise_pred = diffusion.predict_noise(model, x_t, t)

        # L2 loss
        loss = nn.functional.mse_loss(noise_pred, noise)

        optimizer.zero_grad()
        loss.backward()
        optimizer.step()

        total_loss += loss.item()
    return total_loss / len(dataloader)

def evaluate_model(model, diffusion, dataloader, device):
    '''
    Evaluate using MSE on predicted noise to measure progress.
    '''
    model.eval()
    total_loss = 0
    with torch.no_grad():
        for spectrogram in dataloader:
            spectrogram = spectrogram.to(device).float()
```

```python
        t = torch.randint(0, diffusion.n_steps,
        ↪ (spectrogram.size(0),), device=device).long()
        noise = torch.randn_like(spectrogram)
        x_t = diffusion.q_sample(spectrogram, t, noise=noise)
        noise_pred = diffusion.predict_noise(model, x_t, t)
        loss = nn.functional.mse_loss(noise_pred, noise)
        total_loss += loss.item()
    return total_loss / len(dataloader)


# --------------------------------------------------------------
# 6) Sampling function to listen/inspect results
# --------------------------------------------------------------
def sample_and_reconstruct(model, diffusion, device,
↪ guidance_scale=1.0, sample_length=128, sample_rate=16000):
    '''
    Samples random spectrogram from the diffusion model, then
    ↪ attempts
    to invert it back to waveform for listening or saving.
    '''
    model.eval()
    with torch.no_grad():
        # Suppose we want shape = [batch_size=1, channels=1,
        ↪ freq_bins=512, time_frames=?]
        # Let freq_bins and time_frames match typical STFT
        ↪ configuration
        freq_bins = 513   # e.g. with n_fft=1024, freq_bins =
        ↪ n_fft//2 + 1
        x_t = diffusion.p_sample_loop(
            model, shape=(1, 1, freq_bins, sample_length),
            guidance_scale=guidance_scale
        )
        x_t = x_t.clamp(-1.0, 1.0)
        # Convert back to waveform: we can use Griffin-Lim (not
        ↪ perfect but standard).
        # We do an approximate invert with
        ↪ torchaudio.transforms.InverseSpectrogram.

        # The model generated magnitude spectrogram. Real-world
        ↪ usage might need phase approximation.
        # For simplicity, let's do a basic magnitude to complex
        ↪ assumption (phase=0) for demonstration.
        inv_spectro = torchaudio.transforms.InverseSpectrogram(
            n_fft=1024,
            hop_length=256
        )(x_t.squeeze(0).squeeze(0).abs(),
        ↪ torch.zeros_like(x_t.squeeze(0).squeeze(0)))

        # Return as CPU tensor for further usage
        inv_spectro = inv_spectro.cpu().detach().numpy()
        return inv_spectro


# --------------------------------------------------------------
# 7) Main script: load data, initialize model, and train
```

120

```
# --------------------------------------------------------------
def main():
    set_seed(42)
    device = torch.device('cuda' if torch.cuda.is_available() else
    ↪    'cpu')

    # Example config
    audio_dir = 'audio_data'  # Path containing .wav files
    batch_size = 4
    n_steps = 200
    lr = 1e-4
    epochs = 5

    # Create dataset & dataloader
    # Assume audio_dir has .wav files for training
    train_dataset = MusicDataset(audio_dir=audio_dir,
    ↪    transform=None)
    train_loader = DataLoader(train_dataset, batch_size=batch_size,
    ↪    shuffle=True)

    # For demonstration, we use the same dataset as "test"
    test_loader = DataLoader(train_dataset, batch_size=batch_size,
    ↪    shuffle=False)

    # Create the UNet2D model
    model = UNet2D(in_channels=1, out_channels=1, base_channels=32)
    model.device = device
    model = model.to(device)

    # Create diffusion object
    diffusion = Diffusion(n_steps=n_steps, beta_schedule='linear',
    ↪    device=device)

    # Optimizer
    optimizer = optim.Adam(model.parameters(), lr=lr)

    # Training loop
    for epoch in range(epochs):
        train_loss = train_one_epoch(model, diffusion, optimizer,
        ↪    train_loader, device)
        val_loss = evaluate_model(model, diffusion, test_loader,
        ↪    device)
        print(f"Epoch [{epoch+1}/{epochs}] - Train Loss:
        ↪    {train_loss:.4f}, Val Loss: {val_loss:.4f}")

        # Sample a short spectrogram and reconstruct
        reconstructed_audio = sample_and_reconstruct(model,
        ↪    diffusion, device, guidance_scale=1.0)
        # Save or play the 'reconstructed_audio' array if needed
        # For demonstration, we won't actually write out a file
        ↪    here.
```

121

```
    print("Training complete! Your diffusion model is ready to
    ↪  generate new audio textures.")

if __name__ == "__main__":
    main()
```

Key Implementation Details:

- **Forward Diffusion:** We implement `q_sample` to corrupt each spectrogram with noise, controlled by a linear beta schedule. At step t, the amount of added noise is governed by `betas[t]` and the cumulative products of `alphas`.

- **Reverse Diffusion (Sampling):** The function `p_sample_loop` iteratively applies `p_sample` to predict the spectrogram from random noise. Each call computes the mean of the posterior distribution until a clean spectrogram emerges.

- **UNet2D Architecture:** `UNet2D` is adapted for spectrogram shapes, reusing the common encoder-decoder structure with skip connections. Convolutional blocks downsample and upsample time-frequency representations.

- **Training Objective:** We match the model's predicted noise to the actual Gaussian noise. The loss is `MSE` between the model prediction and the ground-truth noise, computed in the spectrogram domain.

- **Reconstruction to Waveform:** After generating spectrograms via the inverse diffusion process, we demonstrate a basic approach (via Griffin-Lim or similar) to convert magnitude spectrograms or partial-complex spectrograms back to an audio waveform, enabling you to audition model outputs.

Chapter 12

Text Generation and Refinement with Diffusion

Adapting diffusion to discrete text data requires careful handling of tokens or embeddings. Common cases include refining incomplete sentences, style correction, or generating short passages. We treat text sequences as token embeddings and add noise in their latent space. Construction involves: (1) converting text to fixed-length token embeddings, (2) defining a noise schedule in embedding space, (3) developing a transformer-based UNet that progressively denoises the corrupted tokens, (4) training to predict the noise at each step using a masked language modeling objective, and (5) sampling new sentences by reversing the diffusion, often starting with random embeddings. An innovative approach relies on continuous relaxation of discrete tokens, enabling more stable training. Additionally, controlling semantic style can be done by adding specialized conditioning vectors that reflect topic or tone preferences.

Python Code Snippet

```
import torch
import torch.nn as nn
import torch.optim as optim
import math
```

```python
import random
from torch.utils.data import Dataset, DataLoader

# ----------------------------------------------------------------
# 1) Utility function: Set random seed for reproducibility
# ----------------------------------------------------------------
def set_seed(seed=42):
    random.seed(seed)
    torch.manual_seed(seed)
    if torch.cuda.is_available():
        torch.cuda.manual_seed_all(seed)


# ----------------------------------------------------------------
# 2) Vocabulary and tokenization
# ----------------------------------------------------------------
class Vocabulary:
    """
    A simple vocabulary class to map tokens to indices and back.
    """
    def __init__(self, special_tokens=["<PAD>", "<MASK>", "<UNK>",
    ↪  "<BOS>", "<EOS>"]):
        self.special_tokens = special_tokens
        self.token2idx = {}
        self.idx2token = {}
        for token in special_tokens:
            self.add_token(token)

    def add_token(self, token):
        if token not in self.token2idx:
            idx = len(self.token2idx)
            self.token2idx[token] = idx
            self.idx2token[idx] = token

    def __len__(self):
        return len(self.token2idx)

    def encode(self, text_tokens):
        """
        Convert a list of text tokens to a list of indices.
        Unknown tokens map to <UNK>.
        """
        return [self.token2idx.get(t, self.token2idx["<UNK>"]) for t
        ↪  in text_tokens]

    def decode(self, indices):
        """
        Convert a list of indices to a list of text tokens.
        """
        return [self.idx2token.get(i, "<UNK>") for i in indices]


# ----------------------------------------------------------------
# 3) Dataset and Dataloader
# ----------------------------------------------------------------
```

124

```python
class TextDataset(Dataset):
    """
    A simple text dataset that returns sequences of token indices,
    all padded/truncated to a fixed length, plus a 'masked' version
    for the diffusion model training.
    """
    def __init__(self, texts, vocab, max_len=10):
        super().__init__()
        self.vocab = vocab
        self.max_len = max_len
        # Tokenize and store
        self.data = []
        for line in texts:
            tokens = line.strip().split()
            tokens = ["<BOS>"] + tokens + ["<EOS>"]
            encoded = vocab.encode(tokens)
            # Pad or truncate to max_len
            encoded = encoded[:max_len] if len(encoded) >= max_len
            ↪   else encoded + [vocab.token2idx["<PAD>"]] * (max_len
            ↪   - len(encoded))
            self.data.append(encoded)

    def __len__(self):
        return len(self.data)

    def __getitem__(self, idx):
        seq = self.data[idx]
        return torch.tensor(seq, dtype=torch.long)

# ----------------------------------------------------------------
# 4) Embedding-based Diffusion Setup
# ----------------------------------------------------------------
def make_beta_schedule(n_timestep, start=1e-4, end=0.02):
    """
    Simple linear beta schedule.
    """
    return torch.linspace(start, end, n_timestep)

class TextDiffusion:
    """
    Handles:
      (1) the forward noising of token embeddings,
      (2) the reverse sampling via a model that predicts noise,
      (3) utility for training.
    """
    def __init__(self, n_steps=100, embed_dim=32):
        self.n_steps = n_steps
        self.betas = make_beta_schedule(n_steps)
        self.alphas = 1.0 - self.betas
        self.alpha_cumprod = torch.cumprod(self.alphas, dim=0)
        self.alpha_cumprod_prev = torch.cat([torch.tensor([1.0]),
        ↪   self.alpha_cumprod[:-1]], dim=0)
```

```python
        self.posterior_variance = self.betas * (1.0 -
        ↪    self.alpha_cumprod_prev) / (1.0 - self.alpha_cumprod)
        self.embed_dim = embed_dim

    def q_sample(self, x_start_emb, t, noise=None):
        """
        Forward diffusion step:
        x_t = sqrt(alpha_cumprod[t]) * x_start_emb + sqrt(1 -
        ↪    alpha_cumprod[t]) * noise
        """
        if noise is None:
            noise = torch.randn_like(x_start_emb)

        # reshape for broadcast if needed
        sqrt_alpha_cumprod_t = self.alpha_cumprod[t].sqrt().view(-1,
        ↪    1, 1)
        sqrt_one_minus_alpha_cumprod_t = (1.0 -
        ↪    self.alpha_cumprod[t]).sqrt().view(-1, 1, 1)
        return sqrt_alpha_cumprod_t * x_start_emb +
        ↪    sqrt_one_minus_alpha_cumprod_t * noise

    def predict_noise(self, model, x_t_emb, t):
        """
        Use the diffusion model to predict the noise added at step
        ↪    t.
        """
        return model(x_t_emb, t)

    def p_sample(self, model, x_t, t):
        """
        Single reverse diffusion step:
        p(x_{t-1} | x_t).
        """
        betas_t = self.betas[t].to(x_t.device)
        alpha_t = self.alphas[t].to(x_t.device)
        alpha_cumprod_t = self.alpha_cumprod[t].to(x_t.device)
        alpha_cumprod_prev_t =
        ↪    self.alpha_cumprod_prev[t].to(x_t.device)

        e_t = self.predict_noise(model, x_t, t)

        # Reconstruct x_0 from x_t
        sqrt_recip_alpha_t = (1.0 / alpha_t).sqrt()
        x_0_hat = (x_t - (1.0 - alpha_t).sqrt() * e_t) *
        ↪    sqrt_recip_alpha_t

        # Compute the coefficients for the mean
        coef1 = (alpha_cumprod_prev_t.sqrt() * betas_t) / (1.0 -
        ↪    alpha_cumprod_t)
        coef2 = ((1.0 - alpha_cumprod_prev_t) * alpha_t.sqrt()) /
        ↪    (1.0 - alpha_cumprod_t)

        mean = coef1 * x_0_hat + coef2 * x_t
```

126

```
        posterior_var = self.posterior_variance[t].to(x_t.device)
        if t > 0:
            noise = torch.randn_like(x_t)
        else:
            noise = torch.zeros_like(x_t)
        x_prev = mean + noise * posterior_var.sqrt()
        return x_prev

    def p_sample_loop(self, model, shape, device):
        """
        Sample an entire sequence from random noise x_T back to x_0.
        shape: (batch_size, seq_len, embed_dim)
        """
        x_t = torch.randn(shape, device=device)
        for i in reversed(range(self.n_steps)):
            t = torch.tensor([i] * shape[0], device=device).long()
            x_t = self.p_sample(model, x_t, t)
        return x_t


# ---------------------------------------------------------------
# 5) Transformer-based "UNet"-ish model
# ---------------------------------------------------------------
class PositionalEncoding(nn.Module):
    """
    Standard positional encoding for tokens in a sequence.
    """
    def __init__(self, d_model, max_len=100):
        super(PositionalEncoding, self).__init__()
        pe = torch.zeros(max_len, d_model)
        position = torch.arange(0, max_len,
        ↪  dtype=torch.float).unsqueeze(1)
        div_term = torch.exp(torch.arange(0, d_model, 2).float() *
        ↪  (-math.log(10000.0) / d_model))
        pe[:, 0::2] = torch.sin(position * div_term)
        pe[:, 1::2] = torch.cos(position * div_term)
        pe = pe.unsqueeze(0)   # shape: (1, max_len, d_model)
        self.register_buffer('pe', pe)

    def forward(self, x):
        """
        x shape: (batch_size, seq_len, d_model)
        We'll add positional encoding up to seq_len for each batch
        ↪  item.
        """
        seq_len = x.size(1)
        return x + self.pe[:, :seq_len, :]

class TransformerDenoiser(nn.Module):
    """
    A simplified transformer-based denoiser for text embeddings.
    The model predicts the noise at each step for the input
    ↪  embeddings.
```

127

```python
    """
    def __init__(self, vocab_size, embed_dim=32, n_heads=2,
    ↪  hidden_dim=64, num_layers=2, max_seq_len=10):
        super().__init__()
        self.vocab_size = vocab_size
        self.embed_dim = embed_dim
        self.token_embed = nn.Embedding(vocab_size, embed_dim)
        self.pos_encoder = PositionalEncoding(embed_dim,
        ↪  max_len=max_seq_len)

        encoder_layer =
        ↪  nn.TransformerEncoderLayer(d_model=embed_dim,
        ↪  nhead=n_heads, dim_feedforward=hidden_dim)
        self.transformer = nn.TransformerEncoder(encoder_layer,
        ↪  num_layers=num_layers)
        self.out = nn.Linear(embed_dim, embed_dim)  # predicts noise
        ↪  in embedding space

        # This embedding is used for time-step conditioning,
        # just a simple trainable lookup
        self.t_embed = nn.Embedding(1000, embed_dim)

    def forward(self, x_t_emb, t):
        """
        x_t_emb: (batch_size, seq_len, embed_dim) at step t
        t: (batch_size,) time steps
        Returns predicted noise (batch_size, seq_len, embed_dim).
        """
        # Add a time embedding to each token embedding
        # broadcast time embedding across seq_len
        t_embedding = self.t_embed(t).unsqueeze(1)  # shape:
        ↪  (batch_size, 1, embed_dim)
        x_t_emb = x_t_emb + t_embedding

        # Apply positional encoding
        x = self.pos_encoder(x_t_emb)

        # Transformer expects (seq_len, batch_size, embed_dim)
        x = x.permute(1, 0, 2)
        x_trans = self.transformer(x)  # shape: (seq_len,
        ↪  batch_size, embed_dim)
        x_trans = x_trans.permute(1, 0, 2)

        # Predict noise
        noise_pred = self.out(x_trans)
        return noise_pred


# ----------------------------------------------------------------
# 6) Training / Evaluation Routines
# ----------------------------------------------------------------
def train_one_epoch(model, diffusion, optimizer, dataloader,
↪  device):
    """
```

```python
    For each batch, we:
    1) Convert tokens to embeddings
    2) Sample a random time step
    3) Forward diffuse the embeddings
    4) Model predicts noise
    5) Compute L2 loss vs. the true noise (masked positions
    ↪   included)
    """
    model.train()
    epoch_loss = 0
    for batch_seq in dataloader:
        batch_seq = batch_seq.to(device)  # shape: (batch_size,
        ↪   seq_len)
        batch_size, seq_len = batch_seq.shape

        # Convert tokens to embeddings
        with torch.no_grad():
            # We'll embed them once for x_0
            x_0_emb = model.token_embed(batch_seq)

        # Sample time steps
        t = torch.randint(0, diffusion.n_steps, (batch_size,),
        ↪   device=device).long()

        # Create random noise
        noise = torch.randn_like(x_0_emb)

        # Forward diffusion
        x_t = diffusion.q_sample(x_0_emb, t, noise=noise)

        # Predict noise
        noise_pred = model(x_t, t)

        loss = nn.functional.mse_loss(noise_pred, noise)

        optimizer.zero_grad()
        loss.backward()
        optimizer.step()

        epoch_loss += loss.item()

    return epoch_loss / len(dataloader)

def evaluate_model(model, diffusion, dataloader, device):
    """
    Compute average L2 error on a validation set for noise
    ↪   prediction.
    """
    model.eval()
    val_loss = 0
    with torch.no_grad():
        for batch_seq in dataloader:
            batch_seq = batch_seq.to(device)
```

```python
        batch_size, seq_len = batch_seq.shape
        x_0_emb = model.token_embed(batch_seq)

        t = torch.randint(0, diffusion.n_steps, (batch_size,),
        ↪   device=device).long()
        noise = torch.randn_like(x_0_emb)
        x_t = diffusion.q_sample(x_0_emb, t, noise=noise)

        noise_pred = model(x_t, t)
        loss = nn.functional.mse_loss(noise_pred, noise)
        val_loss += loss.item()
    return val_loss / len(dataloader)

def sample_text(model, diffusion, vocab, batch_size=2, seq_len=10,
↪   device='cpu'):
    """
    Run reverse diffusion from random noise and decode.
    """
    model.eval()
    with torch.no_grad():
        # Start from x_T (random sample)
        x_T = diffusion.p_sample_loop(model, (batch_size, seq_len,
        ↪   diffusion.embed_dim), device)
        # x_T is our x_0 estimate after all steps, but in practice
        ↪   we treat it as "denoised embeddings"

        # For a simpler approach, we treat x_T as if it were close
        ↪   to x_0
        # Next, we find the closest token in the embedding space to
        ↪   decode:
        # or we can pass them through the model's final
        ↪   "token_embed" weights in reverse.
        token_embeddings = model.token_embed.weight  # shape:
        ↪   (vocab_size, embed_dim)

        # We'll do a naive nearest neighbor in embedding space
        # shape of x_T: (batch_size, seq_len, embed_dim)
        # shape of token_embeddings: (vocab_size, embed_dim)
        # we want to find best matching token for each position
        generated_sequences = []
        for b in range(batch_size):
            tokens_ids = []
            for s in range(seq_len):
                emb = x_T[b, s, :].unsqueeze(0)  # shape: (1,
                ↪   embed_dim)
                # compute L2 distance to each vocab embedding
                dist = torch.norm(token_embeddings - emb, dim=1)  #
                ↪   shape: (vocab_size,)
                closest_token_id = torch.argmin(dist).item()
                tokens_ids.append(closest_token_id)
            generated_sequences.append(tokens_ids)
```

```python
        decoded_sentences = [vocab.decode(seq) for seq in
        ↪   generated_sequences]

    return decoded_sentences

# -----------------------------------------------------------------
# 7) Main function: example usage
# -----------------------------------------------------------------
def main():
    set_seed()
    device = torch.device("cuda" if torch.cuda.is_available() else
    ↪   "cpu")

    # Create a small toy set of sentences
    toy_texts = [
        "cat sat on mat",
        "dog barked loud",
        "i love pizza",
        "birds fly away",
        "the sky is blue",
        "this is a test"
    ]

    # Build vocabulary
    vocab = Vocabulary()
    for line in toy_texts:
        for word in line.strip().split():
            vocab.add_token(word)

    # Create dataset and dataloader
    train_dataset = TextDataset(toy_texts, vocab, max_len=8)
    train_loader = DataLoader(train_dataset, batch_size=2,
    ↪   shuffle=True)

    # We'll reuse the same dataset for 'validation' in this toy
    ↪   example
    val_loader = DataLoader(train_dataset, batch_size=2,
    ↪   shuffle=False)

    # Create diffusion
    embed_dim = 32
    diffusion = TextDiffusion(n_steps=50, embed_dim=embed_dim)

    # Create model
    model = TransformerDenoiser(
        vocab_size=len(vocab),
        embed_dim=embed_dim,
        n_heads=2,
        hidden_dim=64,
        num_layers=2,
        max_seq_len=8
    ).to(device)
```

131

```
optimizer = optim.Adam(model.parameters(), lr=1e-3)

# Train
epochs = 5
for epoch in range(epochs):
    train_loss = train_one_epoch(model, diffusion, optimizer,
    ↪  train_loader, device)
    val_loss = evaluate_model(model, diffusion, val_loader,
    ↪  device)
    print(f"Epoch {epoch+1}/{epochs}, Train Loss:
    ↪  {train_loss:.4f}, Val Loss: {val_loss:.4f}")

    # Sample text
    samples = sample_text(model, diffusion, vocab, batch_size=2,
    ↪  seq_len=8, device=device)
    print("Sampled Sentences:")
    for s in samples:
        print("   ", " ".join(s))

    print("Training complete.")

if __name__ == "__main__":
    main()
```

Key Implementation Details:

- **Forward Diffusion (q_sample):** We sample at each time
  step t by mixing the original token embeddings with random
  noise. The blending coefficients (sqrt(`alpha_cumprod[t]`)
  vs. sqrt(1 - `alpha_cumprod[t]`)) control how much noise
  is added.

- **Reverse Diffusion (p_sample_loop):** We start from random noise and iteratively remove it using our denoiser model.
  Each step requires predicting the noise component in the cur-
  rent noisy embedding, then removing it.

- **TransformerDenoiser Model:** This is a simplified "transformer-
  based UNet" that ingests noisy embeddings, adds a time-step
  embedding, and predicts the noise via a transformer encoder
  stack.

- **Embedding Space Noise Prediction:** By treating text
  tokens in a continuous embedding space, we can apply standard diffusion dynamics (MSE between predicted and true
  noise). A naive nearest-neighbor step then converts final embeddings back to discrete tokens.

132

- **Sampling Decoding:** After reverse diffusion, we obtain denoised embeddings. In this example, we do a simplistic nearest-neighbor lookup in embedding space to decode into tokens, though more sophisticated decoders can improve final text quality.

- **Masked Language Modeling Nuance:** Here, we show a direct noise-prediction scheme. One can incorporate partial masking to refine incomplete sentences or enforce style constraints, aligning with typical masked language modeling protocols in discrete text diffusion.

Chapter 13

Sketch-to-Image Synthesis with Diffusion

Commonly used by artists and designers, sketch-to-image diffusion transforms a simple outline or pencil drawing into a realistic or stylized image. We begin with a dataset of paired sketches and final images, where a forward diffusion corrupts the latter. The network receives a sketch as a conditioning input and predicts how to denoise towards the correct result. Main steps include: (1) collecting sketches coupled with reference images, (2) injecting random noise into the reference image, (3) concatenating the sketch features to the UNet, (4) training to predict the noise at each time step, focusing on structure alignment with the sketches, and (5) synthesizing new images by feeding a user-provided sketch into the reverse process. A novel technique uses edge detection as an intermediate representation, bridging stylistic gaps between the loose sketch lines and the realistic final image.

Python Code Snippet

```python
import os
import random
import math
import glob
import torch
```

```python
import torch.nn as nn
import torchvision
import torch.optim as optim
import numpy as np
from PIL import Image
from torch.utils.data import Dataset, DataLoader
import torchvision.transforms as transforms
import matplotlib.pyplot as plt

# ---------------------------------------------------------------
# 1) Set random seed for reproducibility
# ---------------------------------------------------------------
def set_seed(seed=42):
    random.seed(seed)
    np.random.seed(seed)
    torch.manual_seed(seed)
    if torch.cuda.is_available():
        torch.cuda.manual_seed_all(seed)

# ---------------------------------------------------------------
# 2) Create a dataset that yields paired (sketch, image) examples
# ---------------------------------------------------------------
class SketchImageDataset(Dataset):
    '''
    Expects a directory structure with:
    root/sketches/*.png (or jpg)
    root/images/*.png  (or jpg)
    matching filenames, e.g. 0001.png in sketches and 0001.png in
    ↪  images
    Returns a tuple: (sketch_tensor, image_tensor).
    '''
    def __init__(self, root_dir, transform_sketch=None,
    ↪  transform_image=None):
        super().__init__()
        self.sketch_dir = os.path.join(root_dir, "sketches")
        self.image_dir = os.path.join(root_dir, "images")

        # Gather paths
        self.sketch_paths =
        ↪  sorted(glob.glob(os.path.join(self.sketch_dir, "*")))
        self.image_paths =
        ↪  sorted(glob.glob(os.path.join(self.image_dir, "*")))

        # Basic sanity check
        assert len(self.sketch_paths) == len(self.image_paths), \
            "Number of sketches and images must match!"

        self.transform_sketch = transform_sketch
        self.transform_image = transform_image

    def __len__(self):
        return len(self.sketch_paths)
```

```python
    def __getitem__(self, idx):
        sketch_path = self.sketch_paths[idx]
        image_path = self.image_paths[idx]

        sketch = Image.open(sketch_path).convert("L")  # grayscale
        ↪ sketch
        image = Image.open(image_path).convert("RGB")  # color
        ↪ image

        if self.transform_sketch:
            sketch = self.transform_sketch(sketch)
        if self.transform_image:
            image = self.transform_image(image)

        return sketch, image


# -------------------------------------------------------------
# 3) Define a simple U-Net conditioned on sketch
# -------------------------------------------------------------
class DoubleConv(nn.Module):
    '''
    A helper module that performs two convolutions (each followed by
    ↪ ReLU)
    to reduce boilerplate in the U-Net.
    '''
    def __init__(self, in_channels, out_channels):
        super(DoubleConv, self).__init__()
        self.conv = nn.Sequential(
            nn.Conv2d(in_channels, out_channels, 3, padding=1),
            nn.ReLU(inplace=True),
            nn.Conv2d(out_channels, out_channels, 3, padding=1),
            nn.ReLU(inplace=True)
        )

    def forward(self, x):
        return self.conv(x)


class SketchConditionedUNet(nn.Module):
    '''
    A simplified U-Net architecture that takes (sketch + noisy
    ↪ image)
    as input and outputs predicted noise for the color image.
    - Input channels = (1 for sketch + 3 for noisy RGB) = 4
    - Output channels = 3 (predicted noise for RGB)
    '''
    def __init__(self, in_channels=4, out_channels=3,
    ↪ base_channels=64):
        super(SketchConditionedUNet, self).__init__()

        # Down-sampling (encoder)
        self.down1 = DoubleConv(in_channels, base_channels)
        self.down2 = DoubleConv(base_channels, base_channels*2)
        self.down3 = DoubleConv(base_channels*2, base_channels*4)
```

136

```python
        self.pool = nn.MaxPool2d(2)

        # Bottleneck
        self.bottleneck = DoubleConv(base_channels*4,
        ↪  base_channels*8)

        # Up-sampling (decoder)
        self.up1 = nn.ConvTranspose2d(base_channels*8,
        ↪  base_channels*4, kernel_size=2, stride=2)
        self.conv_up1 = DoubleConv(base_channels*8, base_channels*4)

        self.up2 = nn.ConvTranspose2d(base_channels*4,
        ↪  base_channels*2, kernel_size=2, stride=2)
        self.conv_up2 = DoubleConv(base_channels*4, base_channels*2)

        self.up3 = nn.ConvTranspose2d(base_channels*2,
        ↪  base_channels, kernel_size=2, stride=2)
        self.conv_up3 = DoubleConv(base_channels*2, base_channels)

        # Final output for predicted noise
        self.final_conv = nn.Conv2d(base_channels, out_channels,
        ↪  kernel_size=1)

    def forward(self, sketch, x_noisy):
        # Combine sketch + noisy image as a single 4-channel tensor
        inp = torch.cat([sketch, x_noisy], dim=1)

        # Encoder
        x1 = self.down1(inp)
        x2 = self.pool(x1)

        x2 = self.down2(x2)
        x3 = self.pool(x2)

        x3 = self.down3(x3)
        x4 = self.pool(x3)

        # Bottleneck
        b = self.bottleneck(x4)

        # Decoder
        x = self.up1(b)
        x = torch.cat([x, x3], dim=1)  # skip connection
        x = self.conv_up1(x)

        x = self.up2(x)
        x = torch.cat([x, x2], dim=1)
        x = self.conv_up2(x)

        x = self.up3(x)
        x = torch.cat([x, x1], dim=1)
        x = self.conv_up3(x)
```

```python
        # Final predicted noise
        out = self.final_conv(x)
        return out


# -----------------------------------------------------------------
# 4) Define diffusion schedule and class
# -----------------------------------------------------------------
def make_beta_schedule(schedule_name, n_timestep, start=1e-4,
↪    end=2e-2):
    '''
    Creates a beta schedule for the diffusion process.
    We use a linear schedule as a straightforward example.
    '''
    if schedule_name == "linear":
        return torch.linspace(start, end, n_timestep)
    else:
        raise NotImplementedError("Only 'linear' schedule is
        ↪    implemented in this snippet.")


class Diffusion:
    '''
    A class that encapsulates:
    1) The forward noising process: q(x_t | x_0)
    2) The reverse denoising process: p(x_{t-1} | x_t)
    3) Utility for training and conditional sampling.
    '''
    def __init__(self, n_steps=200, beta_schedule='linear',
    ↪    device='cpu'):
        self.device = device
        self.n_steps = n_steps
        self.betas = make_beta_schedule(beta_schedule,
        ↪    n_steps).to(self.device)
        self.alphas = 1.0 - self.betas
        self.alpha_cumprod = torch.cumprod(self.alphas, dim=0)
        self.alpha_cumprod_prev = torch.cat([torch.tensor([1.0],
        ↪    device=self.device),

                                    ↪    self.alpha_cumprod[:-1]],
                                    ↪    dim=0)

        # Posterior variance term for p(x_{t-1} | x_t, x_0)
        self.posterior_variance = self.betas * (1.0 -
        ↪    self.alpha_cumprod_prev) / (1.0 - self.alpha_cumprod)

    def q_sample(self, x_start, t, noise=None):
        '''
        Forward diffusion: Adds noise to x_start at step t.
        x_t = sqrt(alpha_cumprod[t]) * x_start + sqrt(1 -
        ↪    alpha_cumprod[t]) * noise
        '''
        if noise is None:
            noise = torch.randn_like(x_start)
```

```python
    sqrt_alpha_cumprod_t =
    ↪  self.alpha_cumprod[t].sqrt().unsqueeze(-1).
    unsqueeze(-1).unsqueeze(-1)
    sqrt_one_minus_alpha_cumprod_t = (1 -
    ↪  self.alpha_cumprod[t]).sqrt().unsqueeze(-1).
    unsqueeze(-1).unsqueeze(-1)
    return sqrt_alpha_cumprod_t * x_start +
    ↪  sqrt_one_minus_alpha_cumprod_t * noise

def predict_noise(self, model, sketch, x_t, t):
    '''
    Use the U-Net model (conditioned on sketch) to predict the
    ↪  noise added at step t.
    '''
    return model(sketch, x_t)

def p_sample(self, model, sketch, x_t, t, guidance_scale=1.0):
    '''
    One reverse diffusion step: p(x_{t-1} | x_t).
    The model predicts the noise e_t, and we compute the mean of
    ↪  p(x_{t-1} | x_t, x_0).
    We also allow a "guidance_scale" that can scale the
    ↪  predicted noise.
    '''
    betas_t = self.betas[t]
    alpha_t = self.alphas[t]
    alpha_cumprod_t = self.alpha_cumprod[t]
    alpha_cumprod_prev_t = self.alpha_cumprod_prev[t]

    # Predicted noise
    e_t = self.predict_noise(model, sketch, x_t, t) *
    ↪  guidance_scale

    # Reconstruct x_0:
    sqrt_recip_alpha_t = (1.0 / alpha_t).sqrt()
    x_0_hat = (x_t - (1.0 - alpha_t).sqrt() * e_t) *
    ↪  sqrt_recip_alpha_t

    # Coefficients for the mean
    coef1 = (alpha_cumprod_prev_t.sqrt() * betas_t) / (1.0 -
    ↪  alpha_cumprod_t)
    coef2 = ((1.0 - alpha_cumprod_prev_t) * alpha_t.sqrt()) /
    ↪  (1.0 - alpha_cumprod_t)

    mean = coef1 * x_0_hat + coef2 * x_t

    # Posterior variance
    posterior_var = self.posterior_variance[t]
    if t > 0:
        noise = torch.randn_like(x_t)
    else:
        noise = torch.zeros_like(x_t)
```

```python
        x_prev = mean + noise * posterior_var.sqrt()
        return x_prev

    def p_sample_loop_cond(self, model, sketch, shape,
    ↪  guidance_scale=1.0):
        '''
        Repeatedly apply p_sample to go from x_T ~ N(0,I) to x_0,
        conditioning on the given sketch at each step.
        '''
        x_t = torch.randn(shape, device=self.device)
        for i in reversed(range(self.n_steps)):
            x_t = self.p_sample(model, sketch, x_t, i,
            ↪  guidance_scale=guidance_scale)
        return x_t


# ----------------------------------------------------------------
# 5) Training and sampling routines
# ----------------------------------------------------------------
def train_one_epoch(model, diffusion, optimizer, dataloader,
↪  device):
    '''
    A single training epoch for the conditional diffusion model.
    1) Sample a random time t
    2) Forward diffuse the real image to x_t
    3) Predict the noise given the (sketch, x_t)
    4) Optimize MSE loss between predicted noise and actual noise
    '''
    model.train()
    loss_sum = 0
    for sketch, image in dataloader:
        sketch = sketch.to(device)   # shape: [B, 1, H, W]
        image = image.to(device)     # shape: [B, 3, H, W]

        # Sample a random time step
        t = torch.randint(0, diffusion.n_steps, (image.size(0),),
        ↪  device=device).long()

        # Create random noise
        noise = torch.randn_like(image)

        # Forward diffuse the real image at step t
        x_t = diffusion.q_sample(image, t, noise=noise)

        # Predict the noise with the model
        noise_pred = diffusion.predict_noise(model, sketch, x_t, t)

        # L2 loss to match the real noise
        loss = nn.MSELoss()(noise_pred, noise)

        optimizer.zero_grad()
        loss.backward()
        optimizer.step()
```

```python
        loss_sum += loss.item()

    return loss_sum / len(dataloader)


def evaluate_model(model, diffusion, dataloader, device):
    '''
    Quick evaluation that reports average L2 error on a validation
    ↪  set.
    '''
    model.eval()
    loss_sum = 0
    with torch.no_grad():
        for sketch, image in dataloader:
            sketch = sketch.to(device)
            image = image.to(device)
            t = torch.randint(0, diffusion.n_steps,
            ↪  (image.size(0),), device=device).long()
            noise = torch.randn_like(image)
            x_t = diffusion.q_sample(image, t, noise=noise)
            noise_pred = diffusion.predict_noise(model, sketch, x_t,
            ↪  t)
            loss = nn.MSELoss()(noise_pred, noise)
            loss_sum += loss.item()
    return loss_sum / len(dataloader)


def sample_and_save(model, diffusion, sketch, device, epoch,
↪  guidance_scale=1.0):
    '''
    Use the conditional diffusion sampling process with a single or
    ↪  batch of sketches
    to generate output images and save them to disk for inspection.
    '''
    model.eval()
    with torch.no_grad():
        # We'll assume 'sketch' is either a single image or a batch
        # shape: B x 1 x H x W
        # We want to generate color images: B x 3 x H x W
        shape = (sketch.size(0), 3, sketch.size(2), sketch.size(3))
        # Launch sampling
        x_gen = diffusion.p_sample_loop_cond(model, sketch, shape,
        ↪  guidance_scale=guidance_scale)
        # Convert back to [0,1] range
        x_gen = (x_gen.clamp(-1.0, 1.0) + 1) * 0.5

        grid = torchvision.utils.make_grid(x_gen, nrow=4)
        os.makedirs("results", exist_ok=True)
        plt.figure(figsize=(6,6))
        plt.axis("off")
        plt.imshow(grid.permute(1, 2, 0).cpu().numpy())

        ↪  plt.savefig(f"results/epoch_{epoch}_gs_{guidance_scale}.png")
        plt.close()
```

141

```python
# -----------------------------------------------------------------
# 6) Main script: load data, initialize model, and train
# -----------------------------------------------------------------
def main():
    set_seed(42)
    device = torch.device('cuda' if torch.cuda.is_available() else
    ↪ 'cpu')

    # The data directory must have:
    # root/sketches/...
    # root/images/...
    # with matching file names.
    root_dir = "data/sketch_to_image"  # adjust as needed

    # Define transforms for sketch (grayscale) and image (color)
    transform_sketch = transforms.Compose([
        transforms.Resize((128,128)),
        transforms.ToTensor(),
        # Scale from [0,1] to [-1,1]
        transforms.Normalize((0.5,), (0.5,))
    ])

    transform_image = transforms.Compose([
        transforms.Resize((128,128)),
        transforms.ToTensor(),
        transforms.Normalize((0.5,0.5,0.5), (0.5,0.5,0.5))
    ])

    train_dataset = SketchImageDataset(root_dir,

                                 ↪  transform_sketch=transform_sketch,

                                 ↪  transform_image=transform_image)
    # In a real setup, you may split into train/val sets or have a
    ↪ separate dataset
    train_loader = DataLoader(train_dataset, batch_size=4,
    ↪ shuffle=True)

    # Initialize the U-Net
    model = SketchConditionedUNet(in_channels=4, out_channels=3,
    ↪ base_channels=64).to(device)

    # Create a Diffusion instance
    diffusion = Diffusion(n_steps=200, beta_schedule='linear',
    ↪ device=device)

    # Define optimizer
    optimizer = optim.Adam(model.parameters(), lr=1e-4)

    # Training loop
    epochs = 2  # set higher for real-world usage
    for epoch in range(epochs):
```

142

```
    avg_loss = train_one_epoch(model, diffusion, optimizer,
    ↪   train_loader, device)
    # For brevity, we reuse the same dataset loader for
    ↪   "evaluation"
    val_loss = evaluate_model(model, diffusion, train_loader,
    ↪   device)
    print(f"Epoch [{epoch+1}/{epochs}] - Train Loss:
    ↪   {avg_loss:.4f}, Val Loss: {val_loss:.4f}")

    # Sample using a random batch of sketches from the dataset
    some_sketch_batch, _ = next(iter(train_loader))
    some_sketch_batch = some_sketch_batch.to(device)

    # Generate and save images with different guidance scales
    sample_and_save(model, diffusion, some_sketch_batch, device,
    ↪   epoch, guidance_scale=1.0)
    sample_and_save(model, diffusion, some_sketch_batch, device,
    ↪   epoch, guidance_scale=2.0)

    print("Training complete! Check the 'results' folder for
    ↪   generated samples.")

if __name__ == "__main__":
    main()
```

Key Implementation Details:

- **Forward Diffusion:** We implement `q_sample` to corrupt each reference image with noise, controlled by a simple linear `beta` schedule. At step t, the fraction of noise added is governed by `betas[t]` and the cumulative products of `alphas`.

- **Reverse Diffusion (Sampling):** The function `p_sample_loop_cond` applies the denoising model step by step, starting from random noise. Each call to `p_sample` uses the learned noise prediction alongside the sketch input.

- **Conditioned UNet Architecture:** The `SketchConditionedUNet` in this snippet expects the concatenation of the sketch (1 channel) and the noisy color image (3 channels) as input. Skip connections help preserve structure alignment between sketch and final image.

- **Training Objective:** We directly predict and compare the added noise via a mean-squared error (MSE) loss between the network's prediction and the actual noise at each time step.

- **Edge or Sketch Guidance:** Although our example concatenates sketch and image directly, a common technique is to extract edges or contour lines from the sketch for more robust alignment, especially when the artist's sketches are loose or stylized.

- **Guidance Parameter:** A `guidance_scale` can be used to scale the model's predicted noise, controlling the balance between fidelity to the reference structure and creative freedom in the generated image.

- **End-to-End Pipeline:** The `main` function demonstrates how to load paired sketches and images, define transforms, initialize the diffusion process, train the network, and finally sample realistic or stylized images from a user-provided sketch.

Chapter 14

Face Editing and Restoration via Diffusion

This chapter addresses face-specific tasks such as enhancing low-quality portraits, removing blemishes, or altering attributes like hair color. Commonly used in portrait retouching and content creation, face diffusion leverages specialized facial datasets. Construction steps are: (1) extracting high-quality face images, (2) defining a forward noise process over facial features, (3) building or adapting a UNet to capture fine-grained facial details like eyes and skin texture, (4) training to predict the noise for each time step, and (5) sampling from a degraded or partially masked input to restore or modify the face. A key innovation is the use of facial landmarks or segmentation maps to guide the diffusion, ensuring that changes maintain anatomical consistency. This way, we can achieve controlled edits like changing hairstyles, altering age, or removing imperfections while preserving identity.

Python Code Snippet

```
import os
import random
import math
import glob
import torch
```

```python
import torch.nn as nn
import torch.optim as optim
from torch.utils.data import Dataset, DataLoader
from PIL import Image
import torchvision.transforms as transforms
import matplotlib.pyplot as plt

# -----------------------------------------------------------------
# 1) Utility functions
# -----------------------------------------------------------------
def set_seed(seed=42):
    '''
    Sets random seed for reproducibility across Python, NumPy, and
    ↪  PyTorch.
    '''
    random.seed(seed)
    torch.manual_seed(seed)
    if torch.cuda.is_available():
        torch.cuda.manual_seed_all(seed)


# -----------------------------------------------------------------
# 2) Face dataset loader
# -----------------------------------------------------------------
class FaceDataset(Dataset):
    '''
    A simple dataset class that loads images from a folder.
    Assumes all images are face portraits.

    For demonstration, we do not apply specialized landmark or
    ↪  segmentation.
    But you can insert that logic here for finer control.
    '''
    def __init__(self, folder_path, transform=None):
        super().__init__()
        self.image_paths = glob.glob(os.path.join(folder_path,
        ↪  '*.*'))
        self.transform = transform

    def __len__(self):
        return len(self.image_paths)

    def __getitem__(self, idx):
        img_path = self.image_paths[idx]
        image = Image.open(img_path).convert('RGB')
        if self.transform:
            image = self.transform(image)
        # We omit labels, but you could return identity or
        ↪  attributes here if needed.
        return image, 0


# -----------------------------------------------------------------
```

```python
# 3) Define a UNet-like network for face diffusing tasks
# ----------------------------------------------------------------
class DoubleConv(nn.Module):
    '''
    A helper module with two convolution layers and ReLU activation.
    Used repeatedly in the UNet encoder/decoder blocks.
    '''
    def __init__(self, in_channels, out_channels):
        super(DoubleConv, self).__init__()
        self.layers = nn.Sequential(
            nn.Conv2d(in_channels, out_channels, kernel_size=3,
            ↪  padding=1),
            nn.ReLU(inplace=True),
            nn.Conv2d(out_channels, out_channels, kernel_size=3,
            ↪  padding=1),
            nn.ReLU(inplace=True)
        )

    def forward(self, x):
        return self.layers(x)

class UNet(nn.Module):
    '''
    A simplified UNet architecture that processes 3-channel RGB face
    ↪  images.
    '''
    def __init__(self, in_channels=3, out_channels=3,
    ↪  base_channels=64):
        super(UNet, self).__init__()

        # Encoder
        self.down1 = DoubleConv(in_channels, base_channels)
        self.pool1 = nn.MaxPool2d(2)

        self.down2 = DoubleConv(base_channels, base_channels*2)
        self.pool2 = nn.MaxPool2d(2)

        self.down3 = DoubleConv(base_channels*2, base_channels*4)
        self.pool3 = nn.MaxPool2d(2)

        # Bottleneck
        self.bottleneck = DoubleConv(base_channels*4,
        ↪  base_channels*8)

        # Decoder
        self.up1 = nn.ConvTranspose2d(base_channels*8,
        ↪  base_channels*4, kernel_size=2, stride=2)
        self.conv_up1 = DoubleConv(base_channels*8, base_channels*4)

        self.up2 = nn.ConvTranspose2d(base_channels*4,
        ↪  base_channels*2, kernel_size=2, stride=2)
        self.conv_up2 = DoubleConv(base_channels*4, base_channels*2)
```

147

```python
        self.up3 = nn.ConvTranspose2d(base_channels*2,
         ↪  base_channels, kernel_size=2, stride=2)
        self.conv_up3 = DoubleConv(base_channels*2, base_channels)

        # Final convolution
        self.final_conv = nn.Conv2d(base_channels, out_channels,
         ↪  kernel_size=1)

    def forward(self, x):
        # Encoder
        x1 = self.down1(x)
        x2 = self.pool1(x1)

        x2 = self.down2(x2)
        x3 = self.pool2(x2)

        x3 = self.down3(x3)
        x4 = self.pool3(x3)

        # Bottleneck
        x_b = self.bottleneck(x4)

        # Decoder
        x_ = self.up1(x_b)
        x_ = torch.cat([x_, x3], dim=1)
        x_ = self.conv_up1(x_)

        x_ = self.up2(x_)
        x_ = torch.cat([x_, x2], dim=1)
        x_ = self.conv_up2(x_)

        x_ = self.up3(x_)
        x_ = torch.cat([x_, x1], dim=1)
        x_ = self.conv_up3(x_)

        out = self.final_conv(x_)
        return out


# ----------------------------------------------------------------
# 4) Beta schedule and diffusion steps
# ----------------------------------------------------------------
def make_beta_schedule(schedule_name, n_timestep, start=1e-4,
 ↪  end=2e-2):
    '''
    Builds a beta schedule used in the diffusion process.
    Currently only supports a linear schedule as an example.
    '''
    if schedule_name == "linear":
        return torch.linspace(start, end, n_timestep)
    else:
        raise NotImplementedError("Only 'linear' schedule is
         ↪  implemented in this snippet.")
```

```
class Diffusion:
    '''
    The diffusion class handles:
    - forward noising: q(x_t | x_0)
    - reverse denoising: p(x_{t-1} | x_t)
    - sampling from random noise
    '''

    def __init__(self, n_steps=200, beta_schedule='linear'):
        self.n_steps = n_steps
        self.betas = make_beta_schedule(beta_schedule, n_steps)  #
        ↪  shape: [n_steps]
        self.alphas = 1.0 - self.betas
        self.alpha_cumprod = torch.cumprod(self.alphas, dim=0)  #
        ↪  cumulative product
        self.alpha_cumprod_prev = torch.cat([torch.tensor([1.0]),
        ↪  self.alpha_cumprod[:-1]], dim=0)

        # The variance used in p(x_{t-1} | x_t)
        self.posterior_variance = self.betas * (1.0 -
        ↪  self.alpha_cumprod_prev) / (1.0 - self.alpha_cumprod)

    def q_sample(self, x_start, t, noise=None):
        '''
        Diffuse the image x_start to get x_t at step t.
        x_t = sqrt(alpha_cumprod[t]) * x_start + sqrt(1 -
        ↪  alpha_cumprod[t]) * noise
        '''
        if noise is None:
            noise = torch.randn_like(x_start)
        batch_size = x_start.shape[0]

        # Expand scalars to match batch dimension
        sqrt_alpha_cumprod_t =
        ↪  self.alpha_cumprod[t].sqrt().view(-1,1,1,1)
        sqrt_one_minus_alpha_cumprod_t = (1 -
        ↪  self.alpha_cumprod[t]).sqrt().view(-1,1,1,1)

        # We assume each example in the batch has its own t
        sqrt_alpha_cumprod_t = sqrt_alpha_cumprod_t.repeat(1,
        ↪  x_start.shape[1], x_start.shape[2], x_start.shape[3])
        sqrt_one_minus_alpha_cumprod_t =
        ↪  sqrt_one_minus_alpha_cumprod_t.repeat(1,
        ↪  x_start.shape[1], x_start.shape[2], x_start.shape[3])

        out = sqrt_alpha_cumprod_t * x_start +
        ↪  sqrt_one_minus_alpha_cumprod_t * noise
        return out

    def predict_noise(self, model, x_t, t):
        '''
        Predict the noise given x_t using the UNet model.
        '''
```

```python
    return model(x_t)

def p_sample(self, model, x_t, t, guidance_scale=1.0):
    '''
    One step backward: p(x_{t-1} | x_t).
    Use the model's predicted noise to estimate x_0, then sample
    ↪  x_{t-1}.
    '''
    betas_t = self.betas[t].view(-1,1,1,1)
    alpha_t = self.alphas[t].view(-1,1,1,1)
    alpha_cumprod_t = self.alpha_cumprod[t].view(-1,1,1,1)
    alpha_cumprod_prev_t =
    ↪  self.alpha_cumprod_prev[t].view(-1,1,1,1)

    # scale the noise prediction for demonstration to show
    ↪  controlling variation
    e_t = model(x_t) * guidance_scale

    sqrt_recip_alpha_t = (1.0 / alpha_t).sqrt()
    # x_0_hat = (x_t - sqrt(1 - alpha_t)*e_t ) / sqrt(alpha_t)
    x_0_hat = (x_t - (1.0 - alpha_t).sqrt() * e_t) *
    ↪  sqrt_recip_alpha_t

    coef1 = (alpha_cumprod_prev_t.sqrt() * betas_t) / (1.0 -
    ↪  alpha_cumprod_t)
    coef2 = ((1.0 - alpha_cumprod_prev_t) * alpha_t.sqrt()) /
    ↪  (1.0 - alpha_cumprod_t)

    mean = coef1 * x_0_hat + coef2 * x_t

    posterior_variance_t =
    ↪  self.posterior_variance[t].view(-1,1,1,1)
    if t[0] > 0:
        noise = torch.randn_like(x_t)
    else:
        noise = torch.zeros_like(x_t)

    x_prev = mean + noise * posterior_variance_t.sqrt()
    return x_prev

def p_sample_loop(self, model, shape, device,
↪  guidance_scale=1.0):
    '''
    Repeatedly calls p_sample to move from x_T ~ N(0,I) to x_0.
    '''
    b = shape[0]
    # x_t: random Gaussian noise
    x_t = torch.randn(shape, device=device)

    # We'll create a list of timesteps in descending order
    timesteps = list(range(self.n_steps))[::-1]
```

```python
        # For convenience in this snippet, assume the entire batch
        ↪   uses the same t
        for i in timesteps:
            # create a batch of the same t
            t_batch = torch.tensor([i]*b, device=device).long()
            x_t = self.p_sample(model, x_t, t_batch,
            ↪   guidance_scale=guidance_scale)
        return x_t


# -------------------------------------------------------------------
# 5) Training and evaluation
# -------------------------------------------------------------------
def train_one_epoch(model, diffusion, optimizer, dataloader,
↪   device):
    '''
    One epoch of training the diffusion model:
    1) Sample time t
    2) Forward diffuse x_0 -> x_t
    3) Model predicts the noise
    4) Backprop the MSE loss between predicted and actual noise
    '''
    model.train()
    epoch_loss = 0
    for batch_data, _ in dataloader:
        batch_data = batch_data.to(device)
        b_size = batch_data.size(0)

        # sample random timesteps
        t = torch.randint(0, diffusion.n_steps, (b_size,),
        ↪   device=device).long()
        noise = torch.randn_like(batch_data)

        x_t = diffusion.q_sample(batch_data, t, noise=noise)
        noise_pred = diffusion.predict_noise(model, x_t, t)

        loss = nn.functional.mse_loss(noise_pred, noise)
        optimizer.zero_grad()
        loss.backward()
        optimizer.step()

        epoch_loss += loss.item()

    return epoch_loss / len(dataloader)

def evaluate_model(model, diffusion, dataloader, device):
    '''
    Evaluates the model on a validation set with MSE noise
    ↪   prediction.
    '''
    model.eval()
    val_loss = 0
    with torch.no_grad():
```

```python
        for batch_data, _ in dataloader:
            batch_data = batch_data.to(device)
            b_size = batch_data.size(0)

            t = torch.randint(0, diffusion.n_steps, (b_size,),
            ↪  device=device).long()
            noise = torch.randn_like(batch_data)

            x_t = diffusion.q_sample(batch_data, t, noise=noise)
            noise_pred = diffusion.predict_noise(model, x_t, t)

            loss = nn.functional.mse_loss(noise_pred, noise)
            val_loss += loss.item()

    return val_loss / len(dataloader)

def sample_and_save(model, diffusion, device, epoch,
↪  guidance_scale=1.0, save_folder="results"):
    '''
    Generates a set of samples by reversing from random noise and
    ↪  saves them.
    In actual face editing, you'd start from a partially degraded or
    ↪  masked image
    and run the diffusion steps. For simplicity, we illustrate
    ↪  unconditional sampling.
    '''
    model.eval()
    os.makedirs(save_folder, exist_ok=True)

    with torch.no_grad():
        # We'll sample 4 images for demonstration
        num_samples = 4
        shape = (num_samples, 3, 128, 128)  # RGB, 128x128
        generated = diffusion.p_sample_loop(model, shape, device,
        ↪  guidance_scale=guidance_scale)

        # Convert from [-1,1] to [0,1] if your training used that
        ↪  range
        # For this snippet, we will assume the data is already in
        ↪  [-1,1] range
        out_images = (generated.clamp(-1,1) + 1) * 0.5

        # Save each image
        for idx in range(num_samples):
            arr = out_images[idx].permute(1,2,0).cpu().numpy()
            arr = (arr * 255).astype('uint8')
            pil_img = Image.fromarray(arr)
            pil_img.save(os.path.join(save_folder,
            ↪  f"epoch_{epoch}_sample_{idx}_gs{guidance_scale}.png"))


# -------------------------------------------------------------------
# 6) Main script
```

```python
# ------------------------------------------------------------------
def main():
    set_seed(42)
    device = torch.device('cuda' if torch.cuda.is_available() else
    ↪   'cpu')

    # Suppose we have a folder "face_images" with portrait PNG/JPG
    ↪   files
    data_folder = "face_images"

    # Transform: resize, center-crop, convert to [-1,1]
    transform_ops = transforms.Compose([
        transforms.Resize((128,128)),
        transforms.ToTensor(),
        transforms.Normalize((0.5,0.5,0.5),(0.5,0.5,0.5))
    ])

    dataset = FaceDataset(data_folder, transform=transform_ops)
    dataloader = DataLoader(dataset, batch_size=8, shuffle=True,
    ↪   num_workers=0)

    # Initialize model and diffusion
    model = UNet(in_channels=3, out_channels=3,
    ↪   base_channels=64).to(device)
    diffusion = Diffusion(n_steps=200, beta_schedule='linear')

    optimizer = optim.Adam(model.parameters(), lr=1e-4)

    # We'll run a small number of epochs for demonstration
    epochs = 5

    for epoch in range(epochs):
        train_loss = train_one_epoch(model, diffusion, optimizer,
        ↪   dataloader, device)
        val_loss = evaluate_model(model, diffusion, dataloader,
        ↪   device)

        print(f"Epoch [{epoch+1}/{epochs}] - Train Loss:
        ↪   {train_loss:.4f}, Val Loss: {val_loss:.4f}")

        # Sample from random noise (unconditional generation)
        sample_and_save(model, diffusion, device, epoch,
        ↪   guidance_scale=1.0)
        # Additionally, try a stronger guidance scale
        sample_and_save(model, diffusion, device, epoch,
        ↪   guidance_scale=2.0)

    print("Training complete. Check the 'results' folder for sample
    ↪   outputs!")

if __name__ == "__main__":
    main()
```

153

Key Implementation Details:

- **Forward Diffusion:** We implement `q_sample` to add Gaussian noise at each time step t. This operation is repeated for each training batch to produce noisy face images.

- **Reverse Diffusion (Sampling):** Function `p_sample_loop` applies the learned `UNet` in a stepwise manner to progressively remove noise, starting from pure Gaussian noise. In typical face editing scenarios, we might start from a partially corrupted or masked portrait.

- **UNet Architecture:** This simplified `UNet` is adapted for RGB inputs (3 channels). It captures precise facial details using skip connections that preserve high-frequency information crucial for realistic face restorations.

- **Noise-Prediction Objective:** We compute an MSE between the predicted noise and actual Gaussian noise. This objective guides the model to denoise effectively at each time step.

- **Potential Landmark Guidance:** Although not shown in detail here, you can incorporate facial landmarks or segmentation maps by concatenating them as an auxiliary input or injecting them during the skip connections. This preserves anatomical fidelity while making attribute-level edits.

- **Guidance Scale:** The `guidance_scale` parameter scales the predicted noise, offering a way to steer the model's output between faithful restorations and more diverse or exaggerated edits.

Chapter 15

Style Transfer in Diffusion Models

Style transfer extends beyond standard convolutional neural networks by using diffusion to sample fine-grained style patterns in a target domain. Typical tasks include turning real images into impressionist art or applying abstract design motifs. We begin with a dataset of style images and a dataset of content images, corrupting the style examples via noise injection. The diffusion network learns to model style distributions, which are then fused with content images during sampling. Implementation steps involve: (1) training a style diffusion model on a curated style dataset, (2) capturing content image features through a separate encoder path, (3) injecting content feature maps at each denoising step to guide shape and structure, and (4) reversing the diffusion to generate stylized outputs. An innovative approach includes adaptive style fusion, where multiple style references are blended, enabling layered style transfer effects in a single generation process.

Python Code Snippet

```python
import os
import math
import random
import torch
import torch.nn as nn
import torch.optim as optim
from torch.utils.data import DataLoader, Dataset
```

```python
import torchvision.transforms as transforms
import torchvision
import matplotlib.pyplot as plt


# ----------------------------------------------------------------
# 1) Set random seed for reproducibility
# ----------------------------------------------------------------
def set_seed(seed=42):
    random.seed(seed)
    torch.manual_seed(seed)
    if torch.cuda.is_available():
        torch.cuda.manual_seed_all(seed)


# ----------------------------------------------------------------
# Sample Datasets (Style and Content)
# For demonstration, we use MNIST for content and CIFAR10 for style
# ↪  in this snippet.
# In practice, supply your own style images and content images.
# ----------------------------------------------------------------
class StyleDataset(Dataset):
    def __init__(self, root='data_cifar', download=True):
        super(StyleDataset, self).__init__()
        self.transform = transforms.Compose([
            transforms.Resize((32,32)),
            transforms.ToTensor(),
            transforms.Normalize((0.5,0.5,0.5),(0.5,0.5,0.5))
        ])
        self.dataset = torchvision.datasets.CIFAR10(
            root=root, train=True, download=download,
            ↪  transform=self.transform
        )

    def __len__(self):
        return len(self.dataset)

    def __getitem__(self, idx):
        img, _ = self.dataset[idx]
        return img

class ContentDataset(Dataset):
    def __init__(self, root='data_mnist', download=True):
        super(ContentDataset, self).__init__()
        self.transform = transforms.Compose([
            transforms.Resize((32,32)),
            transforms.ToTensor(),
            transforms.Normalize((0.5,),(0.5,))
        ])
        self.dataset = torchvision.datasets.MNIST(
            root=root, train=True, download=download,
            ↪  transform=self.transform
        )

    def __len__(self):
```

```python
        return len(self.dataset)

    def __getitem__(self, idx):
        img, _ = self.dataset[idx]
        # The MNIST is single-channel, convert to 3-channel to match
        ↪  style dimension
        img_3ch = torch.cat([img, img, img], dim=0)
        return img_3ch


# ---------------------------------------------------------------
# 2) Encoders for style features and content features
# ---------------------------------------------------------------
class StyleEncoder(nn.Module):
    """
    A lightweight encoder to extract style features from a style
    ↪  image.
    """

    def __init__(self, in_channels=3, style_dim=128):
        super(StyleEncoder, self).__init__()
        self.features = nn.Sequential(
            nn.Conv2d(in_channels, 64, kernel_size=4, stride=2,
            ↪  padding=1),
            nn.ReLU(inplace=True),
            nn.Conv2d(64, 128, kernel_size=4, stride=2, padding=1),
            nn.ReLU(inplace=True)
        )
        self.pool = nn.AdaptiveAvgPool2d((1,1))
        self.fc = nn.Linear(128, style_dim)

    def forward(self, x):
        x = self.features(x)
        x = self.pool(x)
        x = x.view(x.size(0), -1)
        x = self.fc(x)
        return x   # style embedding


class ContentEncoder(nn.Module):
    """
    Extract content features (e.g., shape or structure) from a
    ↪  content image.
    """

    def __init__(self, in_channels=3, content_dim=128):
        super(ContentEncoder, self).__init__()
        self.features = nn.Sequential(
            nn.Conv2d(in_channels, 64, kernel_size=4, stride=2,
            ↪  padding=1),
            nn.ReLU(inplace=True),
            nn.Conv2d(64, 128, kernel_size=4, stride=2, padding=1),
            nn.ReLU(inplace=True)
        )
        self.pool = nn.AdaptiveAvgPool2d((1,1))
        self.fc = nn.Linear(128, content_dim)
```

```python
    def forward(self, x):
        x = self.features(x)
        x = self.pool(x)
        x = x.view(x.size(0), -1)
        x = self.fc(x)
        return x  # content embedding


# ----------------------------------------------------------------
# 3) A simplified U-Net that merges style embedding + content
# ↪   embedding
#     into the diffusion denoising steps
# ----------------------------------------------------------------
class DoubleConv(nn.Module):
    '''
    Basic 2D convolution block: Conv -> ReLU -> Conv -> ReLU
    '''
    def __init__(self, in_channels, out_channels):
        super(DoubleConv, self).__init__()
        self.sequence = nn.Sequential(
            nn.Conv2d(in_channels, out_channels, kernel_size=3,
            ↪   padding=1),
            nn.ReLU(inplace=True),
            nn.Conv2d(out_channels, out_channels, kernel_size=3,
            ↪   padding=1),
            nn.ReLU(inplace=True)
        )
    def forward(self, x):
        return self.sequence(x)


class StyleTransferUNet(nn.Module):
    '''
    A U-Net variant that merges style and content embeddings
    at each scale. The style embedding is broadcast as a feature map
    and concatenated, likewise content embedding is broadcast.
    '''
    def __init__(self, in_channels=3, out_channels=3, hidden_dim=64,
    ↪   style_dim=128, content_dim=128):
        super(StyleTransferUNet, self).__init__()
        # Down modules
        self.down1 = DoubleConv(in_channels + 2, hidden_dim)
        self.pool = nn.MaxPool2d(2)
        self.down2 = DoubleConv(hidden_dim + 2, hidden_dim*2)
        self.down3 = DoubleConv(hidden_dim*2 + 2, hidden_dim*4)

        # Bottleneck
        self.bottleneck = DoubleConv(hidden_dim*4 + 2, hidden_dim*8)

        # Up modules
        self.up1 = nn.ConvTranspose2d(hidden_dim*8, hidden_dim*4,
        ↪   kernel_size=2, stride=2)
        self.conv_up1 = DoubleConv(hidden_dim*8 + 2, hidden_dim*4)
```

158

```python
        self.up2 = nn.ConvTranspose2d(hidden_dim*4, hidden_dim*2,
        ↪  kernel_size=2, stride=2)
        self.conv_up2 = DoubleConv(hidden_dim*4 + 2, hidden_dim*2)

        self.up3 = nn.ConvTranspose2d(hidden_dim*2, hidden_dim,
        ↪  kernel_size=2, stride=2)
        self.conv_up3 = DoubleConv(hidden_dim*2 + 2, hidden_dim)

        self.final_conv = nn.Conv2d(hidden_dim, out_channels,
        ↪  kernel_size=1)

        # Mapping from style and content embeddings to a 2-channel
        ↪  map
        self.style_mapper = nn.Linear(style_dim, 1)
        self.content_mapper = nn.Linear(content_dim, 1)

    def forward(self, x, style_emb, content_emb):
        # Convert style and content embeddings into 2D feature maps
        # For simplicity, we create a single-channel from style,
        ↪  single-channel from content
        B, _, H, W = x.shape
        style_w =
        ↪  self.style_mapper(style_emb).unsqueeze(-1).unsqueeze(-1)
        content_w =
        ↪  self.content_mapper(content_emb).unsqueeze(-1).unsqueeze(-1)
        style_map = style_w.repeat(1, 1, H, W)
        content_map = content_w.repeat(1, 1, H, W)

        # Merge into x
        x = torch.cat([x, style_map, content_map], dim=1)
        skip1 = self.down1(x)
        x = self.pool(skip1)

        # at next scale, re-broadcast style, content
        B, _, H2, W2 = x.shape
        style_map2 = style_w.repeat(1, 1, H2, W2)
        content_map2 = content_w.repeat(1, 1, H2, W2)
        x = torch.cat([x, style_map2, content_map2], dim=1)

        skip2 = self.down2(x)
        x = self.pool(skip2)

        B, _, H3, W3 = x.shape
        style_map3 = style_w.repeat(1, 1, H3, W3)
        content_map3 = content_w.repeat(1, 1, H3, W3)
        x = torch.cat([x, style_map3, content_map3], dim=1)

        skip3 = self.down3(x)
        x = self.pool(skip3)

        B, _, H4, W4 = x.shape
        style_map4 = style_w.repeat(1, 1, H4, W4)
        content_map4 = content_w.repeat(1, 1, H4, W4)
```

```python
    x = torch.cat([x, style_map4, content_map4], dim=1)

    # Bottleneck
    bottleneck = self.bottleneck(x)

    # Up stage
    x = self.up1(bottleneck)
    # Re-broadcast at new resolution
    B, _, H_u1, W_u1 = x.shape
    style_map_u1 = style_w.repeat(1, 1, H_u1, W_u1)
    content_map_u1 = content_w.repeat(1, 1, H_u1, W_u1)
    x = torch.cat([x, skip3, style_map_u1, content_map_u1],
    ↪   dim=1)
    x = self.conv_up1(x)

    x = self.up2(x)
    B, _, H_u2, W_u2 = x.shape
    style_map_u2 = style_w.repeat(1, 1, H_u2, W_u2)
    content_map_u2 = content_w.repeat(1, 1, H_u2, W_u2)
    x = torch.cat([x, skip2, style_map_u2, content_map_u2],
    ↪   dim=1)
    x = self.conv_up2(x)

    x = self.up3(x)
    B, _, H_u3, W_u3 = x.shape
    style_map_u3 = style_w.repeat(1, 1, H_u3, W_u3)
    content_map_u3 = content_w.repeat(1, 1, H_u3, W_u3)
    x = torch.cat([x, skip1, style_map_u3, content_map_u3],
    ↪   dim=1)
    x = self.conv_up3(x)

    out = self.final_conv(x)
    return out

# ----------------------------------------------------------------
# 4) Define a linear beta schedule and the forward/backward
↪   diffusion
# ----------------------------------------------------------------
def make_beta_schedule(schedule_name, n_timestep, start=1e-4,
↪   end=2e-2):
    if schedule_name == "linear":
        return torch.linspace(start, end, n_timestep)
    else:
        raise NotImplementedError("Only 'linear' schedule is
        ↪   implemented.")

class Diffusion:
    """
    Encapsulates the forward noising (q_sample) and reverse
    ↪   denoising (p_sample)
    processes for style distribution modeling.
    """
    def __init__(self, n_steps=200, beta_schedule='linear'):
```

```python
        self.n_steps = n_steps
        self.betas = make_beta_schedule(beta_schedule, n_steps)
        self.alphas = 1.0 - self.betas
        self.alpha_cumprod = torch.cumprod(self.alphas, dim=0)
        self.alpha_cumprod_prev = torch.cat(
            [torch.tensor([1.0]), self.alpha_cumprod[:-1]], dim=0
        )

        self.posterior_variance = (
            self.betas * (1.0 - self.alpha_cumprod_prev) / (1.0 -
            ↪ self.alpha_cumprod)
        )

    def q_sample(self, x_start, t, noise=None):
        if noise is None:
            noise = torch.randn_like(x_start)
        sqrt_alpha_cumprod_t =
        ↪ self.alpha_cumprod[t].sqrt().view(-1,1,1,1)
        sqrt_one_minus_alpha_cumprod_t = (1 -
        ↪ self.alpha_cumprod[t]).sqrt().view(-1,1,1,1)
        return sqrt_alpha_cumprod_t * x_start +
        ↪ sqrt_one_minus_alpha_cumprod_t * noise

    def predict_noise(self, model, x_t, style_emb, content_emb, t):
        return model(x_t, style_emb, content_emb)

    def p_sample(self, model, x_t, style_emb, content_emb, t):
        betas_t = self.betas[t]
        alpha_t = self.alphas[t]
        alpha_cumprod_t = self.alpha_cumprod[t]
        alpha_cumprod_prev_t = self.alpha_cumprod_prev[t]

        e_t = model(x_t, style_emb, content_emb)

        sqrt_recip_alpha_t = (1 / alpha_t).sqrt()
        x_0_hat = (x_t - (1 - alpha_t).sqrt() * e_t) *
        ↪ sqrt_recip_alpha_t

        coef1 = (alpha_cumprod_prev_t.sqrt() * betas_t) / (1.0 -
        ↪ alpha_cumprod_t)
        coef2 = ((1.0 - alpha_cumprod_prev_t) * alpha_t.sqrt()) /
        ↪ (1.0 - alpha_cumprod_t)

        mean = coef1 * x_0_hat + coef2 * x_t
        posterior_var = self.posterior_variance[t]
        if t > 0:
            noise = torch.randn_like(x_t)
        else:
            noise = torch.zeros_like(x_t)
        x_prev = mean + noise * posterior_var.sqrt()
        return x_prev
```

```
    def p_sample_loop(self, model, style_emb, content_emb, shape,
    ↪   device):
        x = torch.randn(shape, device=device)
        for i in reversed(range(self.n_steps)):
            x = self.p_sample(model, x, style_emb, content_emb, i)
        return x


# ----------------------------------------------------------------
# 5) Training loop
# ----------------------------------------------------------------
def train_one_epoch(style_loader, content_loader, model, style_enc,
↪   content_enc,
                    diffusion, optimizer, device):
    model.train()
    total_loss = 0.0
    style_iter = iter(style_loader)
    content_iter = iter(content_loader)

    # We assume same length or whichever is shorter for
    ↪   demonstration
    steps = min(len(style_loader), len(content_loader))
    for _ in range(steps):
        try:
            style_imgs = next(style_iter)
        except StopIteration:
            style_iter = iter(style_loader)
            style_imgs = next(style_iter)

        try:
            content_imgs = next(content_iter)
        except StopIteration:
            content_iter = iter(content_loader)
            content_imgs = next(content_iter)

        style_imgs = style_imgs.to(device)
        content_imgs = content_imgs.to(device)

        # Encode style & content
        style_emb = style_enc(style_imgs)
        content_emb = content_enc(content_imgs)

        # Random time step
        t = torch.randint(0, diffusion.n_steps,
        ↪   (style_imgs.size(0),), device=device).long()

        noise = torch.randn_like(style_imgs)
        x_t = diffusion.q_sample(style_imgs, t, noise=noise)

        # Predict noise
        noise_pred = diffusion.predict_noise(model, x_t, style_emb,
        ↪   content_emb, t)

        loss = nn.MSELoss()(noise_pred, noise)
```

```
        optimizer.zero_grad()
        loss.backward()
        optimizer.step()

        total_loss += loss.item()

    return total_loss / steps

# ----------------------------------------------------------------
# 6) Simple evaluation (L2 error on style images)
# ----------------------------------------------------------------
def evaluate_model(style_loader, model, style_enc, content_enc,
↪   diffusion, device):
    model.eval()
    total_loss = 0.0
    with torch.no_grad():
        for style_imgs in style_loader:
            style_imgs = style_imgs.to(device)

            # Use a dummy content here (could be from a small
            ↪   subset)
            dummy_content = style_imgs   # in real setting, load some
            ↪   content images
            style_emb = style_enc(style_imgs)
            content_emb = content_enc(dummy_content)

            t = torch.randint(0, diffusion.n_steps,
            ↪   (style_imgs.size(0),), device=device).long()
            noise = torch.randn_like(style_imgs)
            x_t = diffusion.q_sample(style_imgs, t, noise=noise)
            noise_pred = diffusion.predict_noise(model, x_t,
            ↪   style_emb, content_emb, t)
            loss = nn.MSELoss()(noise_pred, noise)
            total_loss += loss.item()
    return total_loss / len(style_loader)


# ----------------------------------------------------------------
# 7) Sampling and merging style/content
# ----------------------------------------------------------------
def sample_stylized_image(model, style_enc, content_enc, diffusion,
↪   style_img, content_img, device):
    style_img = style_img.unsqueeze(0).to(device)
    content_img = content_img.unsqueeze(0).to(device)

    style_emb = style_enc(style_img)
    content_emb = content_enc(content_img)

    # Start from random noise, reconstruct style distribution while
    ↪   guided by content
    with torch.no_grad():
        generated = diffusion.p_sample_loop(
            model, style_emb, content_emb, style_img.shape, device
```

163

```python
        )
        # Convert from [-1,1] to [0,1] if needed for display
        out = (generated.clamp(-1, 1) + 1) * 0.5
        return out.squeeze(0)


# --------------------------------------------------------------
# 8) Main driver
# --------------------------------------------------------------
def main():
    set_seed(42)
    device = torch.device('cuda' if torch.cuda.is_available() else
    ↪  'cpu')

    # Create style/content datasets
    style_dataset = StyleDataset()
    content_dataset = ContentDataset()

    style_loader = DataLoader(style_dataset, batch_size=8,
    ↪  shuffle=True)
    content_loader = DataLoader(content_dataset, batch_size=8,
    ↪  shuffle=True)

    # Initialize encoders
    style_encoder = StyleEncoder().to(device)
    content_encoder = ContentEncoder().to(device)

    # Initialize UNet
    model = StyleTransferUNet(in_channels=3, out_channels=3,
                              hidden_dim=64, style_dim=128,
                              ↪  content_dim=128).to(device)

    # Diffusion
    diffusion = Diffusion(n_steps=200, beta_schedule='linear')

    # Optimizer
    params = list(model.parameters()) +
    ↪  list(style_encoder.parameters()) +
    ↪  list(content_encoder.parameters())
    optimizer = optim.Adam(params, lr=1e-4)

    # Training
    epochs = 3  # just a small number for example
    for epoch in range(epochs):
        train_loss = train_one_epoch(style_loader, content_loader,
        ↪  model,
                                     style_encoder, content_encoder,
                                     diffusion, optimizer, device)
        val_loss = evaluate_model(style_loader, model,
        ↪  style_encoder, content_encoder, diffusion, device)
        print(f"Epoch [{epoch+1}/{epochs}] - Train Loss:
        ↪  {train_loss:.4f}, Val Loss: {val_loss:.4f}")

        # Demonstration of sampling on a single style/content pair
```

```
style_sample, _ = style_dataset[0].clone(), 0
content_sample, _ = content_dataset[0].clone(), 0
stylized = sample_stylized_image(
    model, style_encoder, content_encoder, diffusion,
    ↪ style_sample, content_sample, device
)

# Save the stylized image
os.makedirs("results_style_transfer", exist_ok=True)
grid = torchvision.utils.make_grid(stylized.unsqueeze(0),
    ↪ nrow=1)
plt.figure(figsize=(3,3))
plt.axis("off")
plt.imshow(grid.permute(1,2,0).cpu().numpy())
plt.savefig(f"results_style_transfer/
stylized_epoch_{epoch+1}.png")
plt.close()

print("Style transfer training complete! Check
↪ 'results_style_transfer' folder for sample outputs.")

if __name__ == "__main__":
    main()
```

Key Implementation Details:

- **Forward Diffusion:** We implement `q_sample` to corrupt style images, where `x_t` is formed by blending the original style image with Gaussian noise based on a linear `beta` schedule.

- **Reverse Diffusion:** Implemented in `p_sample_loop`, the model iteratively denoises from random noise, guided by style and content embeddings.

- **Style & Content Encodings:** The `StyleEncoder` and `ContentEncoder` produce low-dimensional embeddings from style and content images, which are injected into the U-Net at various scales.

- **StyleTransferUNet:** At each scale, we broadcast the style and content embeddings as small feature maps and concatenate them with the intermediate feature maps, providing the necessary conditioning for style transfer during denoising.

- **Training Objective:** We directly predict the noise introduced in the forward diffusion process with a mean-squared

165

error (`MSELoss`) between predicted noise and actual noise.

- **Dataset Details:** In the code example, CIFAR10 images are used as style references and MNIST images as content placeholders. Real-world usage would replace these with specialized style and content datasets (e.g., Monet paintings for style and photographic images for content).

Chapter 16

Colorization of Grayscale Images

Colorizing black-and-white photos is a valuable application for historical image restoration or creative design. Here, diffusion treats grayscale images as the conditioning input while the model learns to inject plausible color details. The forward process randomly corrupts color channels in original training images while preserving luminance. The diffusion network conditions on the grayscale input to estimate and denoise color information step by step. Key implementation details: (1) splitting images into separate luminance and color components, (2) training a diffusion pipeline that progressively corrupts color, (3) concatenating the grayscale channel into the UNet to guide color reconstruction, (4) minimizing a noise prediction loss tailored to the color space, and (5) sampling new colorizations by applying reverse diffusion to a grayscale photograph. An innovative extension is a palette-based sampling scheme that can restrict or alter the color palette for artistic or thematic effects.

Python Code Snippet

```python
import os
import random
import math
import numpy as np
import torch
import torch.nn as nn
```

```python
import torch.optim as optim
from torch.utils.data import DataLoader, Dataset
import torchvision
import torchvision.transforms as T
import matplotlib.pyplot as plt

# ----------------------------------------------------------------
# 1) Utility function: fix seed for reproducibility
# ----------------------------------------------------------------
def set_seed(seed=42):
    random.seed(seed)
    np.random.seed(seed)
    torch.manual_seed(seed)
    if torch.cuda.is_available():
        torch.cuda.manual_seed_all(seed)


# ----------------------------------------------------------------
# 2) Dataset for Colorization
#    We will transform images to a format: [L, C1, C2],
#    where L = grayscale luminance, C1 and C2 are "color difference"
# ↪  channels.
#    For demonstration, we do a simplistic transform:
#      L = 0.299 * R + 0.587 * G + 0.114 * B
#      C1 = R - L
#      C2 = B - L
#    (This is not a true color space like Lab, but suffices here.)
# ----------------------------------------------------------------
class ColorizationDataset(Dataset):
    def __init__(self, root, train=True, transform=None,
    ↪  download=True):
        self.dataset = torchvision.datasets.CIFAR10(
            root=root,
            train=train,
            transform=transform,
            download=download
        )

    def __len__(self):
        return len(self.dataset)

    def __getitem__(self, idx):
        img, _ = self.dataset[idx]
        # img shape: [3, H, W] in [0,1] after transform
        # Convert to grayscale + color difference channels
        with torch.no_grad():
            R = img[0, :, :]
            G = img[1, :, :]
            B = img[2, :, :]

            L = 0.299 * R + 0.587 * G + 0.114 * B
            C1 = R - L
            C2 = B - L
```

168

```python
        # We'll return a 3-channel: [L, C1, C2]
        colorized = torch.stack([L, C1, C2], dim=0)

        return colorized, 0   # We don't need a label here


# ----------------------------------------------------------
# 3) Simple U-Net for colorization
#    in_channels=3 (L, C1, C2), out_channels=3 (predict noise in L,
#    C1, C2).
#     We can later mask the L channel if we only want to add noise to
#     color.
# ----------------------------------------------------------
class DoubleConv(nn.Module):
    '''
    Two consecutive convolutions (with ReLU) in a small block.
    '''

    def __init__(self, in_channels, out_channels):
        super(DoubleConv, self).__init__()
        self.conv = nn.Sequential(
            nn.Conv2d(in_channels, out_channels, kernel_size=3,
                padding=1),
            nn.ReLU(inplace=True),
            nn.Conv2d(out_channels, out_channels, kernel_size=3,
                padding=1),
            nn.ReLU(inplace=True)
        )


    def forward(self, x):
        return self.conv(x)


class UNet(nn.Module):
    '''
    A simplified U-Net with downsampling and upsampling blocks.
    '''

    def __init__(self, in_channels=3, out_channels=3,
        base_channels=64):
        super(UNet, self).__init__()

        # Encoder (down)
        self.down1 = DoubleConv(in_channels, base_channels)
        self.pool1 = nn.MaxPool2d(2)
        self.down2 = DoubleConv(base_channels, base_channels*2)
        self.pool2 = nn.MaxPool2d(2)
        self.down3 = DoubleConv(base_channels*2, base_channels*4)
        self.pool3 = nn.MaxPool2d(2)

        # Bottleneck
        self.bottleneck = DoubleConv(base_channels*4,
            base_channels*8)

        # Decoder (up)
        self.up1 = nn.ConvTranspose2d(base_channels*8,
            base_channels*4, kernel_size=2, stride=2)
```

```python
        self.conv_up1 = DoubleConv(base_channels*8, base_channels*4)

        self.up2 = nn.ConvTranspose2d(base_channels*4,
        ↪  base_channels*2, kernel_size=2, stride=2)
        self.conv_up2 = DoubleConv(base_channels*4, base_channels*2)

        self.up3 = nn.ConvTranspose2d(base_channels*2,
        ↪  base_channels, kernel_size=2, stride=2)
        self.conv_up3 = DoubleConv(base_channels*2, base_channels)

        # Final output
        self.final_conv = nn.Conv2d(base_channels, out_channels,
        ↪  kernel_size=1)

    def forward(self, x):
        # Encode
        x1 = self.down1(x)
        x2 = self.pool1(x1)

        x2 = self.down2(x2)
        x3 = self.pool2(x2)

        x3 = self.down3(x3)
        x4 = self.pool3(x3)

        # Bottleneck
        b = self.bottleneck(x4)

        # Decode
        x = self.up1(b)
        x = torch.cat([x, x3], dim=1)   # skip
        x = self.conv_up1(x)

        x = self.up2(x)
        x = torch.cat([x, x2], dim=1)   # skip
        x = self.conv_up2(x)

        x = self.up3(x)
        x = torch.cat([x, x1], dim=1)   # skip
        x = self.conv_up3(x)

        out = self.final_conv(x)
        return out

# ------------------------------------------------------------
# 4) Diffusion schedule and forward noising
#    We preserve the L channel (channel 0) and only corrupt C1, C2
#    by applying a zero mask to noise for channel 0.
# ------------------------------------------------------------
def make_beta_schedule(schedule_name, n_timestep, start=1e-4,
↪  end=2e-2):
    '''
    Creates a beta schedule for the diffusion process.
```

```
    We use a linear schedule as an example.
    '''
    if schedule_name == "linear":
        return torch.linspace(start, end, n_timestep)
    else:
        raise NotImplementedError("Only 'linear' schedule is
        ↪    supported here.")


class Diffusion:
    def __init__(self, n_steps=200, beta_schedule='linear'):
        self.n_steps = n_steps
        self.betas = make_beta_schedule(beta_schedule, n_steps)
        self.alphas = 1.0 - self.betas
        self.alpha_cumprod = torch.cumprod(self.alphas, dim=0)
        self.alpha_cumprod_prev = torch.cat([torch.tensor([1.0]),
        ↪    self.alpha_cumprod[:-1]], dim=0)

        # Posterior variance for p(x_{t-1} | x_t, x_0)
        self.posterior_variance = self.betas * (1.0 -
        ↪    self.alpha_cumprod_prev) / (1.0 - self.alpha_cumprod)


    def q_sample(self, x_start, t, device, noise=None):
        '''
        Forward diffusion: x_t = sqrt(alpha_cumprod[t]) * x_start +
        ↪    sqrt(1 - alpha_cumprod[t]) * noise
        We apply noise only to channels 1..2, leaving channel 0 (L)
        ↪    uncorrupted.
        '''
        if noise is None:
            noise = torch.randn_like(x_start).to(device)
        # Zero out noise for the L channel
        noise[:, 0, :, :] = 0.0

        sqrt_alpha_cumprod_t =
        ↪    self.alpha_cumprod[t].sqrt().reshape(-1, 1, 1, 1)
        sqrt_one_minus_alpha_cumprod_t = (1 -
        ↪    self.alpha_cumprod[t]).sqrt().reshape(-1, 1, 1, 1)

        # x_t
        x_t = sqrt_alpha_cumprod_t * x_start +
        ↪    sqrt_one_minus_alpha_cumprod_t * noise
        return x_t


    def predict_noise(self, model, x_t, t):
        '''
        Use the model to predict noise from x_t at step t.
        '''
        return model(x_t)


    def p_sample(self, model, x_t, t, device, guidance_scale=1.0):
        '''
        One reverse diffusion step: p(x_{t-1} | x_t).
```

171

```python
    The model predicts noise. We reconstruct x_0, then sample
    ↪   x_{t-1}.
    We preserve the L channel from x_t to anchor grayscale.
    '''
    betas_t = self.betas[t].to(device)
    alpha_t = self.alphas[t].to(device)
    alpha_cumprod_t = self.alpha_cumprod[t].to(device)
    alpha_cumprod_prev_t = self.alpha_cumprod_prev[t].to(device)

    # Predict noise
    e_t = model(x_t) * guidance_scale

    # Force predicted noise on L channel to be zero, ensuring L
    ↪   is not changed
    e_t[:, 0, :, :] = 0.0

    # Reconstruct x_0
    sqrt_recip_alpha_t = (1.0 / alpha_t).sqrt()
    x_0_hat = (x_t - (1.0 - alpha_t).sqrt() * e_t) *
    ↪   sqrt_recip_alpha_t

    # Weighted coefficients
    coef1 = ((alpha_cumprod_prev_t).sqrt() * betas_t) / (1.0 -
    ↪   alpha_cumprod_t)
    coef2 = ((1.0 - alpha_cumprod_prev_t) * alpha_t.sqrt()) /
    ↪   (1.0 - alpha_cumprod_t)

    mean = coef1 * x_0_hat + coef2 * x_t

    # Posterior variance
    posterior_var = self.posterior_variance[t].to(device)
    if t > 0:
        noise = torch.randn_like(x_t).to(device)
        # No noise for L channel again
        noise[:, 0, :, :] = 0.0
    else:
        noise = torch.zeros_like(x_t).to(device)

    x_prev = mean + noise * posterior_var.sqrt()
    return x_prev

def p_sample_loop(self, model, x_init, device,
↪   guidance_scale=1.0):
    '''
    Repeatedly apply p_sample from x_T to x_0.
    x_init is the corrupted image we start with. We only sample
    ↪   color channels.
    For colorization from scratch, x_init can hold the real L
    ↪   channel + random color on C1, C2.
    '''

    x_t = x_init
    for i in reversed(range(self.n_steps)):
```

172

```python
                x_t = self.p_sample(model, x_t, i, device,
                ↪   guidance_scale)
            return x_t


    # ---------------------------------------------------------------
    # 5) Training and sampling routines
    # ---------------------------------------------------------------
    def train_one_epoch(model, diffusion, optimizer, dataloader,
    ↪   device):
        model.train()
        total_loss = 0
        for data, _ in dataloader:
            data = data.to(device)  # shape: [B, 3, H, W] => [L, C1, C2]

            # Sample a random t
            t = torch.randint(0, diffusion.n_steps, (data.size(0),),
            ↪   device=device).long()

            # Create noise only for color channels
            noise = torch.randn_like(data).to(device)
            noise[:, 0, :, :] = 0.0  # L channel not noised

            # Forward diffuse
            x_t = diffusion.q_sample(data, t, device, noise=noise)

            # Predict noise
            noise_pred = diffusion.predict_noise(model, x_t, t)

            # We compute MSE loss only on color channels: 1..2
            loss = ((noise_pred[:, 1:, :, :] - noise[:, 1:, :,
            ↪   :])**2).mean()

            optimizer.zero_grad()
            loss.backward()
            optimizer.step()

            total_loss += loss.item()

        return total_loss / len(dataloader)

    def evaluate_model(model, diffusion, dataloader, device):
        model.eval()
        total_loss = 0
        with torch.no_grad():
            for data, _ in dataloader:
                data = data.to(device)
                t = torch.randint(0, diffusion.n_steps, (data.size(0),),
                ↪   device=device).long()
                noise = torch.randn_like(data).to(device)
                noise[:, 0, :, :] = 0.0
                x_t = diffusion.q_sample(data, t, device, noise=noise)
                noise_pred = diffusion.predict_noise(model, x_t, t)
```

```
                val_loss = ((noise_pred[:, 1:, :, :] - noise[:, 1:, :,
                 ↪    :])**2).mean()
                total_loss += val_loss.item()
        return total_loss / len(dataloader)

def colorize_grayscale_image(model, diffusion, L_channel, device,
 ↪  guidance_scale=1.0):
    '''
    Given a grayscale image (L_channel), generate color channels
     ↪  with diffusion.
    L_channel shape: [1, H, W]
    We create an initial x_init with random color for C1,C2,
     ↪  preserving L.
    Then call p_sample_loop.
    Returns final [L, C1, C2].
    '''
    model.eval()
    with torch.no_grad():
        # Expand to batch dimension=1 to feed model
        L_channel = L_channel.unsqueeze(0).to(device)  # [1, 1, H,
         ↪  W]
        _, _, H, W = L_channel.shape

        # Create random color for channels 1..2
        random_color = torch.randn((1, 2, H, W), device=device)
        # Combine
        x_init = torch.cat([L_channel, random_color], dim=1)  #
         ↪  shape [1,3,H,W]

        # We run p_sample_loop starting from x_init
        x_final = diffusion.p_sample_loop(model, x_init, device,
         ↪  guidance_scale)
        return x_final

def render_to_rgb(tensor_image):
    '''
    Convert the [L, C1, C2] representation back to a simple RGB to
     ↪  visualize.
    L = 0.299*R + 0.587*G + 0.114*B
    C1 = R - L
    C2 = B - L
    => R = C1 + L
       B = C2 + L
       G ~ (L - 0.299R - 0.114B)/0.587
    This is approximate for demonstration.
    '''
    L = tensor_image[0, :, :]
    C1 = tensor_image[1, :, :]
    C2 = tensor_image[2, :, :]

    R = C1 + L
    B = C2 + L
    # We derive G from L = 0.299R + 0.587G + 0.114B
```

174

```python
    # => G = (L - 0.299R - 0.114B)/0.587
    G = (L - 0.299*R - 0.114*B) / 0.587

    rgb = torch.stack([R, G, B], dim=0)
    # Clip to [0,1] just in case
    rgb = torch.clamp(rgb, 0.0, 1.0)
    return rgb

def sample_and_save_colorization(model, diffusion, device, epoch,
↪ dataloader):
    '''
    Take a few grayscale images from the dataloader, colorize them,
    ↪ and save the results.
    '''
    model.eval()
    data_iter = iter(dataloader)
    data, _ = next(data_iter)
    data = data.to(device)

    # We'll take the first 4 images in the batch
    batch_L = data[:4, 0:1, :, :]  # shape [4,1,H,W]

    with torch.no_grad():
        results = []
        for i in range(batch_L.size(0)):
            L_i = batch_L[i]  # [1,H,W]
            colored = colorize_grayscale_image(model, diffusion,
            ↪ L_i, device, guidance_scale=1.5)
            # colored shape [1,3,H,W]
            # Get rid of batch dim
            c_img = colored[0].detach().cpu()
            results.append(c_img)

        fig, axs = plt.subplots(2, batch_L.size(0),
        ↪ figsize=(4*batch_L.size(0), 6))
        for i in range(batch_L.size(0)):
            # Original grayscale
            gray = batch_L[i][0].cpu().numpy()
            axs[0, i].imshow(gray, cmap='gray', vmin=0, vmax=1)
            axs[0, i].set_title("Grayscale (L only)")
            axs[0, i].axis('off')

            # Colorized result -> convert to RGB
            colorized_LC1C2 = results[i]
            rgb_final = render_to_rgb(colorized_LC1C2)
            rgb_numpy = rgb_final.permute(1,2,0).cpu().numpy()
            axs[1, i].imshow(rgb_numpy, vmin=0, vmax=1)
            axs[1, i].set_title("Colorized")
            axs[1, i].axis('off')

        os.makedirs("results_colorize", exist_ok=True)
        plt.tight_layout()
        plt.savefig(f"results_colorize/epoch_{epoch}.png")
```

175

```python
        plt.close()

# ---------------------------------------------------------------
# 6) Main training loop
# ---------------------------------------------------------------
def main():
    set_seed(42)
    device = torch.device("cuda" if torch.cuda.is_available() else
    ↪   "cpu")

    # Transforms: resize, to tensor, scale to [0,1]
    transform = T.Compose([
        T.Resize((32,32)),
        T.ToTensor()
    ])

    train_dataset = ColorizationDataset(root='data_cifar',
                                        train=True,
                                        transform=transform,
                                        download=True)
    test_dataset = ColorizationDataset(root='data_cifar',
                                        train=False,
                                        transform=transform,
                                        download=True)

    train_loader = DataLoader(train_dataset, batch_size=64,
    ↪   shuffle=True)
    test_loader = DataLoader(test_dataset, batch_size=64,
    ↪   shuffle=False)

    # Initialize U-Net, Diffusion
    model = UNet(in_channels=3, out_channels=3,
    ↪   base_channels=64).to(device)
    diffusion = Diffusion(n_steps=200, beta_schedule='linear')

    # Optimizer
    optimizer = optim.Adam(model.parameters(), lr=1e-4)
    epochs = 5

    for epoch in range(epochs):
        train_loss = train_one_epoch(model, diffusion, optimizer,
        ↪   train_loader, device)
        val_loss = evaluate_model(model, diffusion, test_loader,
        ↪   device)
        print(f"Epoch [{epoch+1}/{epochs}] - Train Loss:
        ↪   {train_loss:.4f}, Val Loss: {val_loss:.4f}")

        # We'll colorize a few grayscale images and save them
        sample_and_save_colorization(model, diffusion, device,
        ↪   epoch, test_loader)

    print("Colorization training complete! See 'results_colorize'
    ↪   folder for samples.")
```

```
if __name__ == "__main__":
    main()
```

Key Implementation Details:

- **Splitting Luminance and Color:** We define a color difference scheme inside `ColorizationDataset` by isolating the luminance (L) channel and two difference channels (C1, C2).

- **Forward Diffusion (`q_sample`):** We only add random noise to C1 and C2. The L channel remains uncorrupted, thereby preserving the grayscale structure.

- **Reverse Diffusion (`p_sample`):** The model predicts color noise at each step. The L channel remains untouched, maintaining the original luminance.

- **UNet Architecture:** Our `UNet` has three input channels (`in_channels=3`) and three output channels. The skip connections help preserve spatial detail from input to output.

- **Loss Function:** We use an MSE loss only on the color channels. This ensures the model focuses on predicting the color-related noise without altering luminance.

- **Sampling Procedure (`colorize_grayscale_image`):** For a new grayscale image, we initialize random color channels, then iteratively reverse-diffuse to a realistic colorization.

- **Palette-Based Extension:** In practice, one can constrain the color channels using a palette or histogram technique before the reverse diffusion steps, creating thematic or restricted color trends. This extension builds upon the same diffusion mechanism.

Chapter 17

Data Augmentation for Classification and Detection

Diffusion-generated samples can enhance training sets for image classification or object detection tasks. Common usage includes bolstering underrepresented classes or improving robustness. The model can be trained in an unconditional or class-conditional setting, generating synthetic variations of real-world data. Construction steps are: (1) gathering class-labeled images with bounding boxes if relevant, (2) defining a forward noise schedule and training a diffusion model to produce coherent images, (3) generating new samples in the desired categories or bounding box configurations, and (4) integrating these synthetic samples back into the training pipeline for standard classifiers or detectors. A novel method here is to embed metadata (like bounding box layout) as a separate conditioning input, so that the diffusion network can produce images already aligned with detection tasks.

Python Code Snippet

```python
import os
import random
import math
import torch
import torch.nn as nn
```

```python
import torch.optim as optim
from torch.utils.data import DataLoader
import torchvision
import torchvision.transforms as transforms
import matplotlib.pyplot as plt


# ----------------------------------------------------------------
# 1) Set random seed for reproducibility
# ----------------------------------------------------------------
def set_seed(seed=42):
    random.seed(seed)
    torch.manual_seed(seed)
    if torch.cuda.is_available():
        torch.cuda.manual_seed_all(seed)



# ----------------------------------------------------------------
# 2) Conditional U-Net for image denoising
#     This U-Net supports optional class conditioning via an
# ↪   embedding.
# ----------------------------------------------------------------
class DoubleConv(nn.Module):
    '''
    A helper module that performs two convolutions (each followed by
    ↪   ReLU)
    to reduce block boilerplate in the U-Net.
    '''
    def __init__(self, in_channels, out_channels):
        super(DoubleConv, self).__init__()
        self.conv = nn.Sequential(
            nn.Conv2d(in_channels, out_channels, 3, padding=1),
            nn.ReLU(inplace=True),
            nn.Conv2d(out_channels, out_channels, 3, padding=1),
            nn.ReLU(inplace=True)
        )

    def forward(self, x):
        return self.conv(x)

class ConditionalUNet(nn.Module):
    '''
    A simplified class-conditional U-Net architecture.
    We incorporate a label embedding that is broadcast across the
    ↪   spatial dimensions
    and concatenated with the image as an additional channel.
    For bounding box metadata, one could similarly embed or encode
    ↪   it and
    concatenate it to the input or an intermediate layer.
    '''
    def __init__(self, in_channels=3, num_classes=10,
    ↪   base_channels=64, embed_dim=64):
        super(ConditionalUNet, self).__init__()
```

179

```python
        self.num_classes = num_classes
        self.embed_dim = embed_dim

        # Label embedding
        self.label_emb = nn.Embedding(num_classes, embed_dim)

        # Down-sampling (encoder)
        self.down1 = DoubleConv(in_channels + embed_dim,
        ↪ base_channels)
        self.down2 = DoubleConv(base_channels, base_channels*2)
        self.down3 = DoubleConv(base_channels*2, base_channels*4)

        self.pool = nn.MaxPool2d(2)

        # Bottleneck
        self.bottleneck = DoubleConv(base_channels*4,
        ↪ base_channels*8)

        # Up-sampling (decoder)
        self.up1 = nn.ConvTranspose2d(base_channels*8,
        ↪ base_channels*4, kernel_size=2, stride=2)
        self.conv_up1 = DoubleConv(base_channels*8, base_channels*4)

        self.up2 = nn.ConvTranspose2d(base_channels*4,
        ↪ base_channels*2, kernel_size=2, stride=2)
        self.conv_up2 = DoubleConv(base_channels*4, base_channels*2)

        self.up3 = nn.ConvTranspose2d(base_channels*2,
        ↪ base_channels, kernel_size=2, stride=2)
        self.conv_up3 = DoubleConv(base_channels*2, base_channels)

        # Final output
        self.final_conv = nn.Conv2d(base_channels, in_channels,
        ↪ kernel_size=1)

    def forward(self, x, labels=None):
        '''
        x: B x C x H x W images
        labels: B-sized vector containing class indices
        '''
        B, _, H, W = x.shape

        # If labels are supplied, extract embeddings
        if labels is not None:
            # B x embed_dim
            label_encoding = self.label_emb(labels)
            # Broadcast to B x embed_dim x H x W
            label_map =
            ↪ label_encoding.unsqueeze(-1).unsqueeze(-1).expand(B,
            ↪ self.embed_dim, H, W)
            # Concatenate along channel dimension
            x = torch.cat([x, label_map], dim=1)
        else:
```

180

```python
        # If no labels provided, just add a zero map for the
        ↪   embedding
        # (unconditional scenario)
        zero_map = torch.zeros(B, self.embed_dim, H, W,
        ↪   device=x.device)
        x = torch.cat([x, zero_map], dim=1)

    # Encoder
    x1 = self.down1(x)
    x2 = self.pool(x1)

    x2 = self.down2(x2)
    x3 = self.pool(x2)

    x3 = self.down3(x3)
    x4 = self.pool(x3)

    # Bottleneck
    b = self.bottleneck(x4)

    # Decoder
    x = self.up1(b)
    x = torch.cat([x, x3], dim=1)   # skip connection
    x = self.conv_up1(x)

    x = self.up2(x)
    x = torch.cat([x, x2], dim=1)
    x = self.conv_up2(x)

    x = self.up3(x)
    x = torch.cat([x, x1], dim=1)
    x = self.conv_up3(x)

    # Final
    out = self.final_conv(x)
    return out


# ----------------------------------------------------------------
# 3) Define diffusion schedule and forward process
# ----------------------------------------------------------------
def make_beta_schedule(schedule_name, n_timestep, start=1e-4,
↪   end=2e-2):
    '''
    Creates a beta schedule for the diffusion process.
    We use a linear schedule as a straightforward example.
    '''
    if schedule_name == "linear":
        return torch.linspace(start, end, n_timestep)
    else:
        raise NotImplementedError("Only 'linear' schedule is
        ↪   implemented here.")
```

181

```python
class Diffusion:
    '''
    A class that encapsulates:
    1) The forward noising process: q(x_t | x_0)
    2) The reverse denoising process: p(x_{t-1} | x_t)
    3) Utility for training and sampling in class-conditional or
    ↪  unconditional settings.
    '''

    def __init__(self, n_steps=1000, beta_schedule='linear'):
        self.n_steps = n_steps
        self.betas = make_beta_schedule(beta_schedule, n_steps)
        self.alphas = 1.0 - self.betas
        self.alpha_cumprod = torch.cumprod(self.alphas, dim=0)
        self.alpha_cumprod_prev = torch.cat([torch.tensor([1.0]),
        ↪  self.alpha_cumprod[:-1]], dim=0)

        # Posterior variance term for p(x_{t-1} | x_t, x_0)
        self.posterior_variance = self.betas * (1.0 -
        ↪  self.alpha_cumprod_prev) / (1.0 - self.alpha_cumprod)

    def q_sample(self, x_start, t, noise=None):
        '''
        Forward diffusion: Adds noise to x_start at step t.
        x_t = sqrt(alpha_cumprod[t]) * x_start + sqrt(1 -
        ↪  alpha_cumprod[t]) * noise
        '''
        if noise is None:
            noise = torch.randn_like(x_start)
        shape = x_start.shape

        # Reshape t to broadcast
        sqrt_alpha_cumprod_t =
        ↪  self.alpha_cumprod[t].sqrt().view(-1,1,1,1)
        sqrt_one_minus_alpha_cumprod_t = (1 -
        ↪  self.alpha_cumprod[t]).sqrt().view(-1,1,1,1)

        return sqrt_alpha_cumprod_t * x_start +
        ↪  sqrt_one_minus_alpha_cumprod_t * noise

    def predict_noise(self, model, x_t, t, labels=None):
        '''
        Use the UNet model to predict the noise added at step t.
        Here we can provide optional labels for class conditioning.
        '''
        return model(x_t, labels)

    def p_sample(self, model, x_t, t, labels=None,
    ↪  guidance_scale=1.0):
        '''
        One reverse diffusion step: p(x_{t-1} | x_t).
        The model predicts the noise e_t, and we compute the mean of
        ↪  p(x_{t-1} | x_t, x_0).
```

182

```
    We also demonstrate a "guidance_scale" that scales the
    ↪    predicted noise for
    more or less variation in a simplistic way.
    '''
    betas_t = self.betas[t]
    alpha_t = self.alphas[t]
    alpha_cumprod_t = self.alpha_cumprod[t]
    alpha_cumprod_prev_t = self.alpha_cumprod_prev[t]

    e_t = self.predict_noise(model, x_t, t, labels=labels)
    e_t = e_t * guidance_scale

    sqrt_recip_alpha_t = (1.0 / alpha_t).sqrt()
    # Estimate x_0
    x_0_hat = (x_t - (1.0 - alpha_t).sqrt() * e_t) *
    ↪    sqrt_recip_alpha_t

    # We now compute the mean of the posterior q(x_{t-1} | x_t,
    ↪    x_0_hat)
    coef1 = ((alpha_cumprod_prev_t).sqrt() * betas_t) / (1.0 -
    ↪    alpha_cumprod_t)
    coef2 = ((1.0 - alpha_cumprod_prev_t) * alpha_t.sqrt()) /
    ↪    (1.0 - alpha_cumprod_t)

    mean = coef1 * x_0_hat + coef2 * x_t

    # Posterior variance
    posterior_var = self.posterior_variance[t]
    if t > 0:
        noise = torch.randn_like(x_t)
    else:
        noise = torch.zeros_like(x_t)

    x_prev = mean + noise * posterior_var.sqrt()
    return x_prev

def p_sample_loop(self, model, shape, device, labels=None,
↪    guidance_scale=1.0):
    '''
    Repeatedly apply p_sample to go from x_T ~ N(0,I) to x_0.
    If labels are provided, we do class-conditional sampling;
    ↪    otherwise unconditional.
    '''
    x_t = torch.randn(shape, device=device)
    for i in reversed(range(self.n_steps)):
        x_t = self.p_sample(model, x_t, i, labels=labels,
        ↪    guidance_scale=guidance_scale)
    return x_t


# ---------------------------------------------------------------
# 4) Training and sampling routines
# ---------------------------------------------------------------
```

```python
def train_one_epoch(model, diffusion, optimizer, dataloader, device,
↪    num_classes=10):
    '''
    A single training epoch for the diffusion model.
    We sample a random t, forward diffuse the image, and predict the
    ↪    noise.
    If class labels exist, we pass them to the model for
    ↪    conditioning.
    '''
    model.train()
    loss_sum = 0

    for images, labels in dataloader:
        images, labels = images.to(device), labels.to(device)

        # For each batch, sample a random time step
        t = torch.randint(0, diffusion.n_steps, (images.size(0),),
        ↪    device=device).long()

        # Create random noise
        noise = torch.randn_like(images)

        # Forward diffuse the real image at step t
        # shape: B x C x H x W
        x_t = diffusion.q_sample(images, t, noise=noise)

        # Predict the noise with the model
        noise_pred = diffusion.predict_noise(model, x_t, t,
        ↪    labels=labels)

        # L2 loss to match the real noise
        loss = torch.nn.functional.mse_loss(noise_pred, noise)

        optimizer.zero_grad()
        loss.backward()
        optimizer.step()

        loss_sum += loss.item()

    return loss_sum / len(dataloader)

def evaluate_model(model, diffusion, dataloader, device):
    '''
    A quick evaluation that reports average L2 error on a test set.
    '''
    model.eval()
    loss_sum = 0
    with torch.no_grad():
        for images, labels in dataloader:
            images, labels = images.to(device), labels.to(device)
            t = torch.randint(0, diffusion.n_steps,
            ↪    (images.size(0),), device=device).long()
            noise = torch.randn_like(images)
```

```
                x_t = diffusion.q_sample(images, t, noise=noise)
                noise_pred = diffusion.predict_noise(model, x_t, t,
                ↪    labels=labels)
                loss = torch.nn.functional.mse_loss(noise_pred, noise)
                loss_sum += loss.item()
        return loss_sum / len(dataloader)

def sample_and_save(model, diffusion, device, epoch, num_classes=10,
↪    guidance_scale=1.0):
    '''
    Samples a batch of images from the diffusion model and saves a
    ↪    grid for inspection.
    We randomly choose a label for each sample to demonstrate
    ↪    class-conditional generation.
    '''
    model.eval()
    with torch.no_grad():
        sample_batch_size = 16

        # For demonstration, choose random classes
        random_labels = torch.randint(0, num_classes,
        ↪    (sample_batch_size,), device=device)

        # shape: B x C x H x W
        # Using CIFAR-10 image size: 3 x 32 x 32
        generated = diffusion.p_sample_loop(
            model,
            (sample_batch_size, 3, 32, 32),
            device,
            labels=random_labels,
            guidance_scale=guidance_scale
        )

        # Normalize to [0,1] for visualization
        generated = (generated.clamp(-1.0, 1.0) + 1) * 0.5  # from
        ↪    [-1,1] to [0,1]

        grid = torchvision.utils.make_grid(generated, nrow=4)
        os.makedirs("results", exist_ok=True)
        plt.figure(figsize=(6,6))
        plt.axis("off")
        plt.imshow(grid.permute(1, 2, 0).cpu().numpy())

        ↪    plt.savefig(f"results/epoch_{epoch}_gs_{guidance_scale}.png")
        plt.close()


# ----------------------------------------------------------------
# 5) Main script: load data, initialize model, and train
# ----------------------------------------------------------------
def main():
    set_seed(42)
```

```
device = torch.device('cuda' if torch.cuda.is_available() else
↪   'cpu')

# Load CIFAR-10 (as an example for class-conditional generative
↪   modeling)
transform = transforms.Compose([
    transforms.ToTensor(),
    # Rescale images from [0,1] to [-1,1]
    transforms.Normalize((0.5,0.5,0.5), (0.5,0.5,0.5))
])
train_dataset = torchvision.datasets.CIFAR10(
    root='data_cifar', train=True, download=True,
    ↪   transform=transform
)
test_dataset = torchvision.datasets.CIFAR10(
    root='data_cifar', train=False, download=True,
    ↪   transform=transform
)

train_loader = DataLoader(train_dataset, batch_size=64,
↪   shuffle=True)
test_loader = DataLoader(test_dataset, batch_size=64,
↪   shuffle=False)

# Create Conditional U-Net
model = ConditionalUNet(in_channels=3, num_classes=10,
↪   base_channels=64, embed_dim=64).to(device)

# Diffusion process with 200 time steps and linear schedule
diffusion = Diffusion(n_steps=200, beta_schedule='linear')

# Optimizer
optimizer = optim.Adam(model.parameters(), lr=1e-4)

# Train for a few epochs
epochs = 5
for epoch in range(epochs):
    train_loss = train_one_epoch(model, diffusion, optimizer,
    ↪   train_loader, device, num_classes=10)
    val_loss = evaluate_model(model, diffusion, test_loader,
    ↪   device)
    print(f"Epoch [{epoch+1}/{epochs}] - Train Loss:
    ↪   {train_loss:.4f}, Val Loss: {val_loss:.4f}")

    # Generate samples at the end of each epoch
    sample_and_save(model, diffusion, device, epoch,
    ↪   num_classes=10, guidance_scale=1.0)
    sample_and_save(model, diffusion, device, epoch,
    ↪   num_classes=10, guidance_scale=2.0)

print("Training complete! Check the 'results' folder for
↪   generated samples.")
```

```
if __name__ == "__main__":
    main()
```

Key Implementation Details:

- **Forward Diffusion:** We implement `q_sample` to corrupt each input image with noise, controlled by a linear beta schedule. At step `t`, the fraction of noise added is governed by `betas[t]` and the cumulative products of `alphas`.

- **Reverse Diffusion (Sampling):** The function `p_sample_loop` applies the denoising model step by step, starting from random noise. Each call to `p_sample` uses the learned noise prediction and the diffusion equations to produce a cleaner image.

- **Conditional U-Net Architecture:** `ConditionalUNet` includes an embedding layer for class labels, broadcasting the embedding to match the spatial dimensions and concatenating it with the image. This approach easily generalizes to additional metadata (e.g., bounding boxes).

- **Training Objective:** We directly predict and compare the added noise via an MSE loss between the network's prediction and the actual Gaussian noise. This drives the model to learn how to remove noise at each diffusion step.

- **Guidance Parameter:** A `guidance_scale` (e.g., 2.0 vs. 1.0) can be used to scale the model's predicted noise. While simplistic here, it demonstrates how multiplying noise estimates can adjust between fidelity and diversity in generated images.

- **Data Augmentation Utility:** The trained diffusion model can generate synthetic images and their corresponding class labels. For detection, one can provide bounding box metadata as part of the conditioning, producing images better aligned with detection tasks.

Chapter 18

Anomaly Detection in Visual Inspection

In industrial or medical contexts, identifying anomalies is central to ensuring quality or diagnosing abnormalities. Diffusion-based modeling can learn normal patterns and detect outliers by measuring reconstruction error. The approach typically involves training an unconditional diffusion model on normal data. During evaluation, a test image is corrupted by a series of forward noising steps and then denoised by the trained model. The difference between the reconstructed and original content can reveal anomalies. Implementation steps: (1) collect only normal-class images indicative of healthy or defect-free conditions, (2) train a diffusion model to accurately reconstruct these images, (3) for each new sample, apply partial forward noise, then reverse it using the model, (4) compute the residual or difference map, and (5) classify anomalies based on a threshold. An innovative extension is the integration of attention-based skip connections, which can localize anomalies more precisely in complex or high-resolution data.

Python Code Snippet

```python
import os
import random
import math
import torch
import torch.nn as nn
from torch.utils.data import DataLoader, Subset
```

```python
import torchvision
import torchvision.transforms as transforms
import torch.optim as optim
import matplotlib.pyplot as plt
import numpy as np

# ---------------------------------------------------------------
# 1) Set random seed for reproducibility
# ---------------------------------------------------------------
def set_seed(seed=42):
    random.seed(seed)
    torch.manual_seed(seed)
    if torch.cuda.is_available():
        torch.cuda.manual_seed_all(seed)


# ---------------------------------------------------------------
# 2) Create a simple U-Net-style model
# ---------------------------------------------------------------
class DoubleConv(nn.Module):
    '''
    Two convolutional layers (each followed by ReLU).
    '''
    def __init__(self, in_channels, out_channels):
        super(DoubleConv, self).__init__()
        self.conv = nn.Sequential(
            nn.Conv2d(in_channels, out_channels, 3, padding=1),
            nn.ReLU(inplace=True),
            nn.Conv2d(out_channels, out_channels, 3, padding=1),
            nn.ReLU(inplace=True)
        )

    def forward(self, x):
        return self.conv(x)

class UNet(nn.Module):
    '''
    Simplified U-Net with down-sampling and up-sampling blocks,
    plus skip connections for anomaly detection or reconstruction
    ↪  tasks.
    '''
    def __init__(self, in_channels=1, out_channels=1,
    ↪  base_channels=64):
        super(UNet, self).__init__()

        # Down-sampling (encoder)
        self.down1 = DoubleConv(in_channels, base_channels)
        self.down2 = DoubleConv(base_channels, base_channels * 2)
        self.down3 = DoubleConv(base_channels * 2, base_channels *
        ↪  4)

        self.pool = nn.MaxPool2d(2)

        # Bottleneck
```

```python
        self.bottleneck = DoubleConv(base_channels * 4,
        ↪   base_channels * 8)

        # Up-sampling (decoder)
        self.up1 = nn.ConvTranspose2d(base_channels * 8,
        ↪   base_channels * 4, kernel_size=2, stride=2)
        self.conv_up1 = DoubleConv(base_channels * 8, base_channels
        ↪   * 4)

        self.up2 = nn.ConvTranspose2d(base_channels * 4,
        ↪   base_channels * 2, kernel_size=2, stride=2)
        self.conv_up2 = DoubleConv(base_channels * 4, base_channels
        ↪   * 2)

        self.up3 = nn.ConvTranspose2d(base_channels * 2,
        ↪   base_channels, kernel_size=2, stride=2)
        self.conv_up3 = DoubleConv(base_channels * 2, base_channels)

        # Final output
        self.final_conv = nn.Conv2d(base_channels, out_channels,
        ↪   kernel_size=1)

    def forward(self, x):
        # Encoder
        x1 = self.down1(x)
        x2 = self.pool(x1)

        x2 = self.down2(x2)
        x3 = self.pool(x2)

        x3 = self.down3(x3)
        x4 = self.pool(x3)

        # Bottleneck
        b = self.bottleneck(x4)

        # Decoder
        x = self.up1(b)
        x = torch.cat([x, x3], dim=1)    # skip connection
        x = self.conv_up1(x)

        x = self.up2(x)
        x = torch.cat([x, x2], dim=1)
        x = self.conv_up2(x)

        x = self.up3(x)
        x = torch.cat([x, x1], dim=1)
        x = self.conv_up3(x)

        # Final
        out = self.final_conv(x)
        return out
```

```
# ----------------------------------------------------------
# 3) Define a beta schedule and Diffusion class
# ----------------------------------------------------------
def make_beta_schedule(schedule_name, n_timestep, start=1e-4,
↪   end=2e-2):
    '''
    Creates a beta schedule for the diffusion process (linear in
    ↪   this example).
    '''
    if schedule_name == "linear":
        return torch.linspace(start, end, n_timestep)
    else:
        raise NotImplementedError("Only 'linear' schedule is
            ↪   implemented here.")

class Diffusion:
    '''
    Encapsulates:
    1) The forward noising q(x_t | x_0)
    2) The reverse denoising p(x_{t-1} | x_t)
    3) Training & sampling utilities for anomaly detection.
    '''
    def __init__(self, n_steps=1000, beta_schedule='linear'):
        self.n_steps = n_steps
        self.betas = make_beta_schedule(beta_schedule, n_steps)
        self.alphas = 1.0 - self.betas
        self.alpha_cumprod = torch.cumprod(self.alphas, dim=0)
        self.alpha_cumprod_prev = torch.cat(
            [torch.tensor([1.0]), self.alpha_cumprod[:-1]], dim=0
        )

        # Posterior variance for p(x_{t-1}|x_t, x_0)
        self.posterior_variance = self.betas * (1.0 -
            ↪   self.alpha_cumprod_prev) / (1.0 - self.alpha_cumprod)

    def q_sample(self, x_start, t, noise=None):
        '''
        Forward noising of x_start at step t using:
        x_t = sqrt(alpha_cumprod[t])*x_start +
        ↪   sqrt(1-alpha_cumprod[t])*noise
        '''
        if noise is None:
            noise = torch.randn_like(x_start)
        sqrt_alpha_cumprod_t =
            ↪   self.alpha_cumprod[t].sqrt().view(-1,1,1,1)
        sqrt_one_minus_alpha_cumprod_t = (1 -
            ↪   self.alpha_cumprod[t]).sqrt().view(-1,1,1,1)
        return sqrt_alpha_cumprod_t * x_start +
            ↪   sqrt_one_minus_alpha_cumprod_t * noise

    def predict_noise(self, model, x_t, t):
        '''
        The model predicts the noise component from x_t at step t.
```

```
        '''
        return model(x_t)

    def p_sample(self, model, x_t, t, guidance_scale=1.0):
        '''
        Single reverse diffusion step to get x_{t-1}.
        The model predicts noise e_t, optionally scaled by
        ↪  guidance_scale.
        '''
        betas_t = self.betas[t]
        alpha_t = self.alphas[t]
        alpha_cumprod_t = self.alpha_cumprod[t]
        alpha_cumprod_prev_t = self.alpha_cumprod_prev[t]

        # Predict noise
        e_t = model(x_t) * guidance_scale

        sqrt_recip_alpha_t = (1.0 / alpha_t).sqrt()
        x_0_hat = (x_t - (1.0 - alpha_t).sqrt() * e_t) *
        ↪  sqrt_recip_alpha_t

        coef1 = ((alpha_cumprod_prev_t).sqrt() * betas_t) / (1.0 -
        ↪  alpha_cumprod_t)
        coef2 = ((1.0 - alpha_cumprod_prev_t) * alpha_t.sqrt()) /
        ↪  (1.0 - alpha_cumprod_t)

        mean = coef1 * x_0_hat + coef2 * x_t
        posterior_var = self.posterior_variance[t]

        if t > 0:
            noise = torch.randn_like(x_t)
        else:
            noise = torch.zeros_like(x_t)

        x_prev = mean + noise * posterior_var.sqrt()
        return x_prev

    def p_sample_loop(self, model, shape, device,
    ↪  guidance_scale=1.0):
        '''
        Full reverse process from x_T ~ N(0,I) down to x_0.
        '''
        x_t = torch.randn(shape, device=device)
        for i in reversed(range(self.n_steps)):
            x_t = self.p_sample(model, x_t, i, guidance_scale)
        return x_t

# ----------------------------------------------------------------
# 4) Training and reconstruction-based anomaly detection
# ----------------------------------------------------------------
def train_one_epoch(model, diffusion, optimizer, dataloader,
↪  device):
    model.train()
```

```python
    loss_sum = 0
    for images, _ in dataloader:
        images = images.to(device)

        # Sample random times
        t = torch.randint(0, diffusion.n_steps, (images.size(0),),
        ↪   device=device).long()

        # Create noise
        noise = torch.randn_like(images)

        # Forward diffuse
        x_t = diffusion.q_sample(images, t, noise)

        # Predict noise
        noise_pred = diffusion.predict_noise(model, x_t, t)

        # MSE loss
        loss = nn.functional.mse_loss(noise_pred, noise)

        optimizer.zero_grad()
        loss.backward()
        optimizer.step()

        loss_sum += loss.item()
    return loss_sum / len(dataloader)

def evaluate_model(model, diffusion, dataloader, device):
    '''
    Compute average MSE on normal validation data.
    '''
    model.eval()
    loss_sum = 0
    with torch.no_grad():
        for images, _ in dataloader:
            images = images.to(device)
            t = torch.randint(0, diffusion.n_steps,
            ↪   (images.size(0),), device=device).long()
            noise = torch.randn_like(images)
            x_t = diffusion.q_sample(images, t, noise)
            noise_pred = diffusion.predict_noise(model, x_t, t)
            loss = nn.functional.mse_loss(noise_pred, noise)
            loss_sum += loss.item()
    return loss_sum / len(dataloader)

def compute_residual_map(model, diffusion, x, device, t_step=50):
    '''
    Apply partial forward noise at step t_step, then reverse it.
    Compute the difference between original and reconstructed
    ↪   (x_rec).
    '''
    model.eval()
    with torch.no_grad():
```

```python
    x = x.unsqueeze(0).to(device)   # single sample
    noise = torch.randn_like(x)

    # Forward partial noise
    x_t = diffusion.q_sample(x, torch.tensor([t_step],
    ↪   device=device), noise)

    # Reverse from t_step down to 0
    x_rec = x_t.clone()
    for i in reversed(range(t_step)):
        x_rec = diffusion.p_sample(model, x_rec, i,
        ↪   guidance_scale=1.0)

    residual_map = (x - x_rec).abs()[0]   # remove batch
    ↪   dimension
    return residual_map.cpu()

def compute_threshold(model, diffusion, normal_loader, device,
↪   t_step=50, std_factor=3.0):
    '''
    Estimate a threshold by computing mean + std_factor * std
    over normal samples' average residual error.
    '''
    model.eval()
    all_errors = []
    with torch.no_grad():
        for images, _ in normal_loader:
            images = images.to(device)
            # We only do partial for a subset for speed
            for i in range(images.size(0)):
                x_i = images[i].detach().cpu()
                residual_map = compute_residual_map(model,
                ↪   diffusion, x_i, device, t_step)
                # MSE or L1
                error = residual_map.pow(2).mean().item()
                all_errors.append(error)
    mean_err = np.mean(all_errors)
    std_err = np.std(all_errors)
    threshold = mean_err + std_factor * std_err
    return threshold

def test_for_anomalies(model, diffusion, test_loader, device,
↪   threshold, t_step=50):
    '''
    Classify images as normal or anomaly based on the residual
    ↪   threshold.
    Return simple accuracy metrics for demonstration.
    Assume label 0 => normal, label 1 => anomaly in the test set.
    '''
    model.eval()
    correct = 0
    total = 0
    with torch.no_grad():
```

```
        for images, labels in test_loader:
            for i in range(images.size(0)):
                x_i = images[i].detach().cpu()
                label_i = labels[i].item()

                # Reconstruct
                residual_map = compute_residual_map(model,
                ↪   diffusion, x_i, device, t_step)
                error = residual_map.pow(2).mean().item()

                pred_anomaly = (error > threshold)
                # If label_i == 0 => normal image
                # If label_i == 1 => anomaly
                is_anomaly = (label_i == 1)
                if pred_anomaly == is_anomaly:
                    correct += 1
                total += 1
    acc = (correct / total) * 100.0
    return acc

# --------------------------------------------------------------
# 5) Main script: load data, filter normal vs. anomaly, train,
↪ detect
# --------------------------------------------------------------
def main():
    set_seed(42)
    device = torch.device("cuda" if torch.cuda.is_available() else
    ↪   "cpu")

    # Load MNIST
    transform = transforms.Compose([
        transforms.ToTensor(),
        transforms.Normalize((0.5,), (0.5,))
    ])
    full_train = torchvision.datasets.MNIST(root='data', train=True,
    ↪   download=True, transform=transform)
    full_test = torchvision.datasets.MNIST(root='data', train=False,
    ↪   download=True, transform=transform)

    # Let's define "normal" as digit '0' => label 0, "anomaly" =>
    ↪   digits [1..9] => label 1
    # in a real scenario, you would have actual normal vs. defective
    ↪   data.

    # Filter training set to only keep normal class (digit '0')
    idx_train_normal = [i for i, t in enumerate(full_train) if t[1]
    ↪   == 0]
    train_normal_dataset = Subset(full_train, idx_train_normal)

    # We'll also define a small validation normal subset from the
    ↪   train set for threshold
    val_split = int(len(train_normal_dataset)*0.2)
```

```python
val_normal_dataset = Subset(train_normal_dataset,
↪   range(val_split))
train_normal_dataset = Subset(train_normal_dataset,
↪   range(val_split, len(train_normal_dataset)))

# For test, let's label digit '0' => 0 (normal), everything else
↪   => 1 (anomaly)
test_labels = []
for i, t in enumerate(full_test):
    if t[1] == 0:
        test_labels.append(0)  # normal
    else:
        test_labels.append(1)  # anomaly

# We can assign these new labels to the test set by creating a
↪   custom dataset style:
class MNISTAnomalyWrapper(torch.utils.data.Dataset):
    def __init__(self, dataset, new_labels):
        self.dataset = dataset
        self.new_labels = new_labels
    def __len__(self):
        return len(self.dataset)
    def __getitem__(self, idx):
        img, _ = self.dataset[idx]
        return img, self.new_labels[idx]

test_dataset = MNISTAnomalyWrapper(full_test, test_labels)

# Dataloaders
train_loader = DataLoader(train_normal_dataset, batch_size=64,
↪   shuffle=True)
val_loader = DataLoader(val_normal_dataset, batch_size=64,
↪   shuffle=False)
test_loader = DataLoader(test_dataset, batch_size=64,
↪   shuffle=False)

# Model, Diffusion, Optimizer
model = UNet(in_channels=1, out_channels=1,
↪   base_channels=64).to(device)
diffusion = Diffusion(n_steps=200, beta_schedule='linear')
optimizer = optim.Adam(model.parameters(), lr=1e-4)

# Train for a couple of epochs
epochs = 2
for epoch in range(epochs):
    train_loss = train_one_epoch(model, diffusion, optimizer,
↪   train_loader, device)
    val_loss = evaluate_model(model, diffusion, val_loader,
↪   device)
    print(f"Epoch [{epoch+1}/{epochs}] - Train Loss:
↪   {train_loss:.4f}, Val Loss: {val_loss:.4f}")

# Once trained, compute threshold on normal validation set
```

```
threshold = compute_threshold(model, diffusion, val_loader,
↪   device, t_step=50, std_factor=3.0)
print(f"Threshold for anomaly detection: {threshold:.4f}")

# Test for anomalies
acc = test_for_anomalies(model, diffusion, test_loader, device,
↪   threshold, t_step=50)
print(f"Anomaly Detection Accuracy: {acc:.2f}%")

if __name__ == "__main__":
    main()
```

Key Implementation Details:

- **Forward Diffusion:** The function `q_sample` adds Gaussian noise to images according to a linear schedule. At step t, the fraction of noise is determined by `betas[t]` and the cumulative products of `alphas`.

- **Reverse Diffusion (Sampling):** Within `p_sample`, we compute p(x_t-1|x_t) by predicting the noise component and rebuilding an estimate of x_0, then combining it with a noise term.

- **UNet Architecture:** The `UNet` reconstructs denoised images through downsampling and upsampling paths with skip connections, a structure well-suited for anomaly reconstruction.

- **Anomaly Thresholding:** After training on normal data, we determine a threshold by computing the reconstruction error on a normal validation subset. Images with reconstruction errors above this threshold are classified as anomalies.

- **Partial Forward Noise for Detection:** Our `compute_residual_map` function corrupts the test image at a selected diffusion step (e.g., 50) and then reverses the process to reconstruct the input. The difference (residual map) highlights anomalous regions.

Chapter 19

Motion Planning in Robotics with Diffusion

Diffusion can be applied to motion planning by treating robot trajectories or joint angles as sequences to be denoised. A typical scenario involves generating smooth paths while avoiding obstacles. To construct the model, we: (1) represent motions as a sequence of poses or actions, (2) define a diffusion forward process that adds Gaussian noise to these pose vectors, (3) train a diffusion network—often a temporal UNet or transformer—to predict the noise at each time step, and (4) sample feasible trajectories by reversing the noise process with collision checks or dynamic constraints as partial conditioning. An innovative variant integrates real-world sensor data (e.g., LiDAR) as context, enabling the diffusion process to account for obstacle geometry directly during the sampling procedure, leading to more robust path generation.

Python Code Snippet

```
import math
import random
import torch
import torch.nn as nn
import torch.optim as optim
from torch.utils.data import Dataset, DataLoader

# ------------------------------------------------------------
# 1) Set random seed for reproducibility
```

```python
# --------------------------------------------------------------
def set_seed(seed=42):
    random.seed(seed)
    torch.manual_seed(seed)
    if torch.cuda.is_available():
        torch.cuda.manual_seed_all(seed)


# --------------------------------------------------------------
# 2) Create a synthetic dataset for motion trajectories
#    Each trajectory is a 2D path of length T.
#     We simply interpolate between start & goal + small noise.
# --------------------------------------------------------------
class MotionDataset(Dataset):
    def __init__(self, num_samples=10000, seq_length=20):
        super(MotionDataset, self).__init__()
        self.seq_length = seq_length
        self.data = []
        for _ in range(num_samples):
            start = torch.rand(2) * 2.0 - 1.0      # random start in
            ↪  [-1,1] for x,y
            goal = torch.rand(2) * 2.0 - 1.0       # random goal in
            ↪  [-1,1]
            # linearly interpolate
            trajectory = []
            for t in range(seq_length):
                alpha = t / (seq_length - 1)
                point = (1 - alpha) * start + alpha * goal
                # add small random perturbation
                point += 0.01 * torch.randn(2)
                trajectory.append(point.unsqueeze(0))  # shape
                ↪  [1,2]
            # shape for entire trajectory: [seq_length, 2]
            trajectory = torch.cat(trajectory, dim=0)
            self.data.append(trajectory)
        self.data = torch.stack(self.data, dim=0)  # [num_samples,
        ↪  seq_length, 2]

    def __len__(self):
        return self.data.size(0)

    def __getitem__(self, idx):
        # Return shape: (seq_length, 2)
        traj = self.data[idx]
        # For a diffusion model, we do not need specific labels; we
        ↪  can pass in dummy 0
        return traj, 0


# --------------------------------------------------------------
# 3) A simple 1D U-Net architecture for sequence data
#     We'll treat dimension=2 as "channels" and length=seq_length as
↪  "width".
# --------------------------------------------------------------
class DoubleConv1D(nn.Module):
```

199

```
    ' ' '
    Two 1D convolution layers with ReLU,
    a helper for building the 1D U-Net blocks.
    ' ' '
    def __init__(self, in_ch, out_ch, kernel_size=3, padding=1):
        super(DoubleConv1D, self).__init__()
        self.net = nn.Sequential(
            nn.Conv1d(in_ch, out_ch, kernel_size=kernel_size,
            ↪  padding=padding),
            nn.ReLU(inplace=True),
            nn.Conv1d(out_ch, out_ch, kernel_size=kernel_size,
            ↪  padding=padding),
            nn.ReLU(inplace=True)
        )
    def forward(self, x):
        return self.net(x)

class UNet1D(nn.Module):
    ' ' '
    A simplified 1D U-Net for sequences:
    - We'll use downsample and upsample with stride=2
    - Skip connections between matching layers
    - Input shape: (B, 2, seq_length)
    - Output shape: (B, 2, seq_length)
    ' ' '
    def __init__(self, in_ch=2, base_ch=32):
        super(UNet1D, self).__init__()

        # Down blocks
        self.down1 = DoubleConv1D(in_ch, base_ch)
        self.down2 = DoubleConv1D(base_ch, base_ch*2)
        self.pool = nn.Conv1d(base_ch, base_ch, kernel_size=2,
        ↪  stride=2)
        self.pool2 = nn.Conv1d(base_ch*2, base_ch*2, kernel_size=2,
        ↪  stride=2)

        # Bottleneck
        self.bottleneck = DoubleConv1D(base_ch*2, base_ch*4)

        # Up blocks
        self.up1 = nn.ConvTranspose1d(base_ch*4, base_ch*2,
        ↪  kernel_size=2, stride=2)
        self.conv_up1 = DoubleConv1D(base_ch*4, base_ch*2)

        self.up2 = nn.ConvTranspose1d(base_ch*2, base_ch,
        ↪  kernel_size=2, stride=2)
        self.conv_up2 = DoubleConv1D(base_ch*2, base_ch)

        # Final layer
        self.final_conv = nn.Conv1d(base_ch, in_ch, kernel_size=1)

    def forward(self, x):
        # x shape: [B, 2, T]
```

```python
        # Down
        x1 = self.down1(x)  # [B, base_ch, T]
        x2 = self.pool2(self.down2(self.pool(x1)))  # [B, base_ch*2,
        ↪  T/4]
        # Bottleneck
        b = self.bottleneck(x2)  # [B, base_ch*4, T/4]
        # Up
        x_ = self.up1(b)  # [B, base_ch*2, T/2]
        # Skip conn from down2 block
        x_ = torch.cat([x_, x2], dim=1)  # [B, base_ch*4, T/2]
        x_ = self.conv_up1(x_)

        x_ = self.up2(x_)  # [B, base_ch, T]
        # Skip conn from down1 block
        x_ = torch.cat([x_, x1], dim=1)  # [B, base_ch*2, T]
        x_ = self.conv_up2(x_)
        # Final
        out = self.final_conv(x_)
        return out


# ----------------------------------------------------------------
# 4) Diffusion schedule and forward process
# ----------------------------------------------------------------
def make_beta_schedule(schedule_name, n_timestep, start=1e-4,
↪  end=2e-2):
    '''
    A simple linear beta schedule.
    Beta(t) grows linearly from start to end across n_timestep
    ↪  steps.
    '''
    if schedule_name == "linear":
        return torch.linspace(start, end, n_timestep)
    else:
        raise NotImplementedError("Only 'linear' is implemented
        ↪  here.")


class Diffusion:
    '''
    A class that contains:
    (1) the forward noising process, q(x_t | x_0),
    (2) the reverse denoising process, p(x_{t-1} | x_t),
    (3) training and sampling utilities.
    '''
    def __init__(self, n_steps=100, beta_schedule='linear'):
        self.n_steps = n_steps
        self.betas = make_beta_schedule(beta_schedule, n_steps)
        self.alphas = 1.0 - self.betas
        self.alpha_cumprod = torch.cumprod(self.alphas, dim=0)
        self.alpha_cumprod_prev = torch.cat(
            [torch.tensor([1.0]), self.alpha_cumprod[:-1]], dim=0
        )
        # Posterior variance for diffusion steps:
```

201

```python
        self.posterior_variance = self.betas * (1.0 -
        ↪  self.alpha_cumprod_prev) \
                                    / (1.0 - self.alpha_cumprod)

    def q_sample(self, x_start, t, noise=None):
        '''
        Forward diffusion step:
        x_t = sqrt(alpha_cumprod[t]) * x_start + sqrt(1 -
        ↪  alpha_cumprod[t]) * noise
        '''
        if noise is None:
            noise = torch.randn_like(x_start)
        batch_size = x_start.shape[0]
        shape_ones = (1, 1)
        sqrt_alpha_cumprod_t = self.alpha_cumprod[t].sqrt().view(-1,
        ↪  *[1]*(x_start.ndim-1))
        sqrt_one_minus_alpha_cumprod_t = (1 -
        ↪  self.alpha_cumprod[t]).sqrt().view(
            -1, *[1]*(x_start.ndim-1)
        )
        # gather the correct t for each sample in the batch
        sqrt_alpha_cumprod_t =
        ↪  sqrt_alpha_cumprod_t[0:1].expand(batch_size, -1, -1)
        sqrt_one_minus_alpha_cumprod_t =
        ↪  sqrt_one_minus_alpha_cumprod_t[0:1].expand(batch_size,
        ↪  -1, -1)
        return sqrt_alpha_cumprod_t * x_start +
        ↪  sqrt_one_minus_alpha_cumprod_t * noise

    def predict_noise(self, model, x_t, t):
        '''
        Predict noise at step t using the model.
        '''
        return model(x_t)

    def p_sample(self, model, x_t, t):
        '''
        Single reverse diffusion step:
        p(x_{t-1} | x_t).
        We predict noise using the model, reconstruct x_0, then
        ↪  sample x_{t-1} from the posterior.
        '''
        betas_t = self.betas[t]
        alpha_t = self.alphas[t]
        alpha_cumprod_t = self.alpha_cumprod[t]
        alpha_cumprod_prev_t = self.alpha_cumprod_prev[t]

        e_t = model(x_t)   # predicted noise
        sqrt_recip_alpha_t = (1.0 / alpha_t).sqrt()
        # approximate x_0 from x_t and noise
        x_0_hat = (x_t - (1.0 - alpha_t).sqrt() * e_t) *
        ↪  sqrt_recip_alpha_t
```

```python
        # Weighted coefficients
        coef1 = (alpha_cumprod_prev_t.sqrt() * betas_t) / (1.0 -
        ↪  alpha_cumprod_t)
        coef2 = ((1.0 - alpha_cumprod_prev_t) * alpha_t.sqrt()) /
        ↪  (1.0 - alpha_cumprod_t)

        mean = coef1 * x_0_hat + coef2 * x_t
        posterior_var = self.posterior_variance[t]
        if t > 0:
            noise = torch.randn_like(x_t)
        else:
            noise = torch.zeros_like(x_t)
        x_prev = mean + noise * posterior_var.sqrt()
        return x_prev

    def p_sample_loop(self, model, shape, device):
        '''
        Iteratively apply reverse diffusion from x_T ~ N(0, I) to
        ↪  x_0.
        '''
        x_t = torch.randn(shape, device=device)
        for i in reversed(range(self.n_steps)):
            x_t = self.p_sample(model, x_t, i)
        return x_t


# -----------------------------------------------------------------
# 5) Training and sampling routines
# -----------------------------------------------------------------
def train_one_epoch(model, diffusion, optimizer, dataloader,
↪  device):
    model.train()
    total_loss = 0.0
    for batch_data, _ in dataloader:
        # batch_data shape: [B, seq_length, 2]
        batch_data = batch_data.permute(0, 2, 1).to(device)  # ->
        ↪  [B, 2, seq_length]

        # sample random t
        t = torch.randint(0, diffusion.n_steps,
        ↪  (batch_data.size(0),), device=device).long()

        noise = torch.randn_like(batch_data)
        x_t = diffusion.q_sample(batch_data, t, noise=noise)

        predicted_noise = diffusion.predict_noise(model, x_t, t)
        loss = nn.MSELoss()(predicted_noise, noise)

        optimizer.zero_grad()
        loss.backward()
        optimizer.step()

        total_loss += loss.item()
    return total_loss / len(dataloader)
```

203

```
def sample_trajectory(model, diffusion, device, batch_size=4):
    '''
    Sample random trajectories by reversing from noise.
    Returns a shape [batch_size, seq_length, 2].
    '''
    model.eval()
    with torch.no_grad():
        # shape for [B, 2, seq_length]
        shape = (batch_size, 2, 20)
        x_0 = diffusion.p_sample_loop(model, shape, device)
        # reshape to [B, seq_length, 2]
        trajectories = x_0.permute(0, 2, 1)
    return trajectories

# --------------------------------------------------------------
# 6) Main script: create dataset, model, train, sample
# --------------------------------------------------------------
def main():
    set_seed(42)
    device = torch.device("cuda" if torch.cuda.is_available() else
    ↪    "cpu")

    # Hyperparameters
    seq_length = 20
    train_dataset = MotionDataset(num_samples=8000,
    ↪    seq_length=seq_length)
    test_dataset = MotionDataset(num_samples=2000,
    ↪    seq_length=seq_length)

    train_loader = DataLoader(train_dataset, batch_size=64,
    ↪    shuffle=True)
    test_loader = DataLoader(test_dataset, batch_size=64,
    ↪    shuffle=False)

    # Model and diffusion
    model = UNet1D(in_ch=2, base_ch=32).to(device)
    diffusion = Diffusion(n_steps=100, beta_schedule='linear')

    optimizer = optim.Adam(model.parameters(), lr=1e-3)

    epochs = 5
    for epoch in range(epochs):
        train_loss = train_one_epoch(model, diffusion, optimizer,
        ↪    train_loader, device)

        # Quick evaluation on test set
        model.eval()
        with torch.no_grad():
            val_loss = 0.0
            for batch_data, _ in test_loader:
                batch_data = batch_data.permute(0, 2, 1).to(device)
```

```
                t = torch.randint(0, diffusion.n_steps,
                  ↪  (batch_data.size(0),), device=device).long()
                noise = torch.randn_like(batch_data)
                x_t = diffusion.q_sample(batch_data, t, noise=noise)
                predicted_noise = diffusion.predict_noise(model,
                  ↪  x_t, t)
                loss = nn.MSELoss()(predicted_noise, noise)
                val_loss += loss.item()
            val_loss /= len(test_loader)

        print(f"Epoch [{epoch+1}/{epochs}] - Train Loss:
          ↪  {train_loss:.4f}, Val Loss: {val_loss:.4f}")

    # Sample some trajectories
    sampled_trajs = sample_trajectory(model, diffusion, device,
      ↪  batch_size=4)
    print("Sampled trajectories (first batch):")
    print(sampled_trajs.cpu().numpy())

    print("Motion planning diffusion example complete!")

if __name__ == "__main__":
    main()
```

Key Implementation Details:

- **Trajectory Representation:** We store each motion sample
  as a sequence of 2D waypoints (shape: [seq_length, 2]). In
  the code, this is treated as (B, 2, seq_length) when fed into
  the 1D U-Net.

- **Forward Diffusion:** The function q_sample adds Gaussian
  noise to each trajectory according to the linear beta schedule,
  progressively corruption over time steps.

- **Reverse Diffusion (Sampling):** The function p_sample_loop
  iterates from the last diffusion step to the first, gradually denoising the random initial trajectory into a feasible path using
  the U-Net.

- **1D U-Net Architecture:** UNet1D performs downsampling
  over the temporal dimension (sequence length) and merges
  skip connections during upsampling to preserve fine-grained
  temporal structure.

- **Training Objective:** We directly predict and compare the
  noisy trajectory perturbation via an MSE loss between the

205

network's output and the actual noise added at each step.

- **Potential Collision Checks:** This example demonstrates the diffusion approach to denoising. In practice, you would incorporate sensor data (e.g., LiDAR) and environment constraints to filter or guide the reverse process, ensuring obstacle-free paths.

- **End-to-End Pipeline:** The `main` function covers data loading, training, and eventually sampling new trajectories. The printed results in `sample_trajectory` show how the reverse diffusion can produce smooth paths.

Chapter 20

Navigation Path Generation for Autonomous Systems

Similar to motion planning, navigation path generation can be viewed as a diffusion process over waypoints on a map. Common uses include route planning for drones, cars, or mobile robots in dynamic environments. Building the system involves: (1) encoding the map with relevant features like terrain or road layout, (2) defining a forward schedule that progressively corrupts a path solution, (3) constructing a diffusion network (e.g., a graph-based UNet) that handles spatial adjacency, (4) training to denoise the path by leveraging known feasible routes, and (5) sampling new route solutions starting from random or partially known waypoints. An innovative approach is multi-agent coordination, where parallel diffusion processes for each agent share partial information to yield collaborative navigation paths, improving overall traffic flow in congested environments.

Python Code Snippet

```python
import os
import random
import math
import torch
import torch.nn as nn
```

```python
import numpy as np
import matplotlib.pyplot as plt
from torch.utils.data import Dataset, DataLoader
import torch.optim as optim

# ----------------------------------------------------------------
# 1) Utility: Set random seed for reproducibility
# ----------------------------------------------------------------
def set_seed(seed=42):
    random.seed(seed)
    np.random.seed(seed)
    torch.manual_seed(seed)
    if torch.cuda.is_available():
        torch.cuda.manual_seed_all(seed)


# ----------------------------------------------------------------
# 2) Generate a synthetic 2D map with path
#     Each map is represented as a 2D grid of size n x n:
#     -1 indicates obstacle
#      0 indicates free space
#      1 indicates the path
# ----------------------------------------------------------------
def create_random_path_map(n=32, obstacle_prob=0.2):
    """
    Creates a simple random 'snake-like' path from the left
    edge of the map to the right edge, while placing obstacles
    ↪  randomly.
    """
    grid = np.zeros((n, n), dtype=np.float32)

    # Random initial y for the path
    current_y = random.randint(0, n - 1)
    # Carve out the path across x from 0 to n-1
    for x in range(n):
        grid[current_y, x] = 1.0
        # Random shift up/down by 0 or 1 cell
        shift = random.choice([-1, 0, 1])
        current_y = max(0, min(n - 1, current_y + shift))

    # Place obstacles in the rest of the grid
    for i in range(n):
        for j in range(n):
            if grid[i, j] != 1.0:  # not on the path
                if random.random() < obstacle_prob:
                    grid[i, j] = -1.0  # obstacle

    # Rescale to [-1,1]: we keep path=1, obstacle=-1, free=0
    # Already set properly for the diffusion model
    return grid


# ----------------------------------------------------------------
# 3) Create a custom Dataset to produce random path maps
# ----------------------------------------------------------------
```

```python
class PathDataset(Dataset):
    """
    Generates random path maps on the fly.
    """

    def __init__(self, n_samples=10000, n=32, obstacle_prob=0.2):
        super().__init__()
        self.n_samples = n_samples
        self.n = n
        self.obstacle_prob = obstacle_prob

    def __len__(self):
        return self.n_samples

    def __getitem__(self, idx):
        # Generate a random path map
        grid = create_random_path_map(n=self.n,
        ↪  obstacle_prob=self.obstacle_prob)
        # Convert to torch tensor, shape => (1,n,n)
        tensor_map = torch.from_numpy(grid).unsqueeze(0)  # (C,H,W)
        return tensor_map, 0  # Dummy label to fit standard
        ↪  DataLoader


# ----------------------------------------------------------------
# 4) Define a simplified U-Net for 2D path denoising
# ----------------------------------------------------------------
class DoubleConv(nn.Module):
    """
    A helper module that performs two convolutions (each followed by
    ↪  ReLU)
    to reduce repeated code in the U-Net.
    """

    def __init__(self, in_channels, out_channels):
        super(DoubleConv, self).__init__()
        self.conv = nn.Sequential(
            nn.Conv2d(in_channels, out_channels, 3, padding=1),
            nn.ReLU(inplace=True),
            nn.Conv2d(out_channels, out_channels, 3, padding=1),
            nn.ReLU(inplace=True)
        )

    def forward(self, x):
        return self.conv(x)

class UNet(nn.Module):
    """
    A simplified U-Net for 2D data with down-sampling (encoder),
    bottleneck, and up-sampling (decoder), plus skip connections.
    """
    def __init__(self, in_channels=1, out_channels=1,
    ↪  base_channels=32):
        super(UNet, self).__init__()

        # Down-sampling layers
```

209

```python
        self.down1 = DoubleConv(in_channels, base_channels)
        self.down2 = DoubleConv(base_channels, base_channels * 2)
        self.down3 = DoubleConv(base_channels * 2, base_channels *
        ↪   4)
        self.pool = nn.MaxPool2d(2)

        # Bottleneck
        self.bottleneck = DoubleConv(base_channels * 4,
        ↪   base_channels * 8)

        # Up-sampling layers
        self.up1 = nn.ConvTranspose2d(base_channels * 8,
        ↪   base_channels * 4, 2, stride=2)
        self.conv_up1 = DoubleConv(base_channels * 8, base_channels
        ↪   * 4)

        self.up2 = nn.ConvTranspose2d(base_channels * 4,
        ↪   base_channels * 2, 2, stride=2)
        self.conv_up2 = DoubleConv(base_channels * 4, base_channels
        ↪   * 2)

        self.up3 = nn.ConvTranspose2d(base_channels * 2,
        ↪   base_channels, 2, stride=2)
        self.conv_up3 = DoubleConv(base_channels * 2, base_channels)

        self.final_conv = nn.Conv2d(base_channels, out_channels, 1)

    def forward(self, x):
        # Encoder
        x1 = self.down1(x)
        x2 = self.pool(x1)

        x2 = self.down2(x2)
        x3 = self.pool(x2)

        x3 = self.down3(x3)
        x4 = self.pool(x3)

        # Bottleneck
        b = self.bottleneck(x4)

        # Decoder
        x = self.up1(b)
        x = torch.cat([x, x3], dim=1)
        x = self.conv_up1(x)

        x = self.up2(x)
        x = torch.cat([x, x2], dim=1)
        x = self.conv_up2(x)

        x = self.up3(x)
        x = torch.cat([x, x1], dim=1)
        x = self.conv_up3(x)
```

210

```python
        out = self.final_conv(x)
        return out


# ----------------------------------------------------------------
# 5) Define a linear beta schedule and the Diffusion logic
# ----------------------------------------------------------------
def make_beta_schedule(schedule_name, n_timestep, start=1e-4,
↪   end=2e-2):
    """
    Creates a beta schedule for the diffusion process.
    Here we implement a simple linear schedule.
    """
    if schedule_name == "linear":
        return torch.linspace(start, end, n_timestep)
    else:
        raise NotImplementedError("Only 'linear' schedule is
        ↪   implemented here.")


class Diffusion:
    """
    Encapsulates the forward noising process q(x_t | x_0) and
    the reverse denoising process p(x_{t-1} | x_t), along with
    utilities for training and sampling.
    """
    def __init__(self, n_steps=200, beta_schedule='linear'):
        self.n_steps = n_steps
        self.betas = make_beta_schedule(beta_schedule, n_steps)
        self.alphas = 1.0 - self.betas
        self.alpha_cumprod = torch.cumprod(self.alphas, dim=0)
        self.alpha_cumprod_prev = torch.cat(
            [torch.tensor([1.0]), self.alpha_cumprod[:-1]], dim=0
        )

        # Posterior variance p(x_{t-1} | x_t, x_0)
        self.posterior_variance = self.betas * (1.0 -
        ↪   self.alpha_cumprod_prev) / (1.0 - self.alpha_cumprod)

    def q_sample(self, x_start, t, noise=None):
        """
        Forward diffusion: x_t = sqrt(alpha_cumprod[t]) * x_start
                               + sqrt(1 - alpha_cumprod[t]) * noise
        """
        if noise is None:
            noise = torch.randn_like(x_start)
        shape = x_start.shape
        sqrt_alpha_cumprod_t = self.alpha_cumprod[t].sqrt().view(-1,
        ↪   1, 1, 1)
        sqrt_one_minus_alpha_cumprod_t = (1 -
        ↪   self.alpha_cumprod[t]).sqrt().view(-1, 1, 1, 1)
        # Broadcast to match batch dimensions
        while len(sqrt_alpha_cumprod_t.shape) < len(shape):
```

```python
        sqrt_alpha_cumprod_t =
        ↪   sqrt_alpha_cumprod_t.unsqueeze(-1)
        sqrt_one_minus_alpha_cumprod_t =
        ↪   sqrt_one_minus_alpha_cumprod_t.unsqueeze(-1)

    return sqrt_alpha_cumprod_t * x_start +
    ↪   sqrt_one_minus_alpha_cumprod_t * noise

def predict_noise(self, model, x_t, t):
    """
    Predict the original noise at step t using the model.
    """
    return model(x_t)

def p_sample(self, model, x_t, t, guidance_scale=1.0):
    """
    One reverse diffusion step: p(x_{t-1} | x_t).
    The model predicts noise e_t, and we compute the posterior
    ↪   mean.
    """
    betas_t = self.betas[t]
    alpha_t = self.alphas[t]
    alpha_cumprod_t = self.alpha_cumprod[t]
    alpha_cumprod_prev_t = self.alpha_cumprod_prev[t]

    # Predicted noise
    e_t = model(x_t) * guidance_scale

    # Approximate x_0
    sqrt_recip_alpha_t = (1.0 / alpha_t).sqrt()
    x_0_hat = (x_t - (1.0 - alpha_t).sqrt() * e_t) *
    ↪   sqrt_recip_alpha_t

    # Coefficients for p(x_{t-1} | x_t, x_0_hat)
    coef1 = (alpha_cumprod_prev_t.sqrt() * betas_t) / (1.0 -
    ↪   alpha_cumprod_t)
    coef2 = ((1.0 - alpha_cumprod_prev_t) * alpha_t.sqrt()) /
    ↪   (1.0 - alpha_cumprod_t)
    mean = coef1 * x_0_hat + coef2 * x_t

    # Posterior variance
    posterior_var = self.posterior_variance[t]
    if t > 0:
        noise = torch.randn_like(x_t)
    else:
        noise = torch.zeros_like(x_t)

    x_prev = mean + noise * posterior_var.sqrt()
    return x_prev

def p_sample_loop(self, model, shape, device,
↪   guidance_scale=1.0):
    """
```

```
        Iteratively apply reverse diffusion from x_T ~ N(0,I) to
        ↪  x_0.
        """
        x_t = torch.randn(shape, device=device)
        for i in reversed(range(self.n_steps)):
            x_t = self.p_sample(model, x_t, i,
            ↪  guidance_scale=guidance_scale)
        return x_t


# ----------------------------------------------------------------
# 6) Training and evaluation routines
# ----------------------------------------------------------------
def train_one_epoch(model, diffusion, optimizer, dataloader,
↪  device):
    """
    Train for a single epoch:
    1) Sample random time step
    2) Forward diffuse
    3) Predict noise
    4) Minimize MSE between predicted and actual noise
    """
    model.train()
    total_loss = 0
    for maps, _ in dataloader:
        maps = maps.to(device)
        batch_size = maps.size(0)

        # Random time step [0..n_steps-1]
        t = torch.randint(0, diffusion.n_steps, (batch_size,),
        ↪  device=device).long()

        noise = torch.randn_like(maps)
        x_t = diffusion.q_sample(maps, t, noise=noise)
        noise_pred = diffusion.predict_noise(model, x_t, t)

        loss = nn.functional.mse_loss(noise_pred, noise)
        optimizer.zero_grad()
        loss.backward()
        optimizer.step()
        total_loss += loss.item()
    return total_loss / len(dataloader)

def evaluate_model(model, diffusion, dataloader, device):
    """
    Evaluate model with MSE over a validation set.
    """
    model.eval()
    total_loss = 0
    with torch.no_grad():
        for maps, _ in dataloader:
            maps = maps.to(device)
            batch_size = maps.size(0)
```

213

```
            t = torch.randint(0, diffusion.n_steps, (batch_size,),
            ↪  device=device).long()
            noise = torch.randn_like(maps)
            x_t = diffusion.q_sample(maps, t, noise=noise)
            noise_pred = diffusion.predict_noise(model, x_t, t)
            loss = nn.functional.mse_loss(noise_pred, noise)
            total_loss += loss.item()
    return total_loss / len(dataloader)

def sample_and_save(model, diffusion, device, epoch, n_samples=4,
↪  guidance_scale=1.0):
    """
    Use the diffusion model to sample path solutions from pure
    ↪  noise.
    Saves a grid-like figure with each channel displayed.
    """
    model.eval()
    with torch.no_grad():
        # shape => B x C x H x W
        gen_maps = diffusion.p_sample_loop(
            model, (n_samples, 1, 32, 32), device, guidance_scale
        )
        # Move gen_maps to CPU for plotting
        gen_maps_cpu = gen_maps.detach().cpu().numpy()

    # Plot and save
    fig, axes = plt.subplots(1, n_samples, figsize=(12, 3))
    for i in range(n_samples):
        # Squeeze out channel dimension
        path_map = gen_maps_cpu[i, 0]
        # Show as a heatmap
        axes[i].imshow(path_map, cmap="RdYlBu", vmin=-1, vmax=1)
        axes[i].axis("off")
    os.makedirs("results_paths", exist_ok=True)

    ↪  plt.savefig(f"results_paths/epoch_{epoch}_gs_{guidance_scale}.png")
    plt.close()


# ------------------------------------------------------------
# 7) Main script to tie everything together
# ------------------------------------------------------------
def main():
    set_seed(42)
    device = torch.device('cuda' if torch.cuda.is_available() else
    ↪  'cpu')

    # Create training and test datasets
    train_dataset = PathDataset(n_samples=2000, n=32,
    ↪  obstacle_prob=0.2)
    test_dataset = PathDataset(n_samples=400, n=32,
    ↪  obstacle_prob=0.2)
```

```
train_loader = DataLoader(train_dataset, batch_size=16,
↪   shuffle=True)
test_loader = DataLoader(test_dataset, batch_size=16,
↪   shuffle=False)

# Create UNet model
model = UNet(in_channels=1, out_channels=1,
↪   base_channels=32).to(device)

# Set up Diffusion with 200 time steps and linear schedule
diffusion = Diffusion(n_steps=200, beta_schedule='linear')

# Optimizer
optimizer = optim.Adam(model.parameters(), lr=1e-4)

# Training loop
epochs = 5
for epoch in range(epochs):
    train_loss = train_one_epoch(model, diffusion, optimizer,
    ↪   train_loader, device)
    val_loss = evaluate_model(model, diffusion, test_loader,
    ↪   device)
    print(f"Epoch [{epoch+1}/{epochs}] - Train Loss:
    ↪   {train_loss:.4f}, Val Loss: {val_loss:.4f}")

    # Sample from the diffusion model
    sample_and_save(model, diffusion, device, epoch,
    ↪   n_samples=4, guidance_scale=1.0)
    # Try a second guidance scale to see variation
    sample_and_save(model, diffusion, device, epoch,
    ↪   n_samples=4, guidance_scale=2.0)

    print("Training complete! Generated maps are saved in the
    ↪   'results_paths' folder.")

if __name__ == "__main__":
    main()
```

Key Implementation Details:

- **Random Path Map Creation:** We implement
  `create_random_path_map` to generate synthetic 2D grids with
  a simple "snake-like" path. Obstacles (labeled -1) are placed
  randomly, free space is 0, and the path is 1.

- **U-Net Architecture:** The `UNet` class uses encoder-decoder
  stages with skip connections, allowing the model to capture
  global context and preserve local detail in 2D map data.

215

- **Diffusion Process:** The `Diffusion` class defines the forward noising (`q_sample`) and reverse denoising (`p_sample` and `p_sample_loop`) along a linear beta schedule. The posterior calculation uses the standard diffusion equations to iteratively refine noisy samples toward clean path maps.

- **Training Objective:** The function `train_one_epoch` optimizes a mean-squared error (MSE) loss between the predicted noise and the actual noise, aligning the denoising model for each random diffusion step.

- **Guidance Scale:** During sampling, `guidance_scale` multiplies the model's predicted noise, balancing the trade-off between path fidelity and diversity.

- **Sampling and Visualization:** The `sample_and_save` function generates new path solutions entirely from random noise via reverse diffusion, then saves the results as color-coded 2D grids to illustrate the learned path distributions.

Chapter 21

Protein Structure Sampling and Folding

This chapter explores generating or refining protein structures. A common task is predicting valid 3D conformations from amino acid sequences. We represent the protein backbone or full atomic coordinates as a 3D graph. A forward diffusion corrupts the coordinates with random perturbations, while the model learns to reverse it. Key steps: (1) collect known protein structures from public databases, (2) define a noise schedule that randomly shifts atomic positions, (3) train a graph-based UNet or transformer to predict the coordinate updates, (4) sample new conformations by reversing from random or partially known coordinates, and (5) apply energy or clash constraints to ensure physically valid results. An innovative extension includes integrating co-evolutionary signals or attention layers that capture inter-residue contacts, leading to more biologically plausible folding outcomes.

Python Code Snippet

```
import torch
import torch.nn as nn
import torch.optim as optim
import random
import math
from torch.utils.data import Dataset, DataLoader
import numpy as np
```

```python
# ----------------------------------------------------------------
# 1) Set random seed for reproducibility
# ----------------------------------------------------------------
def set_seed(seed=42):
    random.seed(seed)
    np.random.seed(seed)
    torch.manual_seed(seed)
    if torch.cuda.is_available():
        torch.cuda.manual_seed_all(seed)


# ----------------------------------------------------------------
# 2) Create a toy dataset of protein graphs (3D coordinates)
#     In practice, you would parse real PDB files, build adjacency,
#     and possibly include co-evolutionary signals or residue
# ↪   features.
# ----------------------------------------------------------------
class ProteinGraphDataset(Dataset):
    """
    A minimal synthetic dataset for demonstration.
    Each protein is represented by:
      - node_feats: shape [n_nodes, n_features]
      - coords: shape [n_nodes, 3]
      - adjacency: shape [n_nodes, n_nodes] (binary)
    We'll sample random adjacency and coordinates.
    """

    def __init__(self, num_samples=1000, max_nodes=20, seed=42):
        super().__init__()
        random.seed(seed)
        np.random.seed(seed)
        self.data = []
        for _ in range(num_samples):
            n_nodes = random.randint(5, max_nodes)
            coords = np.random.randn(n_nodes, 3).astype(np.float32)
            adjacency = (np.random.rand(n_nodes, n_nodes) >
                ↪ 0.7).astype(np.float32)
            # make adjacency symmetric and remove self-loops
            adjacency = np.triu(adjacency, k=1)
            adjacency = adjacency + adjacency.T
            adjacency[np.diag_indices_from(adjacency)] = 0
            # random node features (e.g., co-evolutionary signals or
                ↪ residue type embeddings)
            node_feats = np.random.randn(n_nodes,
                ↪ 8).astype(np.float32)
            self.data.append((node_feats, coords, adjacency))

    def __len__(self):
        return len(self.data)

    def __getitem__(self, idx):
        node_feats, coords, adjacency = self.data[idx]
        return (
            torch.from_numpy(node_feats),  # shape [n_nodes,
                ↪ n_feats]
```

```
        torch.from_numpy(coords),      # shape [n_nodes, 3]
        torch.from_numpy(adjacency)    # shape [n_nodes,
        ↪  n_nodes]
    )


# ----------------------------------------------------------------
# 3) Define a simple Graph-based model (GNN) to predict coordinate
↪  updates
#    For real protein folding, more advanced architectures
↪  (Transformers, GVP, etc.) are used.
# ----------------------------------------------------------------
class SimpleGraphGNN(nn.Module):
    """
    A minimal Graph GNN that:
     - Aggregates neighbor features using adjacency matrix
     - Produces a delta in coordinates for each node
    """
    def __init__(self, in_feats=8, hidden_dim=32):
        super(SimpleGraphGNN, self).__init__()
        self.layer1 = nn.Linear(in_feats, hidden_dim)
        self.layer2 = nn.Linear(hidden_dim, hidden_dim)
        self.coord_out = nn.Linear(hidden_dim, 3)  # predict
        ↪  coordinate shifts

        self.relu = nn.ReLU()

    def forward(self, node_feats, adjacency):
        """
        node_feats: shape [batch, n_nodes, in_feats]
        adjacency:  shape [batch, n_nodes, n_nodes]
        Returns predicted coordinate shifts: shape [batch, n_nodes,
        ↪  3]
        """
        # Basic GNN aggregation:
        # out_feats[i] = relu(W sum_j( adjacency[i,j] *
        ↪  node_feats[j] ) + b)
        # Here we do a two-layer approach for demonstration.
        # (No normalization or skip connections for brevity)

        # 1) Weighted neighbor sum
        h = torch.bmm(adjacency, node_feats)
        # 2) Linear + ReLU
        h = self.relu(self.layer1(h))

        h = torch.bmm(adjacency, h)
        h = self.relu(self.layer2(h))

        # 3) Output predicted shift in 3D coords
        coord_shift = self.coord_out(h)  # shape [batch, n_nodes, 3]
        return coord_shift


# ----------------------------------------------------------------
```

```python
# 4) Diffusion schedule and forward/reverse processes for 3D
↪   coordinates
# ------------------------------------------------------------
def make_beta_schedule(schedule_name, n_timestep, start=1e-4,
↪   end=2e-2):
    """
    Creates a beta schedule for the diffusion process.
    We'll keep it linear for simplicity.
    """

    if schedule_name == "linear":
        return torch.linspace(start, end, n_timestep)
    else:
        raise NotImplementedError("Only 'linear' schedule is
        ↪   supported here.")


class ProteinDiffusion:
    """
    Encapsulates forward (q) and reverse (p) diffusion processes for
    ↪   3D coords:
      - q_sample: coords_t = sqrt(alpha_cumprod[t]) * coords_0 +
      ↪   sqrt(1 - alpha_cumprod[t]) * noise
      - p_sample: single step to go from coords_t -> coords_{t-1}
    We treat the GNN model as predicting the noise in 3D coordinate
    ↪   space.
    """

    def __init__(self, n_steps=1000, beta_schedule='linear'):
        self.n_steps = n_steps
        self.betas = make_beta_schedule(beta_schedule, n_steps)
        self.alphas = 1.0 - self.betas
        self.alpha_cumprod = torch.cumprod(self.alphas, dim=0)
        self.alpha_cumprod_prev = torch.cat([torch.tensor([1.0]),
        ↪   self.alpha_cumprod[:-1]], dim=0)

        # Posterior variance term
        self.posterior_variance = self.betas * (1.0 -
        ↪   self.alpha_cumprod_prev) / (1.0 - self.alpha_cumprod)

    def q_sample(self, coords_start, t, noise=None):
        """
        Forward diffusion of coordinates at time step t.
        """

        if noise is None:
            noise = torch.randn_like(coords_start)
        sqrt_alpha_cumprod_t = self.alpha_cumprod[t].sqrt().view(-1,
        ↪   1, 1)
        sqrt_one_minus_alpha_cumprod_t = (1.0 -
        ↪   self.alpha_cumprod[t]).sqrt().view(-1, 1, 1)
        return sqrt_alpha_cumprod_t * coords_start +
        ↪   sqrt_one_minus_alpha_cumprod_t * noise

    def predict_noise(self, model, node_feats, coords_t, adjacency):
        """
```

```python
        Use the GNN model to predict the noise that was added to
        ↪ coords_t.
        The GNN might use node_feats + adjacency + coords if needed.
        """
        # A naive approach: we treat coords as an additional
        ↪ "feature" or pass them separately.
        # For demonstration, we'll just pass node_feats + adjacency.
        # In advanced architectures, coords can also be included as
        ↪ input or used in an iterative loop.
        noise_pred = model(node_feats, adjacency)
        return noise_pred

    def p_sample(self, model, node_feats, coords_t, adjacency, t):
        """
        Single reverse diffusion step.
        """
        betas_t = self.betas[t]
        alpha_t = self.alphas[t]
        alpha_cumprod_t = self.alpha_cumprod[t]
        alpha_cumprod_prev_t = self.alpha_cumprod_prev[t]

        # Model predicts noise in the current coords
        noise_pred = self.predict_noise(model, node_feats, coords_t,
        ↪ adjacency)

        # Reconstruct coords_0 (approx)
        sqrt_recip_alpha_t = (1.0 / alpha_t).sqrt().view(-1, 1, 1)
        coords_0_hat = (coords_t - (1.0 - alpha_t).sqrt().view(-1,
        ↪ 1, 1) * noise_pred) * sqrt_recip_alpha_t

        coef1 = ( (alpha_cumprod_prev_t).sqrt() * betas_t / (1.0 -
        ↪ alpha_cumprod_t) ).view(-1,1,1)
        coef2 = ( (1.0 - alpha_cumprod_prev_t) * alpha_t.sqrt() /
        ↪ (1.0 - alpha_cumprod_t) ).view(-1,1,1)
        mean = coef1 * coords_0_hat + coef2 * coords_t

        posterior_var = self.posterior_variance[t].view(-1,1,1)
        if t > 0:
            noise = torch.randn_like(coords_t)
        else:
            noise = torch.zeros_like(coords_t)

        coords_prev = mean + noise * posterior_var.sqrt()
        return coords_prev

    def p_sample_loop(self, model, node_feats, adjacency, shape,
    ↪ device):
        """
        Repeatedly apply p_sample, starting from random coords ~
        ↪ N(0, I).
        shape: (batch, n_nodes, 3)
        """
        coords_t = torch.randn(shape, device=device)
```

```python
        # We assume adjacency, node_feats are not time-dependent in
        ↪  this naive example.
        for i in reversed(range(self.n_steps)):
            t_tensor = torch.tensor([i]*coords_t.size(0),
            ↪  device=device).long()
            coords_t = self.p_sample(model, node_feats, coords_t,
            ↪  adjacency, t_tensor)
        return coords_t


# ---------------------------------------------------------------
# 5) Training and sampling routines
# ---------------------------------------------------------------
def train_one_epoch(model, diffusion, optimizer, dataloader,
↪  device):
    model.train()
    total_loss = 0
    for node_feats, coords, adjacency in dataloader:
        node_feats, coords, adjacency = (
            node_feats.to(device), coords.to(device),
            ↪  adjacency.to(device)
        )
        batch_size, n_nodes, _ = coords.shape

        # Sample a random time step for each protein in the batch
        t = torch.randint(0, diffusion.n_steps, (batch_size,),
        ↪  device=device).long()

        # Create noise
        noise = torch.randn_like(coords)

        # Forward diffuse
        coords_t = diffusion.q_sample(coords, t, noise)

        # Predict noise at coords_t
        noise_pred = diffusion.predict_noise(model, node_feats,
        ↪  coords_t, adjacency)

        # L2 loss
        loss = nn.functional.mse_loss(noise_pred, noise)

        optimizer.zero_grad()
        loss.backward()
        optimizer.step()

        total_loss += loss.item()

    return total_loss / len(dataloader)

def evaluate_model(model, diffusion, dataloader, device):
    model.eval()
    total_loss = 0
    with torch.no_grad():
        for node_feats, coords, adjacency in dataloader:
```

```python
            node_feats, coords, adjacency = (
                node_feats.to(device), coords.to(device),
                ↪   adjacency.to(device)
            )
            batch_size, n_nodes, _ = coords.shape
            t = torch.randint(0, diffusion.n_steps, (batch_size,),
            ↪   device=device).long()
            noise = torch.randn_like(coords)
            coords_t = diffusion.q_sample(coords, t, noise)
            noise_pred = diffusion.predict_noise(model, node_feats,
            ↪   coords_t, adjacency)
            loss = nn.functional.mse_loss(noise_pred, noise)
            total_loss += loss.item()
    return total_loss / len(dataloader)


def sample_conformations(model, diffusion, dataloader, device):
    """
    Sample new protein conformations from random noise,
    or refine partial coords (not fully showcased here).
    We'll just demonstrate unconditional sampling from noise.
    """
    model.eval()
    node_feats, coords, adjacency = next(iter(dataloader))
    node_feats, coords, adjacency = (
        node_feats.to(device), coords.to(device),
        ↪   adjacency.to(device)
    )
    batch_size, n_nodes, _ = coords.shape
    with torch.no_grad():
        # shape for coords: (batch, n_nodes, 3)
        gen_coords = diffusion.p_sample_loop(
            model,
            node_feats,
            adjacency,
            (batch_size, n_nodes, 3),
            device
        )
    return gen_coords

# ----------------------------------------------------------------
# 6) Main script
# ----------------------------------------------------------------
def main():
    set_seed(42)
    device = torch.device("cuda" if torch.cuda.is_available() else
    ↪   "cpu")

    # Create synthetic dataset
    train_data = ProteinGraphDataset(num_samples=200, max_nodes=15,
    ↪   seed=42)
    test_data = ProteinGraphDataset(num_samples=50, max_nodes=15,
    ↪   seed=999)
```

223

```
train_loader = DataLoader(train_data, batch_size=8,
↪  shuffle=True)
test_loader = DataLoader(test_data, batch_size=8, shuffle=False)

# Initialize model, diffusion schedule
model = SimpleGraphGNN(in_feats=8, hidden_dim=32).to(device)
diffusion = ProteinDiffusion(n_steps=50, beta_schedule='linear')

optimizer = optim.Adam(model.parameters(), lr=1e-3)
epochs = 5
for epoch in range(epochs):
    train_loss = train_one_epoch(model, diffusion, optimizer,
↪      train_loader, device)
    val_loss = evaluate_model(model, diffusion, test_loader,
↪      device)
    print(f"Epoch [{epoch+1}/{epochs}] - Train Loss:
↪      {train_loss:.4f}, Val Loss: {val_loss:.4f}")

    # Sample some conformations for inspection
    sampled_coords = sample_conformations(model, diffusion,
↪      train_loader, device)
    print(f"Sampled coords (one batch) shape:
↪      {sampled_coords.shape}")

print("Training complete. You can now use the diffusion model to
↪  refine or sample new protein structures!")

if __name__ == "__main__":
    main()
```

Key Implementation Details:

- **Forward Diffusion:** We implement `q_sample` to corrupt
  original coordinates by adding Gaussian noise at each step,
  guided by a linear schedule defined in `make_beta_schedule`.

- **Reverse Diffusion (Sampling):** The function `p_sample_loop`
  applies iterative denoising, starting from random 3D coordinates until reaching a potentially valid protein structure.

- **Graph GNN Architecture:** The `SimpleGraphGNN` uses
  adjacency-based neighborhood aggregation to produce a 3D
  coordinate shift (i.e., predicted noise). Advanced methods
  might integrate attention or physically informed message pass-
  ing.

- **Training Objective:** We match the predicted noise to the
  random noise injected in the forward process with an L2 loss

(`mse_loss`).

- **Energy/Clash Constraints:** Though not fully implemented here, one can incorporate additional loss terms or post-processing steps to ensure physically valid sidechain packing and minimal steric clashes.

- **End-to-End Pipeline:** The `main` function ties dataset loading, model initialization, training, and sampling together. In real-world scenarios, input features may include co-evolutionary signals and known partial coordinates to improve biologically plausible folding results.

Chapter 22

Chemical Molecule Generation for Drug Discovery

Diffusion can generate novel molecules by modeling SMILES strings or graph topologies of chemical compounds. Common use cases include generating candidate molecules with desired properties or structural motifs. We begin by representing each molecule as a graph (nodes for atoms, edges for bonds) or a tokenized SMILES string. A forward noise schedule corrupts the graph or string. We use a graph-based or transformer-based UNet to predict the noise for each node or token. Implementation steps include: (1) preparing large datasets of known molecules, (2) applying noise to each molecular graph or token sequence, (3) training the network with a denoising objective, (4) reversing the diffusion to sample new molecules, and (5) optionally incorporating property predictors to guide generation toward target solubility or binding characteristics. A novel method couples property-based classifiers with the diffusion sampling steps to encourage generation of more drug-like compounds.

Python Code Snippet

```
import os
import math
import random
```

```python
import torch
import torch.nn as nn
import torch.optim as optim
from torch.utils.data import Dataset, DataLoader

# 1) Set random seeds for reproducibility
def set_seed(seed=42):
    random.seed(seed)
    torch.manual_seed(seed)
    if torch.cuda.is_available():
        torch.cuda.manual_seed_all(seed)


# ----------------------------------------------------------------
# 2) A toy SMILES dataset and basic tokenization
# ----------------------------------------------------------------
class SmilesDataset(Dataset):
    '''
    A simple dataset that holds SMILES strings.
    In real scenarios, you'll load a large dataset from disk.
    '''
    def __init__(self, smiles_list, max_length=64):
        self.smiles_list = smiles_list
        self.max_length = max_length
        # Build vocabulary from the input SMILES
        self.chars = set()
        for smi in self.smiles_list:
            for ch in smi:
                self.chars.add(ch)
        # Add special tokens
        self.chars = sorted(list(self.chars)) + ['<pad>', '<bos>',
        ↪  '<eos>']
        self.char_to_idx = {c: i for i, c in enumerate(self.chars)}
        self.idx_to_char = {i: c for c, i in
        ↪  self.char_to_idx.items()}

    def __len__(self):
        return len(self.smiles_list)

    def __getitem__(self, idx):
        smi = self.smiles_list[idx]
        # Convert to token indices with <bos> and <eos>
        smi_tokens = ['<bos>'] + list(smi) + ['<eos>']
        # Pad or truncate
        if len(smi_tokens) < self.max_length:
            smi_tokens += ['<pad>'] * (self.max_length -
            ↪  len(smi_tokens))
        else:
            smi_tokens = smi_tokens[:self.max_length]

        token_ids = [self.char_to_idx[ch] for ch in smi_tokens]
        return torch.tensor(token_ids, dtype=torch.long)

    def get_vocab_size(self):
```

```python
        return len(self.chars)

    def decode_tokens(self, token_ids):
        # Convert indices back to string, ignoring padding and
        ↪  special tokens outside of demonstration
        tokens = [self.idx_to_char[int(i)] for i in token_ids]
        # Remove <bos>, <eos>, and any <pad>
        cleaned = []
        for t in tokens:
            if t in ['<bos>', '<eos>', '<pad>']:
                continue
            cleaned.append(t)
        return ''.join(cleaned)


# -----------------------------------------------------------------
# 3) Simple positional encoding for token embeddings
# -----------------------------------------------------------------
class PositionalEncoding(nn.Module):
    '''
    Standard positional encoding for sequence data.
    '''

    def __init__(self, d_model, max_len=5000):
        super(PositionalEncoding, self).__init__()
        pe = torch.zeros(max_len, d_model)
        position = torch.arange(0, max_len,
        ↪  dtype=torch.float).unsqueeze(1)
        div_term = torch.exp(torch.arange(0, d_model, 2).float() *
        ↪  (-math.log(10000.0) / d_model))
        pe[:, 0::2] = torch.sin(position * div_term)
        pe[:, 1::2] = torch.cos(position * div_term)
        self.pe = pe.unsqueeze(0)   # [1, max_len, d_model]

    def forward(self, x):
        # x shape: [batch_size, seq_len, d_model]
        seq_len = x.size(1)
        # Add the embedding directly
        return x + self.pe[:, :seq_len, :].to(x.device)


# -----------------------------------------------------------------
# 4) A simple Transformer model for noise prediction
# -----------------------------------------------------------------
class TransformerModel(nn.Module):
    '''
    A small Transformer-based model that predicts noise over token
    ↪  embeddings.
    '''

    def __init__(self, vocab_size, d_model=128, nhead=4,
    ↪  num_layers=2, max_length=64):
        super(TransformerModel, self).__init__()
        self.d_model = d_model
        self.embedding = nn.Embedding(vocab_size, d_model)
        self.pos_encoder = PositionalEncoding(d_model,
        ↪  max_len=max_length)
```

```
        encoder_layers = nn.TransformerEncoderLayer(d_model=d_model,
        ↪  nhead=nhead, dim_feedforward=256)
        self.transformer_encoder =
        ↪  nn.TransformerEncoder(encoder_layers,
        ↪  num_layers=num_layers)

        # Final linear to predict noise in the same embedding space
        self.fc_out = nn.Linear(d_model, d_model)

    def forward(self, x):
        '''
        x shape: [batch_size, seq_len]
        Returns predicted noise in embedding space: [batch_size,
        ↪  seq_len, d_model]
        '''
        embedded = self.embedding(x) * math.sqrt(self.d_model)
        encoded = self.pos_encoder(embedded)
        out = self.transformer_encoder(encoded)  # shape:
        ↪  [batch_size, seq_len, d_model]
        noise_pred = self.fc_out(out)
        return noise_pred


# ----------------------------------------------------------------
# 5) Diffusion schedule and forward/backward processes
# ----------------------------------------------------------------
def make_beta_schedule(schedule, n_timestep, start=1e-4, end=2e-2):
    if schedule == "linear":
        return torch.linspace(start, end, n_timestep)
    else:
        raise NotImplementedError("Only 'linear' schedule is
        ↪  implemented.")


class MoleculeDiffusion:
    '''
    Encapsulates the forward noising and reverse denoising for token
    ↪  embeddings.
    This is a continuous relaxation: tokens -> embeddings -> add
    ↪  noise -> estimate noise.
    '''
    def __init__(self, n_steps=200, schedule='linear', d_model=128):
        self.n_steps = n_steps
        self.betas = make_beta_schedule(schedule, n_steps)
        self.alphas = 1. - self.betas
        self.alpha_cumprod = torch.cumprod(self.alphas, dim=0)
        self.alpha_cumprod_prev = torch.cat([torch.tensor([1.0]),
        ↪  self.alpha_cumprod[:-1]], dim=0)
        self.posterior_variance = self.betas * (1. -
        ↪  self.alpha_cumprod_prev) / (1. - self.alpha_cumprod)

        self.d_model = d_model

    def q_sample(self, x_start_emb, t, noise=None):
```

```
    '''
    Forward diffusion on embeddings:
    x_t = sqrt(alpha_cumprod[t]) * x_start_emb + sqrt(1 -
    ↪  alpha_cumprod[t]) * noise
    '''
    if noise is None:
        noise = torch.randn_like(x_start_emb)
    sqrt_alpha_cumprod_t = math.sqrt(self.alpha_cumprod[t])
    sqrt_one_minus_alpha_cumprod_t = math.sqrt(1.0 -
    ↪  self.alpha_cumprod[t])
    return sqrt_alpha_cumprod_t * x_start_emb +
    ↪  sqrt_one_minus_alpha_cumprod_t * noise

def predict_noise(self, model, x_t_tokens, t):
    '''
    Use the Transformer to predict noise in the embedding space.
    x_t_tokens = integer tokens, so we need x_t_emb from a prior
    ↪  pass or separate embed net.
    However, for direct demonstration, we embed inside the
    ↪  model. We'll treat x_t_tokens
    as an approximation or placeholder. Real usage would store
    ↪  x_t_emb externally.
    '''
    # We'll pretend that model's input are the same tokens, but
    ↪  in practice,
    # you'd store your x_t_emb and feed it. This is for
    ↪  demonstration simplicity.
    noise_pred = model(x_t_tokens)  # shape: [B, seq_len,
    ↪  d_model]
    return noise_pred

def p_sample(self, model, x_t_emb, x_t_tokens, t,
↪  guidance_scale=1.0):
    '''
    Crystal-ball method: compute x_0 from predicted noise, then
    ↪  sample x_{t-1}.
    We do not do classifier guidance here, but we allow a noise
    ↪  scaling factor for demonstration.
    '''
    betas_t = self.betas[t]
    alpha_t = self.alphas[t]
    alpha_cumprod_t = self.alpha_cumprod[t]
    alpha_cumprod_prev_t = self.alpha_cumprod_prev[t]
    sqrt_recip_alpha_t = math.sqrt(1.0 / alpha_t)

    # Predict the noise
    noise_pred = model(x_t_tokens) * guidance_scale

    # x_0_hat in embedding space
    x_0_hat = (x_t_emb - math.sqrt(1.0 - alpha_t) * noise_pred)
    ↪  * sqrt_recip_alpha_t

    # The posterior mean
```

```
            coef1 = math.sqrt(alpha_cumprod_prev_t) * betas_t / (1.0 -
            ↪  alpha_cumprod_t)
            coef2 = math.sqrt(alpha_t) * (1.0 - alpha_cumprod_prev_t) /
            ↪  (1.0 - alpha_cumprod_t)
            mean = coef1 * x_0_hat + coef2 * x_t_emb

            # Posterior variance
            posterior_var = self.posterior_variance[t]
            if t > 0:
                noise = torch.randn_like(x_t_emb)
            else:
                noise = torch.zeros_like(x_t_emb)

            x_prev_emb = mean + math.sqrt(posterior_var) * noise
            return x_prev_emb


# ------------------------------------------------------------------
# 6) Training loop
# ------------------------------------------------------------------
def train_one_epoch(model, diffusion, optimizer, dataloader,
↪  device):
    model.train()
    total_loss = 0
    for batch in dataloader:
        batch = batch.to(device)                # shape: [B, seq_len]
        optimizer.zero_grad()

        # Random time step
        t = torch.randint(0, diffusion.n_steps, (batch.size(0),),
        ↪  device=device).long()

        # We'll embed the input ourselves for forward noising:
        # Step 1: get the raw tokens from the embedding layer
        with torch.no_grad():
            base_emb = model.embedding(batch)  # shape [B, seq_len,
            ↪  d_model]

        # Step 2: create random noise
        noise = torch.randn_like(base_emb)

        # Step 3: forward diffuse the embeddings
        # Each item in the batch can have a different t, so let's do
        ↪  it one by one
        x_t_list = []
        for i in range(batch.size(0)):
            x_t_list.append(diffusion.q_sample(base_emb[i], t[i],
            ↪  noise=noise[i]))
        x_t_emb = torch.stack(x_t_list, dim=0)  # shape [B, seq_len,
        ↪  d_model]

        # Step 4: The model sees only the discrete tokens "batch" in
        ↪  this simple demo
        noise_pred = model(batch)
```

```python
        # We want to measure MSE between noise_pred and the actual
        ↪  noise added
        # But noise_pred, x_t_emb, and base_emb must align in shape
        # noise_pred is [B, seq_len, d_model]
        # actual noise is (x_t_emb - sqrt(alpha_cumprod[t]) *
        ↪  base_emb) / sqrt(1-alpha_cumprod[t]) for each sample
        # We'll just do a direct MSE with the "noise" in a naive
        ↪  approach:
        loss = (noise_pred - noise).pow(2).mean()

        loss.backward()
        optimizer.step()

        total_loss += loss.item()
    return total_loss / len(dataloader)


@torch.no_grad()
def evaluate_model(model, diffusion, dataloader, device):
    model.eval()
    total_loss = 0
    for batch in dataloader:
        batch = batch.to(device)

        # Random time step
        t = torch.randint(0, diffusion.n_steps, (batch.size(0),),
        ↪  device=device).long()

        with torch.no_grad():
            base_emb = model.embedding(batch)
            noise = torch.randn_like(base_emb)

        x_t_list = []
        for i in range(batch.size(0)):
            x_t_list.append(diffusion.q_sample(base_emb[i], t[i],
            ↪  noise=noise[i]))
        x_t_emb = torch.stack(x_t_list, dim=0)

        noise_pred = model(batch)
        loss = (noise_pred - noise).pow(2).mean()
        total_loss += loss.item()
    return total_loss / len(dataloader)


# ------------------------------------------------------------
# 7) Sampling routine (reverse diffusion)
# ------------------------------------------------------------
@torch.no_grad()
def sample_molecules(model, diffusion, dataset, device,
↪  num_samples=4, guidance_scale=1.0):
    '''
    Start from random embeddings x_T and iteratively sample x_0 in
    ↪  embedding space.
    Then decode the final embeddings to tokens (naive approach).
```

```
    In practice, you might do argmax or sampling in discrete space
    ↪   guided by x_0.
    '''
    model.eval()
    vocab_size = dataset.get_vocab_size()

    # Initialize random tokens or embeddings
    seq_len = dataset.max_length

    # We'll create random tokens to feed the model at each step
    # (this is a naive approach for demonstration).
    x_t_tokens = torch.randint(0, vocab_size, (num_samples,
    ↪   seq_len), device=device)

    # We'll also maintain a random embedding to represent x_t
    x_t_emb = torch.randn(num_samples, seq_len, diffusion.d_model,
    ↪   device=device)

    for step in reversed(range(diffusion.n_steps)):
        x_t_emb = diffusion.p_sample(model, x_t_emb, x_t_tokens,
        ↪   step, guidance_scale=guidance_scale)

    # After full reverse diffusion, we interpret x_0_hat as a
    ↪   "clean" embedding.
    # For demonstration, let's do a naive nearest-token approach
    ↪   (not truly accurate).
    with torch.no_grad():
        # We'll pass x_0_hat to model.fc_out^-1 if that existed,
        # but we only have forward transforms. We'll do a naive
        ↪   approach:
        # 1) Find the token with the highest similarity to the final
        ↪   embeddings.
        # This is approximate, but suffices as an example.

        final_smiles = []
        # We can access the token embedding matrix
        token_emb_matrix = model.embedding.weight.data   # shape
        ↪   [vocab_size, d_model]

        for i in range(num_samples):
            token_ids = []
            for j in range(seq_len):
                # x_0_hat for one token
                token_vec = x_t_emb[i, j, :].unsqueeze(0)   # shape
                ↪   [1, d_model]
                # compute similarity to each token embedding
                sims = torch.matmul(token_vec, token_emb_matrix.T)
                ↪   # [1, vocab_size]
                chosen_id = torch.argmax(sims, dim=1).item()
                token_ids.append(chosen_id)
            # decode
            token_ids = torch.tensor(token_ids).cpu().numpy()
            smiles_str = dataset.decode_tokens(token_ids)
```

```
        final_smiles.append(smiles_str)

    return final_smiles

# ----------------------------------------------------------------
# 8) Main function to tie everything together
# ----------------------------------------------------------------
def main():
    set_seed(42)
    device = torch.device("cuda" if torch.cuda.is_available() else
    ↪  "cpu")

    # Your real dataset might be loaded from a file.
    # For illustration, we create a tiny set of example SMILES
    ↪  strings.
    example_smiles = [
        "CCO",          # ethanol
        "C1=CC=CC=C1",  # benzene
        "CC(=O)OC1=CC=CC=C1C(=O)OC",  # aspirin
        "CCCC",         # butane
        "NC(=O)C",      # simple amide
        "CCN(CC)CC"     # triethylamine
    ]

    # Expand artificially for training
    example_smiles = example_smiles * 100  # replicate for a bigger
    ↪  dataset

    dataset = SmilesDataset(example_smiles, max_length=20)
    train_loader = DataLoader(dataset, batch_size=16, shuffle=True)
    val_loader = DataLoader(dataset, batch_size=16, shuffle=False)

    # Build a model
    model = TransformerModel(
        vocab_size=dataset.get_vocab_size(),
        d_model=128,
        nhead=4,
        num_layers=2,
        max_length=20
    ).to(device)

    # Define diffusion
    diffusion = MoleculeDiffusion(n_steps=100, schedule='linear',
    ↪  d_model=128)

    # Optimizer
    optimizer = optim.Adam(model.parameters(), lr=1e-4)

    # Training
    epochs = 5
    for epoch in range(epochs):
        train_loss = train_one_epoch(model, diffusion, optimizer,
        ↪  train_loader, device)
```

```
    val_loss = evaluate_model(model, diffusion, val_loader,
    ↪  device)
    print(f"Epoch [{epoch+1}/{epochs}] - Train Loss:
    ↪  {train_loss:.4f}, Val Loss: {val_loss:.4f}")

    # Sampling
    sampled = sample_molecules(model, diffusion, dataset, device,
    ↪  num_samples=5, guidance_scale=1.5)
    print("\nSampled SMILES strings:")
    for s in sampled:
        print(f"  {s}")

if __name__ == "__main__":
    main()
```

Key Implementation Details:

- **Token Embeddings and Continuous Noise:** SMILES are tokenized, embedded, and treated as continuous vectors. The forward diffusion adds Gaussian noise to these embeddings at each step.

- **Transformer Noise Predictor:** The `TransformerModel` predicts the noise in the embedding space, analogous to how an image `UNet` predicts noise for pixels.

- **Forward Diffusion:** We corrupt the embedding of each token with noise based on a time-dependent beta schedule.

- **Reverse Diffusion (Sampling):** We iteratively remove noise, starting from random embeddings, guided by the model's noise predictions. A "guidance scale" can intensify or reduce the model's corrections.

- **Reconstruction to Tokens:** For demonstration, we use a naive token-embedding similarity to recover discrete tokens. Real applications integrate more advanced decoding or sampling from a discrete distribution.

- **End-to-End Pipeline:** The `main` function shows the entire workflow—loading a SMILES dataset, training the diffusion model, and sampling new hypothetical compounds that match the learned distribution. Property-based filters or auxiliary networks can be integrated for more drug-like molecule generation.

Chapter 23

Therapeutic Protein and Ligand Co-Design

This specialized application combines protein structure sampling and ligand generation to propose new binding interactions. Common use cases involve rational drug design to optimize ligand binding. Construction requires: (1) modeling protein-ligand pairs, either in 3D space or as separate data streams, (2) applying forward noise to both protein structures and ligands, (3) training a dual-stream diffusion network that co-denoises the molecular complex, preserving interaction interfaces, (4) sampling new protein-ligand combinations from random or partially guided seeds, and (5) incorporating scoring functions to evaluate binding affinity. An innovative approach is to condition on region-of-interest maps inside the protein's active site, steering the diffusion to produce ligands that fit the pocket geometry and complement the protein's structure.

Python Code Snippet

```python
import torch
import torch.nn as nn
import torch.optim as optim
from torch.utils.data import Dataset, DataLoader
import random
import math
import numpy as np

# --------------------------------------------------------------
```

```python
# 1) Set random seed for reproducibility
# ------------------------------------------------------------
def set_seed(seed=42):
    random.seed(seed)
    np.random.seed(seed)
    torch.manual_seed(seed)
    if torch.cuda.is_available():
        torch.cuda.manual_seed_all(seed)


# ------------------------------------------------------------
# 2) Create a simple synthetic Protein-Ligand dataset
#    For demonstration, we randomly generate coordinates
#    to mimic protein and ligand 3D positions.
# ------------------------------------------------------------
class ProteinLigandDataset(Dataset):
    '''
    Returns synthetic pairs of protein coordinates (B x P x 3)
    and ligand coordinates (B x L x 3). For demonstration,
    these are randomly generated 3D points.
    In practice, one would load real structures from PDB files or
    ↪ similar.
    '''
    def __init__(self, num_samples=10000,
                 n_protein_atoms=50,
                 n_ligand_atoms=10):
        super().__init__()
        self.num_samples = num_samples
        self.n_protein_atoms = n_protein_atoms
        self.n_ligand_atoms = n_ligand_atoms

    def __len__(self):
        return self.num_samples

    def __getitem__(self, idx):
        # Random 3D positions in [-1, 1]
        protein_coords = np.random.uniform(-1, 1,
                                (self.n_protein_atoms,
                                 ↪ 3)).astype(np.float32)
        ligand_coords  = np.random.uniform(-1, 1,
                                (self.n_ligand_atoms,
                                 ↪ 3)).astype(np.float32)

        # In a real scenario, region_of_interest might be a 3D
        ↪ volume or
        # assignment of which protein residues are critical. Here,
        ↪ we'll use
        # a placeholder vector with random floats.
        region_of_interest = np.random.uniform(-1, 1,
            ↪ 10).astype(np.float32)

        return protein_coords, ligand_coords, region_of_interest

# ------------------------------------------------------------
```

```python
# 3) Define a dual-stream feed-forward network (MLP)
#    that predicts noise for both protein and ligand.
#    For real 3D data, specialized architectures (e.g. GNNs)
#    might be more suitable. This is a simplified demonstration.
# -------------------------------------------------------------
class DualStreamModel(nn.Module):
    '''
    A simple MLP that flattens protein and ligand coordinates
    along with a region_of_interest vector, then outputs
    predicted noise for protein+ligand coords.
    '''
    def __init__(self, n_protein_atoms=50, n_ligand_atoms=10,
    ↪ roi_dim=10, hidden_size=256):
        super(DualStreamModel, self).__init__()
        self.n_protein_atoms = n_protein_atoms
        self.n_ligand_atoms  = n_ligand_atoms
        self.roi_dim = roi_dim

        # Flattened dimension:
        #    protein coords (n_protein_atoms*3) +
        #    ligand coords (n_ligand_atoms*3) +
        #    region_of_interest dimension
        input_dim = self.n_protein_atoms*3 + self.n_ligand_atoms*3 +
        ↪ self.roi_dim

        # Outputs noise for all coords combined
        output_dim = self.n_protein_atoms*3 + self.n_ligand_atoms*3

        self.net = nn.Sequential(
            nn.Linear(input_dim, hidden_size),
            nn.ReLU(),
            nn.Linear(hidden_size, hidden_size),
            nn.ReLU(),
            nn.Linear(hidden_size, output_dim)
        )

    def forward(self, protein_coords, ligand_coords, roi):
        # Flatten inputs
        B = protein_coords.shape[0]
        protein_flat = protein_coords.view(B, -1)   # (B, P*3)
        ligand_flat  = ligand_coords.view(B, -1)    # (B, L*3)
        # region_of_interest is already (B, roi_dim)

        # Concatenate everything
        combined = torch.cat([protein_flat, ligand_flat, roi],
        ↪ dim=1)
        noise_pred = self.net(combined)

        # Reshape noise back into protein and ligand coords
        protein_noise = noise_pred[:, :self.n_protein_atoms*3]
        ligand_noise  = noise_pred[:, self.n_protein_atoms*3:]
```

```python
        protein_noise = protein_noise.view(B, self.n_protein_atoms,
        ↪   3)
        ligand_noise  = ligand_noise.view(B, self.n_ligand_atoms, 3)

        return protein_noise, ligand_noise

# -------------------------------------------------------------
# 4) Define a Diffusion class that handles
#    forward noise addition and reverse sampling
#    for dual-stream (protein+ligand) data.
# -------------------------------------------------------------
def make_beta_schedule(schedule_name, n_timestep, start=1e-4,
↪   end=2e-2):
    '''
    Creates a beta schedule for the diffusion process.
    We use a linear schedule as a straightforward example.
    '''
    if schedule_name == "linear":
        return torch.linspace(start, end, n_timestep)
    else:
        raise NotImplementedError("Only 'linear' schedule is
        ↪   implemented here.")

class DualStreamDiffusion:
    '''
    Manages forward (q_sample) and reverse (p_sample) steps
    for protein-ligand coordinate data.
    '''
    def __init__(self, n_steps=200, beta_schedule='linear'):
        self.n_steps = n_steps
        self.betas = make_beta_schedule(beta_schedule, n_steps)  #
        ↪   shape: (n_steps)
        self.alphas = 1.0 - self.betas
        self.alpha_cumprod = torch.cumprod(self.alphas, dim=0)  #
        ↪   shape: (n_steps)
        alpha_cumprod_prev = torch.cat([
            torch.tensor([1.0]),
            self.alpha_cumprod[:-1]
        ], dim=0)

        self.alpha_cumprod_prev = alpha_cumprod_prev
        self.posterior_variance = (
            self.betas * (1.0 - alpha_cumprod_prev) / (1.0 -
            ↪   self.alpha_cumprod)
        )

    def q_sample(self, x_start, t, noise=None):
        '''
        Forward diffusion: x_start -> x_t
        x_start: (protein_coords, ligand_coords)
        Each is shape (B, N, 3).
        We add noise scaled by self.alpha_cumprod[t].
        '''
```

```python
    protein_x0, ligand_x0 = x_start
    bsz = protein_x0.shape[0]

    if noise is None:
        # We add noise for both protein and ligand
        noise_protein = torch.randn_like(protein_x0)
        noise_ligand  = torch.randn_like(ligand_x0)
    else:
        noise_protein, noise_ligand = noise

    sqrt_alpha_cumprod_t = self.alpha_cumprod[t].sqrt().view(
        -1, 1, 1
    ) # shape: (bsz,1,1) after expand
    sqrt_one_minus_alpha_cumprod_t = (1 -
    ↪ self.alpha_cumprod[t]).sqrt().view(
        -1, 1, 1
    )

    # Expand for broadcasting
    sqrt_alpha_cumprod_t = sqrt_alpha_cumprod_t.expand(bsz,
    ↪ protein_x0.size(1), protein_x0.size(2))
    sqrt_one_minus_alpha_cumprod_t =
    ↪ sqrt_one_minus_alpha_cumprod_t.expand(bsz,
    ↪ protein_x0.size(1), protein_x0.size(2))

    protein_xt = sqrt_alpha_cumprod_t * protein_x0 + \
                 sqrt_one_minus_alpha_cumprod_t * noise_protein

    # For ligand
    sqrt_alpha_cumprod_t_lig = sqrt_alpha_cumprod_t[:,
    ↪ :ligand_x0.size(1), :]
    sqrt_one_minus_alpha_cumprod_t_lig =
    ↪ sqrt_one_minus_alpha_cumprod_t[:, :ligand_x0.size(1), :]

    ligand_xt = sqrt_alpha_cumprod_t_lig * ligand_x0 + \
                sqrt_one_minus_alpha_cumprod_t_lig *
                ↪ noise_ligand

    return protein_xt, ligand_xt

def predict_noise(self, model, x_t, roi):
    '''
    Model predicts noise given current x_t (protein+ligand) and
    ↪ region_of_interest.
    '''
    protein_xt, ligand_xt = x_t
    return model(protein_xt, ligand_xt, roi)

def p_sample(self, model, x_t, t, roi, guidance_scale=1.0):
    '''
    One reverse diffusion step: x_{t} -> x_{t-1}.
    We compute x_0 estimate, then sample x_{t-1}.
    '''
```

```python
# Extract sets
protein_xt, ligand_xt = x_t

# Predicted noise
protein_noise_pred, ligand_noise_pred = model(protein_xt,
↪  ligand_xt, roi)
protein_noise_pred = protein_noise_pred * guidance_scale
ligand_noise_pred  = ligand_noise_pred  * guidance_scale

betas_t = self.betas[t]
alpha_t = self.alphas[t]
alpha_cumprod_t = self.alpha_cumprod[t]
alpha_cumprod_prev_t = self.alpha_cumprod_prev[t]

# Compute x_0 estimate for protein
sqrt_recip_alpha_t = (1.0 / alpha_t).sqrt()
protein_x0_hat = (protein_xt - (1.0 - alpha_t).sqrt() *
↪  protein_noise_pred) * sqrt_recip_alpha_t
# Posterior mean
coef1 = (alpha_cumprod_prev_t.sqrt() * betas_t) / (1.0 -
↪  alpha_cumprod_t)
coef2 = ((1.0 - alpha_cumprod_prev_t) * alpha_t.sqrt()) /
↪  (1.0 - alpha_cumprod_t)
protein_mean = coef1 * protein_x0_hat + coef2 * protein_xt

# For ligand
ligand_x0_hat = (ligand_xt - (1.0 - alpha_t).sqrt() *
↪  ligand_noise_pred) * sqrt_recip_alpha_t
ligand_mean = coef1 * ligand_x0_hat + coef2 * ligand_xt

# Posterior variance
posterior_var = self.posterior_variance[t]
if t > 0:
    noise_protein = torch.randn_like(protein_xt)
    noise_ligand  = torch.randn_like(ligand_xt)
else:
    noise_protein = torch.zeros_like(protein_xt)
    noise_ligand  = torch.zeros_like(ligand_xt)

protein_x_prev = protein_mean + noise_protein *
↪  posterior_var.sqrt()
ligand_x_prev  = ligand_mean  + noise_ligand  *
↪  posterior_var.sqrt()

return protein_x_prev, ligand_x_prev

def p_sample_loop(self, model, shape, device, roi,
↪  guidance_scale=1.0):
    '''
    Sample from x_T ~ N(0,I) down to x_0 using repeated
    ↪  p_sample.
    shape: tuple (batch_size, n_prot_atoms, 3) and (batch_size,
    ↪  n_lig_atoms, 3)
```

241

```
        '''
        bsz, n_prot, _ = shape[0]
        _, n_lig, _    = shape[1]

        protein_xt = torch.randn(bsz, n_prot, 3, device=device)
        ligand_xt  = torch.randn(bsz, n_lig, 3, device=device)

        for i in reversed(range(self.n_steps)):
            protein_xt, ligand_xt = self.p_sample(
                model, (protein_xt, ligand_xt), i, roi,
                ↪   guidance_scale
            )
        return protein_xt, ligand_xt

# ---------------------------------------------------------------
# 5) Training routines
# ---------------------------------------------------------------
def train_one_epoch(model, diffusion, optimizer, dataloader,
↪ device):
    model.train()
    epoch_loss = 0.0
    for protein_coords, ligand_coords, roi in dataloader:
        protein_coords = protein_coords.to(device)
        ligand_coords  = ligand_coords.to(device)
        roi            = roi.to(device)

        bsz = protein_coords.size(0)
        t = torch.randint(0, diffusion.n_steps, (bsz,),
        ↪   device=device).long()

        # Create random noise
        noise_protein = torch.randn_like(protein_coords)
        noise_ligand  = torch.randn_like(ligand_coords)

        # Forward diffusion
        protein_xt, ligand_xt = diffusion.q_sample((protein_coords,
        ↪   ligand_coords), t,

                                            ↪   noise=(noise_protein,
                                            ↪   noise_ligand))

        # Predict noise
        protein_noise_pred, ligand_noise_pred =
        ↪   diffusion.predict_noise(model,

                                            ↪   (protein_xt,
                                            ↪   ligand_xt),
                                            ↪   roi)

        # Compute MSE loss
        loss = ( (protein_noise_pred - noise_protein)**2 ).mean() +
        ↪   \
            ( (ligand_noise_pred  - noise_ligand)**2 ).mean()
```

242

```
                optimizer.zero_grad()
                loss.backward()
                optimizer.step()

                epoch_loss += loss.item()

        return epoch_loss / len(dataloader)

def evaluate_model(model, diffusion, dataloader, device):
    '''
    Reports average MSE on a validation set.
    '''
    model.eval()
    val_loss = 0.0
    with torch.no_grad():
        for protein_coords, ligand_coords, roi in dataloader:
            protein_coords = protein_coords.to(device)
            ligand_coords  = ligand_coords.to(device)
            roi            = roi.to(device)

            bsz = protein_coords.size(0)
            t = torch.randint(0, diffusion.n_steps, (bsz,),
            ↪  device=device).long()

            noise_protein = torch.randn_like(protein_coords)
            noise_ligand  = torch.randn_like(ligand_coords)

            protein_xt, ligand_xt =
            ↪  diffusion.q_sample((protein_coords, ligand_coords),
            ↪  t,
                                        noise=(noise_protein,
                                        ↪  noise_ligand))

            protein_noise_pred, ligand_noise_pred =
            ↪  diffusion.predict_noise(model,
                        (protein_xt, ligand_xt), roi)

            loss = ( (protein_noise_pred - noise_protein)**2
            ↪  ).mean() + \
                    ( (ligand_noise_pred  - noise_ligand)**2 ).mean()
            val_loss += loss.item()
    return val_loss / len(dataloader)


# ------------------------------------------------------------
# 6) Sampling demonstration
#    We create random region_of_interest for each sample,
#    then let the diffusion model sample random complex coordinates.
# ------------------------------------------------------------
def sample_complexes(model, diffusion, device, batch_size=4,
                    n_protein_atoms=50, n_ligand_atoms=10,
                    roi_dim=10, guidance_scale=1.0):
    model.eval()
```

243

```python
    with torch.no_grad():
        # We'll treat ROI as random for demonstration
        roi = torch.randn(batch_size, roi_dim, device=device)

        # shapes for protein and ligand
        protein_shape = (batch_size, n_protein_atoms, 3)
        ligand_shape  = (batch_size, n_ligand_atoms, 3)

        protein_final, ligand_final = diffusion.p_sample_loop(
            model, (protein_shape, ligand_shape), device, roi,
            ↪  guidance_scale=guidance_scale
        )
    return protein_final, ligand_final, roi

# ---------------------------------------------------------------
# 7) Main script
# ---------------------------------------------------------------
def main():
    set_seed(42)
    device = torch.device('cuda' if torch.cuda.is_available() else
    ↪  'cpu')

    # Create synthetic dataset
    train_dataset = ProteinLigandDataset(num_samples=2000,
                                         n_protein_atoms=50,
                                         n_ligand_atoms=10)
    val_dataset   = ProteinLigandDataset(num_samples=200,
                                         n_protein_atoms=50,
                                         n_ligand_atoms=10)
    train_loader = DataLoader(train_dataset, batch_size=32,
    ↪  shuffle=True)
    val_loader   = DataLoader(val_dataset, batch_size=32,
    ↪  shuffle=False)

    # Create model and diffusion
    model = DualStreamModel(n_protein_atoms=50,
                            n_ligand_atoms=10,
                            roi_dim=10,
                            hidden_size=256).to(device)

    diffusion = DualStreamDiffusion(n_steps=200,
    ↪  beta_schedule='linear')

    # Optimizer
    optimizer = optim.Adam(model.parameters(), lr=1e-4)

    # Train for a few epochs
    epochs = 5
    for epoch in range(epochs):
        train_loss = train_one_epoch(model, diffusion, optimizer,
        ↪  train_loader, device)
        val_loss   = evaluate_model(model, diffusion, val_loader,
        ↪  device)
```

```
      print(f"Epoch [{epoch+1}/{epochs}] - Train Loss:
      ↪ {train_loss:.4f}, Val Loss: {val_loss:.4f}")

   print("Training complete! Now sampling new protein-ligand
   ↪ complexes.")

   # Sample a few complexes
   protein_gen, ligand_gen, roi_used = sample_complexes(
      model, diffusion, device, batch_size=3,
      n_protein_atoms=50, n_ligand_atoms=10, guidance_scale=2.0
   )

   # The coordinates are in protein_gen and ligand_gen.
   # In practice, you'd evaluate with a docking score or visualize
   ↪ in 3D software.
   print("Sampled protein coords:", protein_gen)
   print("Sampled ligand coords:", ligand_gen)
   print("Random ROI used:", roi_used)

if __name__ == "__main__":
   main()
```

Key Implementation Details:

- **Forward Diffusion:** We implement `q_sample` to corrupt
  protein and ligand coordinates step by step with Gaussian
  noise, scaled by a linear beta schedule.

- **Reverse Diffusion (Sampling):** Repeated calls to `p_sample`
  denoise from random Gaussian initialization, leveraging the
  learned model to reconstruct coherent protein-ligand structures.

- **Dual-Stream Modeling:** The `DualStreamModel` is a simplified MLP that predicts noise for both protein and ligand
  coordinates, optionally conditioned on a `region_of_interest`.

- **Training Objective:** We sum the mean-squared error between the predicted noise and the actual noise across protein
  and ligand streams, guiding the model to accurately invert
  the forward corruption process.

- **Guidance Parameter:** A `guidance_scale` can enhance or
  reduce variability in sampled structures. Higher scales can
  sometimes drive the model to produce more distinct outputs.

- **End-to-End Pipeline:** The `main` function simulates a dataset, trains the diffusion model for a few epochs, and then samples new protein-ligand complexes, which can be further refined or scored via docking tools in real-world applications.

Chapter 24

Partial Differential Equation Solvers with Diffusion

Diffusion models can approximate solutions to PDEs like heat diffusion, fluid flow, or electromagnetic fields. The method trains on known solutions, treating each PDE solution field as data to be corrupted. The diffusion network learns to reverse the corruption and can then generate or approximate new solutions under various conditions (e.g., boundary conditions or initial states). Key steps are: (1) defining a discretized PDE domain (mesh or grid), (2) applying a noise schedule that distorts the solution fields, (3) building a UNet (potentially 3D or multi-dimensional) to predict the noise at each grid point, (4) training with known PDE solutions from simulations or analytical methods, and (5) generating new fields by reversing the diffusion with user-specified boundary or initial conditions. An innovative technique is to fuse a physics-based PDE solver with the diffusion process, refining approximate numeric solutions for increased accuracy.

Python Code Snippet

```python
import torch
import torch.nn as nn
import torch.optim as optim
from torch.utils.data import Dataset, DataLoader
```

```python
import matplotlib.pyplot as plt
import numpy as np
import random
import os

# ----------------------------------------------------------------
# 1) Utility: Set random seeds for reproducibility
# ----------------------------------------------------------------
def set_seed(seed=42):
    random.seed(seed)
    np.random.seed(seed)
    torch.manual_seed(seed)
    if torch.cuda.is_available():
        torch.cuda.manual_seed_all(seed)


# ----------------------------------------------------------------
# 2) Generate synthetic PDE data (2D Heat Equation)
# ----------------------------------------------------------------
def solve_2d_heat_equation(nx=32, ny=32, nt=50, alpha=1.0):
    """
    A simple forward-time central-space scheme for the 2D heat
    ↪ equation:
    u_t = alpha * (u_xx + u_yy).
    This function starts with random initial conditions and
    returns the final solution after nt time steps.
    Boundary conditions: Dirichlet=0 on all sides (for simplicity).
    """
    # Initialize temperature field
    u = np.random.rand(nx, ny).astype(np.float32) * 1.0  # random
    ↪ initial condition

    dx = 1.0 / nx    # assume domain [0,1] x [0,1]
    dy = 1.0 / ny
    dt = 0.2 * dx * dy / alpha  # a stable time step guess

    for _ in range(nt):
        u_new = u.copy()
        # Apply finite difference in the interior
        for i in range(1, nx-1):
            for j in range(1, ny-1):
                u_xx = (u[i+1, j] - 2*u[i, j] + u[i-1, j]) / (dx*dx)
                u_yy = (u[i, j+1] - 2*u[i, j] + u[i, j-1]) / (dy*dy)
                u_new[i, j] = u[i, j] + alpha * dt * (u_xx + u_yy)
        # Update with boundary conditions = 0
        u_new[0, :]  = 0.0
        u_new[-1, :] = 0.0
        u_new[:, 0]  = 0.0
        u_new[:, -1] = 0.0
        u = u_new
    return u

class PDE_Dataset(Dataset):
    """
```

248

```python
    A dataset class that stores PDE solutions generated by
    ↪   solve_2d_heat_equation.
    """
    def __init__(self, size=2000, nx=32, ny=32, nt=50, alpha=1.0):
        super().__init__()
        self.data = []
        for _ in range(size):
            sol = solve_2d_heat_equation(nx, ny, nt, alpha)
            # Expand dims to match (C,H,W) format for UNet
            self.data.append(np.expand_dims(sol, axis=0))
        self.data = np.array(self.data)  # shape: [size, 1, nx, ny]

    def __len__(self):
        return len(self.data)

    def __getitem__(self, idx):
        # We can treat the PDE solution as a single-channel "image"
        return torch.from_numpy(self.data[idx]).float(), 0  # dummy
        ↪   label


# -----------------------------------------------------------
# 3) Define a simple 2D UNet for denoising PDE solutions
# -----------------------------------------------------------
class DoubleConv(nn.Module):
    '''
    A helper module that performs two convolutions (each followed by
    ↪   ReLU)
    for simplicity in U-Net blocks.
    '''
    def __init__(self, in_channels, out_channels):
        super(DoubleConv, self).__init__()
        self.conv = nn.Sequential(
            nn.Conv2d(in_channels, out_channels, 3, padding=1),
            nn.ReLU(inplace=True),
            nn.Conv2d(out_channels, out_channels, 3, padding=1),
            nn.ReLU(inplace=True)
        )

    def forward(self, x):
        return self.conv(x)

class UNet(nn.Module):
    '''
    A simplified 2D U-Net architecture suitable for PDE field
    ↪   denoising.
    '''
    def __init__(self, in_channels=1, out_channels=1,
    ↪   base_channels=32):
        super(UNet, self).__init__()

        # Encoder (downsampling)
        self.down1 = DoubleConv(in_channels, base_channels)
        self.pool1 = nn.MaxPool2d(2)
```

```python
        self.down2 = DoubleConv(base_channels, base_channels*2)
        self.pool2 = nn.MaxPool2d(2)

        # Bottleneck
        self.bottleneck = DoubleConv(base_channels*2,
        ↪  base_channels*4)

        # Decoder (upsampling)
        self.up1 = nn.ConvTranspose2d(base_channels*4,
        ↪  base_channels*2, kernel_size=2, stride=2)
        self.conv_up1 = DoubleConv(base_channels*4, base_channels*2)

        self.up2 = nn.ConvTranspose2d(base_channels*2,
        ↪  base_channels, kernel_size=2, stride=2)
        self.conv_up2 = DoubleConv(base_channels*2, base_channels)

        # Final output
        self.final_conv = nn.Conv2d(base_channels, out_channels,
        ↪  kernel_size=1)

    def forward(self, x):
        # Down
        x1 = self.down1(x)
        x2 = self.pool1(x1)

        x2 = self.down2(x2)
        x3 = self.pool2(x2)

        # Bottleneck
        b = self.bottleneck(x3)

        # Up
        x = self.up1(b)
        x = torch.cat([x, x2], dim=1)
        x = self.conv_up1(x)

        x = self.up2(x)
        x = torch.cat([x, x1], dim=1)
        x = self.conv_up2(x)

        out = self.final_conv(x)
        return out


# -------------------------------------------------------------
# 4) Diffusion utilities and schedule
# -------------------------------------------------------------
def make_beta_schedule(schedule_name, n_timestep, start=1e-4,
↪  end=2e-2):
    '''
    Creates a beta schedule for the diffusion process (linear
    ↪  example).
    '''
```

```python
    if schedule_name == "linear":
        return torch.linspace(start, end, n_timestep)
    else:
        raise NotImplementedError("Only 'linear' schedule is
        ↪   implemented.")

class Diffusion:
    '''
    Manages forward noising and reverse sampling for PDE fields.
    '''
    def __init__(self, n_steps=100, beta_schedule='linear'):
        self.n_steps = n_steps
        self.betas = make_beta_schedule(beta_schedule, n_steps)
        self.alphas = 1.0 - self.betas
        self.alpha_cumprod = torch.cumprod(self.alphas, dim=0)
        self.alpha_cumprod_prev = torch.cat(
            [torch.tensor([1.0]), self.alpha_cumprod[:-1]], dim=0)

        self.posterior_variance = self.betas * (1.0 -
        ↪   self.alpha_cumprod_prev) / (1.0 - self.alpha_cumprod)

    def q_sample(self, x_start, t, noise=None):
        '''
        Forward diffusion step: x_t = sqrt(alpha_cumprod[t]) *
        ↪   x_start +
                                sqrt(1-alpha_cumprod[t]) * noise
        '''
        if noise is None:
            noise = torch.randn_like(x_start)
        sqrt_alpha_cumprod_t =
        ↪   self.alpha_cumprod[t].sqrt().view(-1,1,1,1)
        sqrt_one_minus_alpha_cumprod_t = (1 -
        ↪   self.alpha_cumprod[t]).sqrt().view(-1,1,1,1)
        return sqrt_alpha_cumprod_t * x_start +
        ↪   sqrt_one_minus_alpha_cumprod_t * noise

    def predict_noise(self, model, x_t, t):
        '''
        Model predicts the added noise in x_t.
        '''
        return model(x_t)

    def p_sample(self, model, x_t, t):
        '''
        Reverse diffusion: p(x_{t-1} | x_t).
        '''
        betas_t = self.betas[t]
        alpha_t = self.alphas[t]
        alpha_cumprod_t = self.alpha_cumprod[t]
        alpha_cumprod_prev_t = self.alpha_cumprod_prev[t]

        e_t = self.predict_noise(model, x_t, t)
```

251

```python
        sqrt_recip_alpha_t = (1.0 / alpha_t).sqrt()
        x_0_hat = (x_t - (1.0 - alpha_t).sqrt() * e_t) *
        ↪   sqrt_recip_alpha_t

        coef1 = (alpha_cumprod_prev_t.sqrt() * betas_t) / (1.0 -
        ↪   alpha_cumprod_t)
        coef2 = ((1.0 - alpha_cumprod_prev_t) * alpha_t.sqrt()) /
        ↪   (1.0 - alpha_cumprod_t)
        mean = coef1 * x_0_hat + coef2 * x_t

        posterior_var = self.posterior_variance[t]
        if t > 0:
            noise = torch.randn_like(x_t)
        else:
            noise = torch.zeros_like(x_t)

        x_prev = mean + noise * posterior_var.sqrt()
        return x_prev

    def p_sample_loop(self, model, shape, device):
        '''
        Iteratively calls p_sample to go from x_T ~ N(0, I) to x_0.
        '''
        x_t = torch.randn(shape, device=device)
        for i in reversed(range(self.n_steps)):
            x_t = self.p_sample(model, x_t, i)
        return x_t

# ---------------------------------------------------------------
# 5) Training and evaluation routines
# ---------------------------------------------------------------
def train_one_epoch(model, diffusion, optimizer, dataloader,
↪   device):
    model.train()
    total_loss = 0.0
    for x, _ in dataloader:
        x = x.to(device)
        # random t in [0, n_steps)
        t = torch.randint(0, diffusion.n_steps, (x.size(0),),
        ↪   device=device).long()
        noise = torch.randn_like(x)
        x_t = diffusion.q_sample(x, t, noise=noise)

        noise_pred = diffusion.predict_noise(model, x_t, t)
        loss = nn.MSELoss()(noise_pred, noise)

        optimizer.zero_grad()
        loss.backward()
        optimizer.step()

        total_loss += loss.item()
    return total_loss / len(dataloader)
```

```python
def evaluate_model(model, diffusion, dataloader, device):
    model.eval()
    total_loss = 0.0
    with torch.no_grad():
        for x, _ in dataloader:
            x = x.to(device)
            t = torch.randint(0, diffusion.n_steps, (x.size(0),),
            ↪  device=device).long()
            noise = torch.randn_like(x)
            x_t = diffusion.q_sample(x, t, noise=noise)
            noise_pred = diffusion.predict_noise(model, x_t, t)
            loss = nn.MSELoss()(noise_pred, noise)
            total_loss += loss.item()
    return total_loss / len(dataloader)


def sample_and_plot(model, diffusion, device, epoch):
    model.eval()
    with torch.no_grad():
        sample_batch_size = 8
        # shape: [batch_size, 1, nx, ny]
        generated = diffusion.p_sample_loop(model,
        ↪  (sample_batch_size, 1, 32, 32), device)
        # We can plot a few of these PDE fields
        generated = generated.cpu().numpy()

        fig, axs = plt.subplots(2, 4, figsize=(10, 5))
        axs = axs.flatten()
        for i in range(sample_batch_size):
            axs[i].imshow(generated[i, 0], cmap='jet')
            axs[i].axis('off')
        os.makedirs("pde_results", exist_ok=True)
        plt.tight_layout()
        plt.savefig(f"pde_results/epoch_{epoch}.png")
        plt.close(fig)


# -------------------------------------------------------------
# 6) Main script: generate PDE dataset, train the model, sample
# -------------------------------------------------------------
def main():
    set_seed(42)
    device = torch.device("cuda" if torch.cuda.is_available() else
    ↪  "cpu")

    # Generate synthetic PDE dataset
    train_dataset = PDE_Dataset(size=1000, nx=32, ny=32, nt=50,
    ↪  alpha=1.0)
    test_dataset  = PDE_Dataset(size=200, nx=32, ny=32, nt=50,
    ↪  alpha=1.0)

    train_loader = DataLoader(train_dataset, batch_size=16,
    ↪  shuffle=True)
    test_loader  = DataLoader(test_dataset, batch_size=16,
    ↪  shuffle=False)
```

253

```
# Create UNet model
model = UNet(in_channels=1, out_channels=1,
↪    base_channels=32).to(device)

# Create Diffusion instance
diffusion = Diffusion(n_steps=100, beta_schedule='linear')

# Optimizer
optimizer = optim.Adam(model.parameters(), lr=1e-4)

# Training loop
epochs = 5
for epoch in range(epochs):
    train_loss = train_one_epoch(model, diffusion, optimizer,
↪        train_loader, device)
    val_loss = evaluate_model(model, diffusion, test_loader,
↪        device)
    print(f"Epoch [{epoch+1}/{epochs}] - Train Loss:
↪        {train_loss:.4f}, Val Loss: {val_loss:.4f}")

    # Sample PDE fields
    sample_and_plot(model, diffusion, device, epoch)

print("Training complete! Generated samples are saved in the
↪    'pde_results' folder.")

if __name__ == "__main__":
    main()
```

Key Implementation Details:

- **Synthetic PDE Data Generation:** The function
  `solve_2d_heat_equation` uses a finite-difference scheme to
  produce a variety of 2D heat diffusion solutions from random
  initial states. These solutions form the training and testing
  data for our diffusion model.

- **Forward Diffusion:** In `q_sample`, we corrupt each PDE
  solution with noise based on a linear beta schedule. The
  fraction of noise inserted is controlled by `betas[t]` and cumulative products of `alphas`.

- **Reverse Diffusion (Sampling):** `p_sample_loop` iterates
  backward from random noise to produce a refined PDE solution. The model's noise prediction is used to compute the
  mean of the posterior distribution p(x_{t-1} | x_t, x_0).

254

- **UNet Architecture:** Our simplified `UNet` captures multi-scale context. Downsampling blocks extract broader features, while transposed convolutions and skip connections restore spatial structure essential to PDE fields.

- **Training Objective:** The network directly predicts the noise added during forward diffusion, and we minimize the mean-squared error between predicted noise and true noise.

- **Sampling PDE Solutions:** The `sample_and_plot` function shows how to generate new solutions by reversing the diffusion process. The resulting fields can be visualized as color maps to interpret fluid or heat distributions.

Chapter 25

Climate Data Modeling and Forecasting

Diffusion models can handle high-dimensional climate and weather data, capturing spatiotemporal correlations. Common tasks include forecasting temperature grids, precipitation fields, or more complex atmospheric patterns. The training pipeline involves: (1) encoding climate variables—often multi-channel spatial maps—over historical time steps, (2) adding noise to these maps across time, (3) using a 3D or 4D UNet (where time is treated as an extra dimension) to learn the reverse denoising process, and (4) sampling future climate states from partial or randomized initial conditions. An innovative approach includes conditioning on global teleconnection indices (e.g., ENSO phases), allowing the diffusion model to incorporate large-scale climate signals in its generative forecasts. This improves accuracy for extended time horizons and complex atmospheric phenomena.

Python Code Snippet

```
import os
import random
import math
import torch
import torch.nn as nn
import torch.optim as optim
from torch.utils.data import DataLoader, Dataset
import matplotlib.pyplot as plt
```

```python
# ------------------------------------------------------------------
# 1) Set random seed for reproducibility
# ------------------------------------------------------------------
def set_seed(seed=42):
    random.seed(seed)
    torch.manual_seed(seed)
    if torch.cuda.is_available():
        torch.cuda.manual_seed_all(seed)


# ------------------------------------------------------------------
# 2) Create 3D U-Net components for spatiotemporal data
# ------------------------------------------------------------------
class DoubleConv3D(nn.Module):
    '''
    A helper module that performs two 3D convolutions (each followed
    ↪  by ReLU)
    to reduce code repetition in the U-Net.
    '''

    def __init__(self, in_channels, out_channels):
        super(DoubleConv3D, self).__init__()
        self.conv = nn.Sequential(
            nn.Conv3d(in_channels, out_channels, kernel_size=3,
            ↪  padding=1),
            nn.ReLU(inplace=True),
            nn.Conv3d(out_channels, out_channels, kernel_size=3,
            ↪  padding=1),
            nn.ReLU(inplace=True)
        )
    def forward(self, x):
        return self.conv(x)


class Down3D(nn.Module):
    '''
    Downscaling with maxpool then double 3D conv.
    '''

    def __init__(self, in_channels, out_channels):
        super(Down3D, self).__init__()
        self.pool = nn.MaxPool3d(kernel_size=2)
        self.double_conv = DoubleConv3D(in_channels, out_channels)
    def forward(self, x):
        x = self.pool(x)
        x = self.double_conv(x)
        return x


class Up3D(nn.Module):
    '''
    Upscaling then double 3D conv, with skip connections.
    '''

    def __init__(self, in_channels, out_channels):
        super(Up3D, self).__init__()
        self.up = nn.ConvTranspose3d(
            in_channels, out_channels, kernel_size=2, stride=2
```

257

```python
        )
        self.conv = DoubleConv3D(out_channels*2, out_channels)
    def forward(self, x, skip):
        x = self.up(x)
        # Concatenate skip connection
        x = torch.cat([x, skip], dim=1)
        x = self.conv(x)
        return x

class UNet3D(nn.Module):
    '''
    A simplified 3D U-Net for spatiotemporal climate data.
    Accepts input of shape [B, C, T, H, W].
    '''
    def __init__(self, in_channels=1, out_channels=1,
    ↪ base_channels=8):
        super(UNet3D, self).__init__()

        # Encoder
        self.inc = DoubleConv3D(in_channels, base_channels)
        self.down1 = Down3D(base_channels, base_channels*2)
        self.down2 = Down3D(base_channels*2, base_channels*4)

        # Bottleneck
        self.bottleneck = DoubleConv3D(base_channels*4,
        ↪ base_channels*8)

        # Decoder
        self.up1 = Up3D(base_channels*8, base_channels*4)
        self.up2 = Up3D(base_channels*4, base_channels*2)
        self.up3 = Up3D(base_channels*2, base_channels)

        self.outc = nn.Conv3d(base_channels, out_channels,
        ↪ kernel_size=1)

    def forward(self, x):
        # Encoder
        x1 = self.inc(x)
        x2 = self.down1(x1)
        x3 = self.down2(x2)

        # Bottleneck
        b = self.bottleneck(x3)

        # Decoder
        x = self.up1(b, x3)
        x = self.up2(x, x2)
        x = self.up3(x, x1)

        # Output
        out = self.outc(x)
        return out
```

```python
# ----------------------------------------------------------------
# 3) Define diffusion schedule and forward process
# ----------------------------------------------------------------
def make_beta_schedule(schedule_name, n_timestep, start=1e-4,
↪   end=2e-2):
    '''
    Creates a beta schedule for the diffusion process (1D tensor).
    For demonstration, we implement a linear schedule.
    '''

    if schedule_name == "linear":
        return torch.linspace(start, end, n_timestep)
    else:
        raise NotImplementedError("Only 'linear' schedule is
        ↪   implemented in this snippet.")


class Diffusion:
    '''
    Encapsulates:
    1) The forward noising process q(x_t | x_0)
    2) The reverse denoising process p(x_{t-1} | x_t)
    3) Utility for training and sampling with a spatiotemporal
    ↪   U-Net.
    '''

    def __init__(self, n_steps=1000, beta_schedule='linear'):
        self.n_steps = n_steps
        self.betas = make_beta_schedule(beta_schedule, n_steps)
        self.alphas = 1.0 - self.betas
        self.alpha_cumprod = torch.cumprod(self.alphas, dim=0)
        self.alpha_cumprod_prev = torch.cat(
            [torch.tensor([1.0]), self.alpha_cumprod[:-1]], dim=0
        )

        # Posterior variance term for p(x_{t-1} | x_t, x_0)
        self.posterior_variance = self.betas * (1.0 -
        ↪   self.alpha_cumprod_prev) / (1.0 - self.alpha_cumprod)

    def q_sample(self, x_start, t, noise=None):
        '''
        Forward diffusion: Adds noise to x_start at step t.
        x_t = sqrt(alpha_cumprod[t]) * x_start + sqrt(1 -
        ↪   alpha_cumprod[t]) * noise
        '''

        if noise is None:
            noise = torch.randn_like(x_start)

        # The shape of x_start is [B, C, T, H, W], so we need to
        ↪   broadcast t properly.
        batch_size = x_start.shape[0]
        shape_broadcast = (batch_size, 1, 1, 1, 1)

        sqrt_alpha_cumprod_t =
        ↪   self.alpha_cumprod[t].sqrt().view(shape_broadcast)
```

```python
        sqrt_one_minus_alpha_cumprod_t = (1 -
        ↪  self.alpha_cumprod[t]).sqrt().view(shape_broadcast)

        return sqrt_alpha_cumprod_t * x_start +
        ↪  sqrt_one_minus_alpha_cumprod_t * noise

    def predict_noise(self, model, x_t, t):
        '''
        Use the UNet3D model to predict the noise added at step t.
        We reshape t for potential embedding if needed, but
        for simplicity, we'll just directly feed x_t to the model
        ↪  here.
        '''
        return model(x_t)

    def p_sample(self, model, x_t, t, guidance_scale=1.0):
        '''
        One reverse diffusion step: p(x_{t-1} | x_t).
        The model predicts the noise e_t, and we compute the mean of
        p(x_{t-1} | x_t, x_0). We also include a "guidance_scale"
        to showcase how one might adjust the predicted noise.
        '''
        betas_t = self.betas[t]
        alpha_t = self.alphas[t]
        alpha_cumprod_t = self.alpha_cumprod[t]
        alpha_cumprod_prev_t = self.alpha_cumprod_prev[t]

        # Model's noise estimate
        e_t = model(x_t) * guidance_scale

        # Reconstruct x_0 from x_t and e_t:
        sqrt_recip_alpha_t = (1.0 / alpha_t).sqrt()
        # x_0_hat = (x_t - sqrt(1-alpha_t)*e_t) / sqrt(alpha_t)
        x_0_hat = (x_t - (1.0 - alpha_t).sqrt() * e_t) *
        ↪  sqrt_recip_alpha_t

        # Posterior mean coefficients
        coef1 = ((alpha_cumprod_prev_t).sqrt() * betas_t) / (1.0 -
        ↪  alpha_cumprod_t)
        coef2 = ((1.0 - alpha_cumprod_prev_t) * alpha_t.sqrt()) /
        ↪  (1.0 - alpha_cumprod_t)

        mean = coef1 * x_0_hat + coef2 * x_t

        # Posterior variance
        posterior_var = self.posterior_variance[t]
        if t > 0:
            noise = torch.randn_like(x_t)
        else:
            noise = torch.zeros_like(x_t)

        x_prev = mean + noise * posterior_var.sqrt()
        return x_prev
```

```python
    def p_sample_loop(self, model, shape, device,
    ↪    guidance_scale=1.0):
        '''
        Repeatedly apply p_sample to go from x_T ~ N(0, I) to x_0.
        shape is [batch_size, channels, time, height, width].
        '''
        x_t = torch.randn(shape, device=device)
        for i in reversed(range(self.n_steps)):
            x_t = self.p_sample(model, x_t, i,
            ↪    guidance_scale=guidance_scale)
        return x_t


# ----------------------------------------------------------------
# 4) A synthetic dataset for demonstration
# ----------------------------------------------------------------
class RandomClimateDataset(Dataset):
    '''
    Generates random spatiotemporal climate-like data
    of shape [1, T, H, W] for demonstration.
    '''
    def __init__(self, length=1000, time_steps=4, height=32,
    ↪    width=32):
        super(RandomClimateDataset, self).__init__()
        self.length = length
        self.time_steps = time_steps
        self.height = height
        self.width = width

    def __len__(self):
        return self.length

    def __getitem__(self, idx):
        # Example: single channel, T frames, HxW grid
        x = torch.randn(1, self.time_steps, self.height, self.width)
        # Label is a dummy placeholder
        return x, 0


# ----------------------------------------------------------------
# 5) Training and evaluation routines
# ----------------------------------------------------------------
def train_one_epoch(model, diffusion, optimizer, dataloader,
↪    device):
    '''
    A single training epoch for the diffusion model on climate data.
    We sample a random t, forward diffuse the data, and predict the
    ↪    noise.
    '''
    model.train()
    total_loss = 0.0
    for data, _ in dataloader:
        data = data.to(device)
```

```python
        # Random time step for each sample
        t = torch.randint(0, diffusion.n_steps, (data.size(0),),
        ↪   device=device).long()

        # Random noise
        noise = torch.randn_like(data)

        # Forward diffuse
        x_t = diffusion.q_sample(data, t, noise=noise)

        # Predict the noise
        noise_pred = diffusion.predict_noise(model, x_t, t)

        # Compute MSE loss
        loss = nn.functional.mse_loss(noise_pred, noise)

        optimizer.zero_grad()
        loss.backward()
        optimizer.step()

        total_loss += loss.item()

    return total_loss / len(dataloader)

def evaluate_model(model, diffusion, dataloader, device):
    '''
    Computes average MSE across the dataset to gauge model
    ↪   performance.
    '''
    model.eval()
    total_loss = 0.0
    with torch.no_grad():
        for data, _ in dataloader:
            data = data.to(device)
            t = torch.randint(0, diffusion.n_steps, (data.size(0),),
            ↪   device=device).long()
            noise = torch.randn_like(data)
            x_t = diffusion.q_sample(data, t, noise=noise)
            noise_pred = diffusion.predict_noise(model, x_t, t)
            loss = nn.functional.mse_loss(noise_pred, noise)
            total_loss += loss.item()
    return total_loss / len(dataloader)

# ----------------------------------------------------------------
# 6) Sampling routine
# ----------------------------------------------------------------
def sample_and_save(model, diffusion, device, epoch,
↪   guidance_scale=1.0):
    '''
    Samples a batch of spatiotemporal cubes from the diffusion model
    and saves slices for inspection.
    '''
    model.eval()
```

262

```python
    with torch.no_grad():
        sample_batch_size = 4
        shape = (sample_batch_size, 1, 4, 32, 32)  # B, C, T, H, W
        generated = diffusion.p_sample_loop(model, shape, device,
        ↪  guidance_scale=guidance_scale)

        # For demonstration, visualize the middle time slice (e.g.
        ↪  T//2)
        # by flattening it into a 2D image grid.
        # We'll choose the second time slice (index=1) as an
        ↪  example.
        time_slice = 1
        # We map from [-some, +some] to [0,1]
        generated_slice = generated[:, :, time_slice, :, :].clone()
        generated_slice = (generated_slice - generated_slice.min())
        ↪  / (generated_slice.max() - generated_slice.min() + 1e-7)

        # Create a simple grid horizontally
        # We'll place them side by side as separate images
        import matplotlib.pyplot as plt
        import numpy as np

        grid_rows = 1
        grid_cols = sample_batch_size
        fig, axes = plt.subplots(grid_rows, grid_cols,
        ↪  figsize=(4*grid_cols, 4))

        if sample_batch_size == 1:
            axes = [axes]

        for i in range(sample_batch_size):
            ax = axes[i] if sample_batch_size > 1 else axes[0]
            img_np = generated_slice[i, 0].cpu().numpy()
            ax.imshow(img_np, cmap='coolwarm')
            ax.set_title(f"Sample {i}, T-slice={time_slice}")
            ax.axis("off")

        os.makedirs("results_climate", exist_ok=True)
        plt.tight_layout()
        plt.savefig(f"results_climate/
        epoch_{epoch}_gs_{guidance_scale}.png")
        plt.close()


# -------------------------------------------------------------------
# 7) Main training loop
# -------------------------------------------------------------------
def main():
    set_seed(42)
    device = torch.device("cuda" if torch.cuda.is_available() else
    ↪  "cpu")

    # Create random synthetic climate dataset
```

```python
    train_dataset = RandomClimateDataset(length=500, time_steps=4,
    ↪  height=32, width=32)
    val_dataset = RandomClimateDataset(length=100, time_steps=4,
    ↪  height=32, width=32)

    train_loader = DataLoader(train_dataset, batch_size=8,
    ↪  shuffle=True)
    val_loader = DataLoader(val_dataset, batch_size=8,
    ↪  shuffle=False)

    # Create 3D UNet
    model = UNet3D(in_channels=1, out_channels=1,
    ↪  base_channels=8).to(device)

    # Diffusion process with 200 steps, linear schedule
    diffusion = Diffusion(n_steps=200, beta_schedule='linear')

    # Optimizer
    optimizer = optim.Adam(model.parameters(), lr=1e-4)

    # Train for a few epochs
    epochs = 2
    for epoch in range(epochs):
        train_loss = train_one_epoch(model, diffusion, optimizer,
        ↪  train_loader, device)
        val_loss = evaluate_model(model, diffusion, val_loader,
        ↪  device)

        print(f"Epoch [{epoch+1}/{epochs}] - Train Loss:
        ↪  {train_loss:.4f}, Val Loss: {val_loss:.4f}")

        # Sample for qualitative inspection
        sample_and_save(model, diffusion, device, epoch,
        ↪  guidance_scale=1.0)
        sample_and_save(model, diffusion, device, epoch,
        ↪  guidance_scale=2.0)

    print("Training complete! Check the 'results_climate' folder for
    ↪  generated samples.")

if __name__ == "__main__":
    main()
```

Key Implementation Details:

- **Forward Diffusion**: In the function `q_sample`, we corrupt
  the original data with noise proportionally determined by
  `betas` over time steps. Although the data here is 5D ($[B,C,T,H,W]$),
  the formulation stays the same.

- **Reverse Diffusion (Sampling)**: `p_sample_loop` iteratively applies the reverse step, estimating noise with the 3D U-Net and subtracting it to reconstruct a cleaner real-valued climate field.

- **3D U-Net Architecture**: The `UNet3D` class uses 3D convolutions to handle spatiotemporal volumes. Each down/up-sampling uses a `Down3D` or `Up3D` layer paired with skip connections, allowing the network to capture both local and global context.

- **Training Objective**: We directly predict and match the added noise (`noise_pred` vs. the true noise) using an MSE loss, a straightforward approach for diffusion-based denoising.

- **Data Loading**: `RandomClimateDataset` simulates small patches of climate data with random values, demonstrating the workflow without requiring a large real-world dataset.

- **End-to-End Pipeline**: The `main` function stitches everything together—initializing the synthetic dataset, creating the U-Net and Diffusion objects, training with minibatches, and periodically sampling 3D volumes to visualize slices over time.

- **Guidance Parameter**: The `guidance_scale` is available to scale the predicted noise during sampling, offering a way to trade off between diversity and fidelity of generated climate fields.

Chapter 26

Financial Time Series Forecasting and Simulation

Diffusion provides a robust method for generating realistic time series data for market simulation and forecasting. Common use cases include stress testing, scenario analysis, and data augmentation. We represent price series or multiple signals (e.g., open, high, low, close) as a temporal sequence, applying Gaussian noise in the forward process. A temporal UNet or transformer-based architecture then learns to remove the noise step by step, capturing temporal dependencies. Construction details: (1) gather historical financial datasets, (2) scale and normalize the price or volumetric signals, (3) corrupt these signals with noise over multiple steps, (4) train a denoising model to reconstruct valid time series, and (5) sample new plausible scenarios for risk assessment. An innovation is to add conditional variables, such as macroeconomic indicators or sentiment data, to guide the generative process toward specific market conditions.

Python Code Snippet

```
import os
import math
import random
import numpy as np
```

```python
import torch
import torch.nn as nn
import torch.optim as optim
import matplotlib.pyplot as plt
from torch.utils.data import Dataset, DataLoader

# ----------------------------------------------------------------
# 1) Set random seed for reproducibility
# ----------------------------------------------------------------
def set_seed(seed=42):
    random.seed(seed)
    np.random.seed(seed)
    torch.manual_seed(seed)
    if torch.cuda.is_available():
        torch.cuda.manual_seed_all(seed)


# ----------------------------------------------------------------
# 2) Create a synthetic Dataset for time series data
# ----------------------------------------------------------------
class SyntheticTimeSeriesDataset(Dataset):
    """
    A simple synthetic dataset that generates random
    time series signals, optionally with sinusoidal patterns.
    """
    def __init__(self, num_samples=1000, seq_len=60):
        super().__init__()
        self.seq_len = seq_len
        self.data = []
        for _ in range(num_samples):
            # Combine random noise + a sine wave
            freq = random.choice([1, 2, 4])
            x = np.linspace(0, 2 * math.pi, seq_len)
            sin_wave = np.sin(freq * x) + 0.1 *
            ↪  np.random.randn(seq_len)
            self.data.append(sin_wave.astype(np.float32))

        self.data = np.array(self.data)  # shape: [num_samples,
        ↪  seq_len]

    def __len__(self):
        return self.data.shape[0]

    def __getitem__(self, idx):
        # Return (time_series, None) to mimic (data, label)
        return self.data[idx], 0

# ----------------------------------------------------------------
# 3) A 1D UNet for time series denoising
# ----------------------------------------------------------------
class DoubleConv1D(nn.Module):
    """
    Performs two consecutive 1D convolutions, each followed by ReLU.
    """
```

```python
    def __init__(self, in_channels, out_channels):
        super(DoubleConv1D, self).__init__()
        self.conv = nn.Sequential(
            nn.Conv1d(in_channels, out_channels, kernel_size=3,
            ↪   padding=1),
            nn.ReLU(inplace=True),
            nn.Conv1d(out_channels, out_channels, kernel_size=3,
            ↪   padding=1),
            nn.ReLU(inplace=True)
        )

    def forward(self, x):
        return self.conv(x)

class UNet1D(nn.Module):
    """
    A simplified 1D U-Net architecture with down-sampling (encoder)
    and up-sampling (decoder) blocks, plus skip connections.
    Useful for time series denoising.
    """
    def __init__(self, in_channels=1, out_channels=1,
    ↪   base_channels=64):
        super(UNet1D, self).__init__()

        # Down-sampling (encoder)
        self.down1 = DoubleConv1D(in_channels, base_channels)
        self.pool1 = nn.MaxPool1d(2)

        self.down2 = DoubleConv1D(base_channels, base_channels * 2)
        self.pool2 = nn.MaxPool1d(2)

        self.down3 = DoubleConv1D(base_channels * 2, base_channels *
        ↪   4)
        self.pool3 = nn.MaxPool1d(2)

        # Bottleneck
        self.bottleneck = DoubleConv1D(base_channels * 4,
        ↪   base_channels * 8)

        # Up-sampling (decoder)
        self.up1 = nn.ConvTranspose1d(base_channels*8,
        ↪   base_channels*4, kernel_size=2, stride=2)
        self.conv_up1 = DoubleConv1D(base_channels*8,
        ↪   base_channels*4)

        self.up2 = nn.ConvTranspose1d(base_channels*4,
        ↪   base_channels*2, kernel_size=2, stride=2)
        self.conv_up2 = DoubleConv1D(base_channels*4,
        ↪   base_channels*2)

        self.up3 = nn.ConvTranspose1d(base_channels*2,
        ↪   base_channels, kernel_size=2, stride=2)
        self.conv_up3 = DoubleConv1D(base_channels*2, base_channels)
```

```python
        # Final output
        self.final_conv = nn.Conv1d(base_channels, out_channels,
        ↪  kernel_size=1)

    def forward(self, x):
        # Encoder
        x1 = self.down1(x)        # [B, base_channels, L]
        x2 = self.pool1(x1)       # [B, base_channels, L/2]

        x2 = self.down2(x2)       # [B, base_channels*2, L/2]
        x3 = self.pool2(x2)       # [B, base_channels*2, L/4]

        x3 = self.down3(x3)       # [B, base_channels*4, L/4]
        x4 = self.pool3(x3)       # [B, base_channels*4, L/8]

        # Bottleneck
        b = self.bottleneck(x4) # [B, base_channels*8, L/8]

        # Decoder
        x_ = self.up1(b)          # [B, base_channels*4, L/4]
        x_ = torch.cat([x_, x3], dim=1)  # skip connection
        x_ = self.conv_up1(x_)

        x_ = self.up2(x_)         # [B, base_channels*2, L/2]
        x_ = torch.cat([x_, x2], dim=1)
        x_ = self.conv_up2(x_)

        x_ = self.up3(x_)         # [B, base_channels, L]
        x_ = torch.cat([x_, x1], dim=1)
        x_ = self.conv_up3(x_)

        out = self.final_conv(x_)
        return out


# ----------------------------------------------------------------
# 4) Define the diffusion schedule and forward process
# ----------------------------------------------------------------
def make_beta_schedule(schedule_name, n_timestep, start=1e-4,
↪  end=2e-2):
    """
    Creates a beta schedule for the diffusion process.
    Here we only implement a simple linear schedule as an example.
    """
    if schedule_name == "linear":
        return torch.linspace(start, end, n_timestep)
    else:
        raise NotImplementedError("Only 'linear' schedule is
        ↪  supported for this example.")


class Diffusion:
    """
    This class encapsulates:
```

```
    1) The forward noising process: q(x_t | x_0)
    2) The reverse denoising process: p(x_{t-1} | x_t)
    3) The training & sampling utility for time series.
"""
def __init__(self, n_steps=50, beta_schedule='linear'):
    self.n_steps = n_steps
    self.betas = make_beta_schedule(beta_schedule, n_steps)
    self.alphas = 1.0 - self.betas
    self.alpha_cumprod = torch.cumprod(self.alphas, dim=0)
    self.alpha_cumprod_prev = torch.cat(
        [torch.tensor([1.0]), self.alpha_cumprod[:-1]], dim=0
    )

    # Posterior variance used in p(x_{t-1} | x_t, x_0)
    self.posterior_variance = self.betas * (1.0 -
    ↪  self.alpha_cumprod_prev) / (1.0 - self.alpha_cumprod)

def q_sample(self, x_start, t, noise=None):
    """
    Forward diffusion: x_t = sqrt(alpha_cumprod[t]) * x_start +
    ↪  sqrt(1 - alpha_cumprod[t]) * noise
    """
    if noise is None:
        noise = torch.randn_like(x_start)
    sqrt_alpha_cumprod_t =
    ↪  self.alpha_cumprod[t].sqrt().view(-1,1,1)
    sqrt_one_minus_alpha_cumprod_t = (1.0 -
    ↪  self.alpha_cumprod[t]).sqrt().view(-1,1,1)

    # We assume x_start has shape [B, 1, L], t has shape [B]
    # We expand t to match [B, 1, L] as needed
    # This requires index into self.alpha_cumprod using each
    ↪  t[i]

    # Build factors for each batch element
    sqrt_alpha_cumprod_t =
    ↪  sqrt_alpha_cumprod_t[x_start.shape[0]*[0]]
    sqrt_one_minus_alpha_cumprod_t =
    ↪  sqrt_one_minus_alpha_cumprod_t[x_start.shape[0]*[0]]

    return sqrt_alpha_cumprod_t * x_start +
    ↪  sqrt_one_minus_alpha_cumprod_t * noise

def predict_noise(self, model, x_t, t):
    """
    Uses the model to predict the noise in x_t (the intermediate
    ↪  corrupted input).
    """
    return model(x_t)

def p_sample(self, model, x_t, t, guidance_scale=1.0):
    """
    One reverse diffusion step: p(x_{t-1} | x_t).
```

270

```
    The model predicts e_t (noise), which we use to refine x_t
    ↪   down to x_{t-1}.
    """
    betas_t = self.betas[t]
    alpha_t = self.alphas[t]
    alpha_cumprod_t = self.alpha_cumprod[t]
    alpha_cumprod_prev_t = self.alpha_cumprod_prev[t]

    e_t = model(x_t) * guidance_scale

    # Reconstruct x_0 from x_t and the predicted noise
    sqrt_recip_alpha_t = (1.0 / alpha_t).sqrt()
    x_0_hat = (x_t - (1.0 - alpha_t).sqrt() * e_t) *
    ↪   sqrt_recip_alpha_t

    # Posterior mean
    coef1 = (alpha_cumprod_prev_t.sqrt() * betas_t) / (1.0 -
    ↪   alpha_cumprod_t)
    coef2 = ((1.0 - alpha_cumprod_prev_t) * alpha_t.sqrt()) /
    ↪   (1.0 - alpha_cumprod_t)
    mean = coef1 * x_0_hat + coef2 * x_t

    # Posterior variance
    posterior_var = self.posterior_variance[t]

    if t > 0:
        noise = torch.randn_like(x_t)
    else:
        noise = torch.zeros_like(x_t)

    x_prev = mean + noise * posterior_var.sqrt()
    return x_prev

def p_sample_loop(self, model, shape, device,
↪   guidance_scale=1.0):
    """
    Applies reverse diffusion from x_T ~ N(0, I) to x_0 step by
    ↪   step.
    shape is (batch_size, 1, seq_length).
    """
    x_t = torch.randn(shape, device=device)
    for i in reversed(range(self.n_steps)):
        # For each item in the batch, we want to pick i
        ↪   individually
        # But here we do a single t for the entire batch
        t_tensor = torch.tensor([i]*shape[0], device=device)
        x_t = self.p_sample(model, x_t, t_tensor,
        ↪   guidance_scale=guidance_scale)
    return x_t

# ----------------------------------------------------------------
# 5) Training, evaluation, and sampling routines
# ----------------------------------------------------------------
```

271

```
def train_one_epoch(model, diffusion, optimizer, dataloader,
↪  device):
    """
    A single training epoch for the diffusion model.
    We sample a random t, corrupt the time series with noise, then
    ↪  predict that noise.
    """
    model.train()
    total_loss = 0.0

    for real_series, _ in dataloader:
        real_series = real_series.unsqueeze(1).to(device)  # shape:
        ↪  [B, 1, L]

        # pick a random time step t for each sample in batch
        t = torch.randint(0, diffusion.n_steps,
        ↪  (real_series.size(0),), device=device).long()

        # create random noise
        noise = torch.randn_like(real_series)

        # forward diffuse
        x_t = diffusion.q_sample(real_series, t, noise=noise)

        # predict noise
        noise_pred = diffusion.predict_noise(model, x_t, t)

        # MSE loss
        loss = nn.functional.mse_loss(noise_pred, noise)

        optimizer.zero_grad()
        loss.backward()
        optimizer.step()

        total_loss += loss.item()

    return total_loss / len(dataloader)

def evaluate_model(model, diffusion, dataloader, device):
    """
    Evaluate model with average MSE on noise prediction.
    """
    model.eval()
    total_loss = 0.0
    with torch.no_grad():
        for real_series, _ in dataloader:
            real_series = real_series.unsqueeze(1).to(device)
            t = torch.randint(0, diffusion.n_steps,
            ↪  (real_series.size(0),), device=device).long()
            noise = torch.randn_like(real_series)
            x_t = diffusion.q_sample(real_series, t, noise=noise)
            noise_pred = diffusion.predict_noise(model, x_t, t)
            loss = nn.functional.mse_loss(noise_pred, noise)
```

```
                total_loss += loss.item()
        return total_loss / len(dataloader)


def sample_and_plot(model, diffusion, device, epoch, seq_len=60,
↪   guidance_scale=1.0, num_samples=8):
        """
        Generate new time series via reverse diffusion and plot them.
        """
        model.eval()
        with torch.no_grad():
            # shape: [num_samples, 1, seq_len]
            generated = diffusion.p_sample_loop(model, (num_samples, 1,
            ↪   seq_len), device, guidance_scale=guidance_scale)
            generated = generated.squeeze(1).cpu().numpy()   # shape:
            ↪   [num_samples, seq_len]

            # Plot each sample
            fig, axs = plt.subplots(num_samples, 1, figsize=(8,
            ↪   num_samples*2))
            if num_samples == 1:
                axs = [axs]
            for idx, ax in enumerate(axs):
                ax.plot(generated[idx], label=f"Sample {idx}")
                ax.legend(loc="upper right")
            plt.tight_layout()

            os.makedirs("timeseries_results", exist_ok=True)
            plt.savefig(f"timeseries_results/
            epoch_{epoch}_gs_{guidance_scale}.png")
            plt.close()


# ---------------------------------------------------------------
# 6) Main training loop
# ---------------------------------------------------------------
def main():
    set_seed(42)
    device = torch.device('cuda' if torch.cuda.is_available() else
    ↪   'cpu')

    # Prepare dataset (synthetic for example)
    train_dataset = SyntheticTimeSeriesDataset(num_samples=2000,
    ↪   seq_len=60)
    test_dataset = SyntheticTimeSeriesDataset(num_samples=500,
    ↪   seq_len=60)

    train_loader = DataLoader(train_dataset, batch_size=32,
    ↪   shuffle=True)
    test_loader = DataLoader(test_dataset, batch_size=32,
    ↪   shuffle=False)

    # Create UNet1D model
    model = UNet1D(in_channels=1, out_channels=1,
    ↪   base_channels=32).to(device)
```

273

```
# Diffusion with 50 steps, linear beta schedule
diffusion = Diffusion(n_steps=50, beta_schedule='linear')

# Optimizer
optimizer = optim.Adam(model.parameters(), lr=1e-3)

# Training config
epochs = 10

for epoch in range(epochs):
    train_loss = train_one_epoch(model, diffusion, optimizer,
    ↪ train_loader, device)
    val_loss = evaluate_model(model, diffusion, test_loader,
    ↪ device)
    print(f"Epoch [{epoch+1}/{epochs}] - Train Loss:
    ↪ {train_loss:.4f}, Val Loss: {val_loss:.4f}")

    # Sample new time series and save a plot
    sample_and_plot(model, diffusion, device, epoch, seq_len=60,
    ↪ guidance_scale=1.0, num_samples=5)
    # Optionally sample with a higher guidance scale
    sample_and_plot(model, diffusion, device, epoch, seq_len=60,
    ↪ guidance_scale=2.0, num_samples=5)

    print("Training complete! Check the 'timeseries_results' folder
    ↪ for generated plots.")

if __name__ == "__main__":
    main()
```

Key Implementation Details:

- **Forward Diffusion:** We implement `q_sample` to add noise
  to each time series at a randomly chosen step. At step `t`, the
  fraction of noise is controlled by `betas` and `alpha_cumprod`.

- **Reverse Diffusion (Sampling):** The function `p_sample_loop`
  applies the learned reverse denoising step-by-step starting
  from random noise, yielding a plausible time series.

- **Temporal UNet:** The `UNet1D` uses 1D convolutions and
  skip connections to aggregate context across the temporal
  dimension. Convolutional downsampling captures long-range
  dependencies; transposed convolutions restore resolution.

- **Training Objective:** We predict the noise (via an MSE loss)
  that was injected at a given step `t`, encouraging the network

to learn how to remove noise and thereby reconstruct valid signals.

- **Conditional Variables (Optional):** You can extend `UNet1D` to accept extra features such as macroeconomic indicators or sentiment scores, influencing the diffusion sampling toward desired market conditions.

- **Practical Pipeline:** The `main` function brings everything together—building a synthetic dataset, creating the diffusion schedule, training over multiple epochs, and finally generating new time series samples for inspection.

Chapter 27

Generating Synthetic Tabular Data for Privacy and Analysis

Many industries need to share or analyze data in ways that protect sensitive information. Diffusion-based synthetic data generation offers a solution by producing realistic but anonymized tabular samples. We convert each row into a feature vector and define a diffusion process adding noise. A feed-forward or transformer-based network is trained to denoise these vectors step by step. Implementation steps: (1) collecting real tabular data, (2) applying normalization or encoding for categorical features, (3) injecting Gaussian noise according to a time-dependent schedule, (4) training the network to predict noise across each feature dimension, and (5) generating new rows by reversing the process from random vectors. The innovative aspect is using differential privacy techniques that clip gradient norms or add noise during training, ensuring that no individual's data can be reverse-engineered from the model.

Python Code Snippet

```python
import torch
import torch.nn as nn
import torch.optim as optim
import torch.utils.data as data
import numpy as np
```

```python
import random

# -----------------------------------------------------------------
# 1) Set random seed for reproducibility
# -----------------------------------------------------------------
def set_seed(seed=42):
    random.seed(seed)
    np.random.seed(seed)
    torch.manual_seed(seed)
    if torch.cuda.is_available():
        torch.cuda.manual_seed_all(seed)


# -----------------------------------------------------------------
# 2) Synthetic tabular dataset generation and preprocessing
# -----------------------------------------------------------------
class TabularDataset(data.Dataset):
    '''
    A simple synthetic dataset for demonstration. We create
    both numerical and categorical columns, then one-hot encode
    the categorical columns.
    '''
    def __init__(self, n_samples=5000, n_num_features=6,
    ↪    n_cat_features=2, cat_cardinality=4):
        super().__init__()
        # For numeric features, just sample from a normal
        ↪    distribution
        numeric_data = np.random.randn(n_samples, n_num_features)

        # For categorical features, sample discrete values
        # Each categorical feature has 'cat_cardinality' possible
        ↪    categories
        cat_data = []
        for _ in range(n_cat_features):
            cat_values = np.random.randint(0, cat_cardinality,
            ↪    size=(n_samples,))
            cat_data.append(cat_values.reshape(-1, 1))
        cat_data = np.concatenate(cat_data, axis=1)  # shape:
        ↪    (n_samples, n_cat_features)

        # One-hot encode the categorical columns
        # We assume each cat feature has the same cardinality for
        ↪    simplicity
        encoded_cat_list = []
        for i in range(n_cat_features):
            one_hot = np.eye(cat_cardinality)[cat_data[:, i]]
            encoded_cat_list.append(one_hot)
        encoded_cat = np.concatenate(encoded_cat_list, axis=1)  #
        ↪    shape: (n_samples, n_cat_features * cat_cardinality)

        # Combine numeric + encoded categorical
        self.data = np.concatenate([numeric_data, encoded_cat],
        ↪    axis=1).astype(np.float32)
```

```
            # Optionally, we could apply normalization across numeric
            ↪  features here.
            # For demonstration, we assume numeric data is roughly
            ↪  zero-mean, unit-variance.
            # If you load real data, consider using standard scalers or
            ↪  min-max normalization.

            self.data = torch.tensor(self.data)

    def __len__(self):
        return self.data.size(0)

    def __getitem__(self, idx):
        return self.data[idx]

def get_dataloaders(batch_size=64):
    '''
    Utility to create train and validation dataloaders from
    ↪  synthetic data.
    '''
    # We'll create a train and a validation set
    train_dataset = TabularDataset(n_samples=5000)
    val_dataset   = TabularDataset(n_samples=1000)

    train_loader = data.DataLoader(train_dataset,
    ↪  batch_size=batch_size, shuffle=True)
    val_loader   = data.DataLoader(val_dataset,
    ↪  batch_size=batch_size, shuffle=False)

    return train_loader, val_loader

# ------------------------------------------------------------
# 3) Define a simple MLP for denoising tabular data
# ------------------------------------------------------------
class TabularMLP(nn.Module):
    '''
    A small feed-forward neural network with skip connections
    to predict the noise in each feature of the data vector.
    Assumes input and output dimensions are the same.
    '''
    def __init__(self, input_dim=14, hidden_dim=64):
        super().__init__()
        self.net = nn.Sequential(
            nn.Linear(input_dim, hidden_dim),
            nn.ReLU(inplace=True),
            nn.Linear(hidden_dim, hidden_dim),
            nn.ReLU(inplace=True),
            nn.Linear(hidden_dim, input_dim)
        )

    def forward(self, x):
        return self.net(x)
```

278

```
# ----------------------------------------------------------------
# 4) Create a beta schedule, define diffusion processes
# ----------------------------------------------------------------
def make_beta_schedule(schedule_name, n_timestep, start=1e-4,
↪    end=2e-2):
    '''
    Creates a beta schedule for the diffusion process.
    Linear schedule is used here as a simple example.
    '''
    if schedule_name == "linear":
        return torch.linspace(start, end, n_timestep)
    else:
        raise NotImplementedError("Only 'linear' schedule is
        ↪    implemented here.")


class TabularDiffusion:
    '''
    1) The forward noising process: q(x_t | x_0)
    2) The reverse denoising process: p(x_{t-1} | x_t)
    3) Utilities for training and sampling
    '''
    def __init__(self, n_steps=200, beta_schedule='linear',
    ↪    device='cpu'):
        self.n_steps = n_steps
        self.device = device
        self.betas = make_beta_schedule(beta_schedule,
        ↪    n_steps).to(device)
        self.alphas = 1.0 - self.betas
        self.alpha_cumprod = torch.cumprod(self.alphas, dim=0)
        self.alpha_cumprod_prev = torch.cat([torch.tensor([1.0],
        ↪    device=device), self.alpha_cumprod[:-1]], dim=0)

        # Posterior variance term for p(x_{t-1} | x_t, x_0)
        self.posterior_variance = self.betas * (1.0 -
        ↪    self.alpha_cumprod_prev) / (1.0 - self.alpha_cumprod)

    def q_sample(self, x_start, t, noise=None):
        '''
        Forward diffusion: Adds noise to x_start at step t.
        x_t = sqrt(alpha_cumprod[t]) * x_start + sqrt(1 -
        ↪    alpha_cumprod[t]) * noise
        '''
        if noise is None:
            noise = torch.randn_like(x_start)
        sqrt_alpha_cumprod_t =
        ↪    self.alpha_cumprod[t].sqrt().unsqueeze(-1)
        sqrt_one_minus_alpha_cumprod_t = (1 -
        ↪    self.alpha_cumprod[t]).sqrt().unsqueeze(-1)
        return sqrt_alpha_cumprod_t * x_start +
        ↪    sqrt_one_minus_alpha_cumprod_t * noise

    def predict_noise(self, model, x_t, t):
        '''
```

```
    Use the MLP model to predict the noise added at step t.
    We pass t to the model if it was conditional, but here
    we keep it simple and feed only x_t.
    '''
    return model(x_t)

def p_sample(self, model, x_t, t, guidance_scale=1.0):
    '''
    One reverse diffusion step: p(x_{t-1} | x_t).
    The model predicts the noise e_t, and we compute the mean.
    "guidance_scale" can amplify or reduce the predicted noise.
    '''
    betas_t = self.betas[t]
    alpha_t = self.alphas[t]
    alpha_cumprod_t = self.alpha_cumprod[t]
    alpha_cumprod_prev_t = self.alpha_cumprod_prev[t]

    e_t = model(x_t) * guidance_scale   # scaled noise estimate

    sqrt_recip_alpha_t = (1.0 / alpha_t).sqrt()
    # approximate x_0 from x_t and predicted noise
    x_0_hat = (x_t - (1.0 - alpha_t).sqrt() * e_t) *
    ↪  sqrt_recip_alpha_t

    coef1 = (alpha_cumprod_prev_t.sqrt() * betas_t) / (1.0 -
    ↪  alpha_cumprod_t)
    coef2 = ((1.0 - alpha_cumprod_prev_t) * alpha_t.sqrt()) /
    ↪  (1.0 - alpha_cumprod_t)

    mean = coef1 * x_0_hat + coef2 * x_t
    posterior_var = self.posterior_variance[t]

    if t > 0:
        noise = torch.randn_like(x_t)
    else:
        noise = torch.zeros_like(x_t)

    x_prev = mean + noise * posterior_var.sqrt()
    return x_prev

def p_sample_loop(self, model, shape, guidance_scale=1.0):
    '''
    Repeatedly apply p_sample to go from x_T ~ N(0,I) to x_0.
    For tabular data, shape = (batch_size, num_features).
    '''
    x_t = torch.randn(shape, device=self.device)
    for i in reversed(range(self.n_steps)):
        x_t = self.p_sample(model, x_t, i,
        ↪  guidance_scale=guidance_scale)
    return x_t

# ------------------------------------------------------------
# 5) Training routines
```

280

```python
# -----------------------------------------------------------------
def train_one_epoch(model, diffusion, optimizer, dataloader,
 ↪ device):
    '''
    A single training epoch: sample random t, forward-diffuse data,
    and predict the noise with MSE loss.
    '''
    model.train()
    loss_sum = 0
    for batch in dataloader:
        batch = batch.to(device)

        # Random time step
        t = torch.randint(0, diffusion.n_steps, (batch.size(0),),
         ↪ device=device).long()

        # True noise
        noise = torch.randn_like(batch)

        # Forward diffuse
        x_t = diffusion.q_sample(batch, t, noise)

        # Predict noise
        noise_pred = diffusion.predict_noise(model, x_t, t)

        # MSE loss
        loss = nn.functional.mse_loss(noise_pred, noise)

        optimizer.zero_grad()
        loss.backward()

        # Example of gradient clipping for differential privacy
        # (can be combined with noise addition if desired)
        torch.nn.utils.clip_grad_norm_(model.parameters(),
         ↪ max_norm=1.0)

        optimizer.step()
        loss_sum += loss.item()

    return loss_sum / len(dataloader)

def evaluate_model(model, diffusion, dataloader, device):
    '''
    Compute average L2 error for a validation set.
    '''
    model.eval()
    loss_sum = 0
    with torch.no_grad():
        for batch in dataloader:
            batch = batch.to(device)
            t = torch.randint(0, diffusion.n_steps,
             ↪ (batch.size(0),), device=device).long()
            noise = torch.randn_like(batch)
```

281

```python
            x_t = diffusion.q_sample(batch, t, noise)
            noise_pred = diffusion.predict_noise(model, x_t, t)
            loss = nn.functional.mse_loss(noise_pred, noise)
            loss_sum += loss.item()
    return loss_sum / len(dataloader)

def sample_synthetic_data(model, diffusion, num_samples=16,
↪   guidance_scale=1.0):
    '''
    Generates new synthetic rows by reversing diffusion from pure
    ↪   noise.
    '''
    model.eval()
    with torch.no_grad():
        shape = (num_samples, model.net[0].in_features)  #
        ↪   input_dim
        samples = diffusion.p_sample_loop(model, shape=shape,
        ↪   guidance_scale=guidance_scale)
    return samples


# --------------------------------------------------------------
# 6) Main training script
# --------------------------------------------------------------
def main():
    set_seed(42)
    device = torch.device("cuda" if torch.cuda.is_available() else
    ↪   "cpu")

    # Create data loaders
    train_loader, val_loader = get_dataloaders(batch_size=64)

    # MLP for tabular data
    # input_dim = numeric_features(6) + 2 cat_features x
    ↪   cardinality(4) = 14
    model = TabularMLP(input_dim=14, hidden_dim=64).to(device)

    # Diffusion process
    diffusion = TabularDiffusion(n_steps=200,
    ↪   beta_schedule='linear', device=device)

    # Optimizer
    optimizer = optim.Adam(model.parameters(), lr=1e-3)

    # Training
    epochs = 5
    for epoch in range(epochs):
        train_loss = train_one_epoch(model, diffusion, optimizer,
        ↪   train_loader, device)
        val_loss = evaluate_model(model, diffusion, val_loader,
        ↪   device)
        print(f"Epoch [{epoch+1}/{epochs}] - Train Loss:
        ↪   {train_loss:.4f}, Val Loss: {val_loss:.4f}")
```

```python
# Sample synthetic rows at the end of each epoch
synthetic_rows = sample_synthetic_data(model, diffusion,
↪  num_samples=5, guidance_scale=1.0)
print("Sampled Synthetic Data (guidance_scale=1.0):")
print(synthetic_rows.cpu().numpy())

# Optionally try a higher guidance scale to see changes in
↪  diversity
synthetic_rows_g2 = sample_synthetic_data(model, diffusion,
↪  num_samples=5, guidance_scale=2.0)
print("Sampled Synthetic Data (guidance_scale=2.0):")
print(synthetic_rows_g2.cpu().numpy())
print("-" * 50)

    print("Training complete. Synthetic data generation is
↪  demonstrated above.")

if __name__ == "__main__":
    main()
```

Key Implementation Details:

- **Forward Diffusion:** We implement `q_sample` to corrupt each row by mixing original tabular values with Gaussian noise, controlled by a linear `beta` schedule. At step t, the fraction of noise is determined by the cumulative product of `alphas[t]`.

- **Reverse Diffusion (Sampling):** The function `p_sample_loop` applies the MLP-based model in a stepwise manner, gradually removing noise starting from a random Gaussian initialization. Each call to `p_sample` refines the data closer toward realistic tabular values.

- **MLP Architecture:** The `TabularMLP` uses dense (fully connected) layers to handle tabular inputs. It predicts the noise in each feature dimension using an MSE loss criterion.

- **Training Objective:** We train by matching the model's noise prediction to the actual Gaussian noise injected at each step. This "predict the noise" approach aligns with modern diffusion-based objectives.

- **Differential Privacy:** In this snippet, we demonstrate gradient clipping to help prevent large updates that could leak individual data details. Adding noise to gradients is another

283

step often taken to achieve formal differential privacy guarantees.

- **End-to-End Pipeline:** The `main` function orchestrates data loading, model initialization, training across epochs, and finally sampling synthetic rows at multiple guidance scales to observe variations in the generated data.

Chapter 28

Domain Adaptation in Vision with Diffusion

In cross-domain tasks—such as adapting synthetic images to real-world imagery—diffusion can smooth the domain gap. Common usage includes aligning simulation data to real photographs for robotics or AR applications. The construction modifies standard image-to-image diffusion, conditioning on the source domain image while learning to match the target domain distribution. Implementation steps: (1) gather paired or unpaired datasets from source and target domains, (2) apply a forward noise schedule to target-domain images, (3) condition the UNet on the source-domain image, (4) train a noise prediction objective, forcing the network to converge toward target domain semantics, and (5) generate adapted images by reversing the diffusion from partially noisy source data. An innovative approach is multi-domain adaptation: the model can simultaneously adapt images from various source domains toward multiple target styles, switching styles dynamically during sampling.

Python Code Snippet

```python
import os
import random
import math
import torch
import torch.nn as nn
import torchvision
```

```python
import torchvision.transforms as transforms
from torch.utils.data import Dataset, DataLoader
import torch.optim as optim
import matplotlib.pyplot as plt
from PIL import Image
import glob

# ---------------------------------------------------------------
# 1) Set random seed for reproducibility
# ---------------------------------------------------------------
def set_seed(seed=42):
    random.seed(seed)
    torch.manual_seed(seed)
    if torch.cuda.is_available():
        torch.cuda.manual_seed_all(seed)


# ---------------------------------------------------------------
# 2) Paired Domain Dataset: returns (source_image, target_image).
#    Replace file paths with real data for actual domain adaptation.
# ---------------------------------------------------------------
class PairedDomainDataset(Dataset):
    '''
    This dataset expects two folders: one for source domain
    ↪  (synthetic) images
    and another for target domain (real) images. For a paired
    ↪  approach,
    the file ordering in each folder should match, or you can
    ↪  implement
    your own pairing logic.
    '''
    def __init__(self, source_dir, target_dir, transform=None):
        super().__init__()
        self.source_files =
        ↪  sorted(glob.glob(os.path.join(source_dir, "*.jpg")))
        self.target_files =
        ↪  sorted(glob.glob(os.path.join(target_dir, "*.jpg")))
        self.transform = transform

    def __len__(self):
        return min(len(self.source_files), len(self.target_files))

    def __getitem__(self, idx):
        source_img_path = self.source_files[idx]
        target_img_path = self.target_files[idx]

        source_img = Image.open(source_img_path).convert("RGB")
        target_img = Image.open(target_img_path).convert("RGB")

        if self.transform:
            source_img = self.transform(source_img)
            target_img = self.transform(target_img)

        return source_img, target_img
```

```
# ------------------------------------------------------------
# 3) A U-Net that conditions on the source image + noised target
↪ image
#   So input channels = 6 (3 for source, 3 for noised target),
↪ output = predicted noise (3 channels).
# ------------------------------------------------------------
class DoubleConv(nn.Module):
    '''
    A helper module that performs two convolutions (each followed by
    ↪ ReLU).
    Used as a building block in the U-Net.
    '''
    def __init__(self, in_channels, out_channels):
        super(DoubleConv, self).__init__()
        self.conv = nn.Sequential(
            nn.Conv2d(in_channels, out_channels, 3, padding=1),
            nn.ReLU(inplace=True),
            nn.Conv2d(out_channels, out_channels, 3, padding=1),
            nn.ReLU(inplace=True)
        )

    def forward(self, x):
        return self.conv(x)

class ConditionUNet(nn.Module):
    '''
    A U-Net that takes (source_image, noised_target_image) as a
    ↪ 6-channel input
    and predicts the added noise for the target domain (3 channels).
    '''
    def __init__(self, in_channels=6, out_channels=3,
    ↪ base_channels=64):
        super(ConditionUNet, self).__init__()

        # Down-sampling (encoder)
        self.down1 = DoubleConv(in_channels, base_channels)
        self.pool1 = nn.MaxPool2d(2)

        self.down2 = DoubleConv(base_channels, base_channels*2)
        self.pool2 = nn.MaxPool2d(2)

        self.down3 = DoubleConv(base_channels*2, base_channels*4)
        self.pool3 = nn.MaxPool2d(2)

        # Bottleneck
        self.bottleneck = DoubleConv(base_channels*4,
        ↪ base_channels*8)

        # Up-sampling (decoder)
        self.up1 = nn.ConvTranspose2d(base_channels*8,
        ↪ base_channels*4, kernel_size=2, stride=2)
        self.conv_up1 = DoubleConv(base_channels*8, base_channels*4)
```

```python
        self.up2 = nn.ConvTranspose2d(base_channels*4,
        ↪  base_channels*2, kernel_size=2, stride=2)
        self.conv_up2 = DoubleConv(base_channels*4, base_channels*2)

        self.up3 = nn.ConvTranspose2d(base_channels*2,
        ↪  base_channels, kernel_size=2, stride=2)
        self.conv_up3 = DoubleConv(base_channels*2, base_channels)

        # Final output
        self.final_conv = nn.Conv2d(base_channels, out_channels,
        ↪  kernel_size=1)

    def forward(self, source_img, noised_target):
        # Concatenate along channel dimension
        x = torch.cat([source_img, noised_target], dim=1)  # B x 6 x
        ↪  H x W

        # Encoder
        x1 = self.down1(x)
        x2 = self.pool1(x1)

        x2 = self.down2(x2)
        x3 = self.pool2(x2)

        x3 = self.down3(x3)
        x4 = self.pool3(x3)

        # Bottleneck
        b = self.bottleneck(x4)

        # Decoder
        x = self.up1(b)
        x = torch.cat([x, x3], dim=1)
        x = self.conv_up1(x)

        x = self.up2(x)
        x = torch.cat([x, x2], dim=1)
        x = self.conv_up2(x)

        x = self.up3(x)
        x = torch.cat([x, x1], dim=1)
        x = self.conv_up3(x)

        # Final output
        out = self.final_conv(x)
        return out

# ------------------------------------------------------------
# 4) Diffusion schedule, forward process, and sampling logic
# ------------------------------------------------------------
def make_beta_schedule(schedule_name, n_timestep, start=1e-4,
↪  end=2e-2):
```

```python
    '''
    Creates a beta schedule for the diffusion process.
    Using a linear schedule as the default example.
    '''
    if schedule_name == "linear":
        return torch.linspace(start, end, n_timestep)
    else:
        raise NotImplementedError("Only 'linear' schedule is
        ↪    implemented here.")


class Diffusion:
    '''
    A class that encapsulates:
    1) The forward noising process: q(x_t | x_0)
    2) The reverse denoising process: p(x_{t-1} | x_t)
    3) Utility for training and sampling, adapted for domain
    ↪    adaptation.
    '''

    def __init__(self, n_steps=200, beta_schedule='linear'):
        self.n_steps = n_steps
        self.betas = make_beta_schedule(beta_schedule, n_steps)
        self.alphas = 1.0 - self.betas
        self.alpha_cumprod = torch.cumprod(self.alphas, dim=0)
        self.alpha_cumprod_prev = torch.cat(
            [torch.tensor([1.0]), self.alpha_cumprod[:-1]], dim=0
        )

        # Posterior variance term for p(x_{t-1} | x_t, x_0)
        self.posterior_variance = self.betas * (1.0 -
        ↪    self.alpha_cumprod_prev) / (1.0 - self.alpha_cumprod)

    def q_sample(self, x_start, t, noise=None):
        '''
        Forward diffusion: Adds noise to x_start at step t.
        x_t = sqrt(alpha_cumprod[t]) * x_start + sqrt(1 -
        ↪    alpha_cumprod[t]) * noise
        '''
        if noise is None:
            noise = torch.randn_like(x_start)
        sqrt_alpha_cumprod_t =
        ↪    self.alpha_cumprod[t].sqrt().unsqueeze(-1).
        unsqueeze(-1).unsqueeze(-1)
        sqrt_one_minus_alpha_cumprod_t = (1 -
        ↪    self.alpha_cumprod[t]).sqrt().unsqueeze(-1).
        unsqueeze(-1).unsqueeze(-1)
        return sqrt_alpha_cumprod_t * x_start +
        ↪    sqrt_one_minus_alpha_cumprod_t * noise

    def predict_noise(self, model, source, x_t, t):
        '''
        Use the condition-aware UNet model to predict the noise
        ↪    added at step t.
        source: source domain image
```

289

```
    x_t: noised target domain image
    '''
    return model(source, x_t)

def p_sample(self, model, source, x_t, t, guidance_scale=1.0):
    '''
    One reverse diffusion step: p(x_{t-1} | x_t).
    The model predicts the noise e_t, and we compute the mean of
    ↪   p(x_{t-1} | x_t, x_0).
    We also demonstrate a "guidance_scale" that scales the
    ↪   predicted noise
    for more or less variation or stylization.
    '''
    betas_t = self.betas[t]
    alpha_t = self.alphas[t]
    alpha_cumprod_t = self.alpha_cumprod[t]
    alpha_cumprod_prev_t = self.alpha_cumprod_prev[t]

    # Predicted noise
    e_t = model(source, x_t) * guidance_scale

    # Reconstruct x_0:
    sqrt_recip_alpha_t = (1.0 / alpha_t).sqrt()
    x_0_hat = (x_t - (1.0 - alpha_t).sqrt() * e_t) *
    ↪   sqrt_recip_alpha_t

    # Coefficients for mean computation
    coef1 = (alpha_cumprod_prev_t.sqrt() * betas_t) / (1.0 -
    ↪   alpha_cumprod_t)
    coef2 = ((1.0 - alpha_cumprod_prev_t) * alpha_t.sqrt()) /
    ↪   (1.0 - alpha_cumprod_t)

    mean = coef1 * x_0_hat + coef2 * x_t

    # Posterior variance
    posterior_var = self.posterior_variance[t]
    if t > 0:
        noise = torch.randn_like(x_t)
    else:
        noise = torch.zeros_like(x_t)

    x_prev = mean + noise * posterior_var.sqrt()
    return x_prev

def p_sample_loop(self, model, source, shape, device,
↪   guidance_scale=1.0):
    '''
    Repeatedly apply p_sample to go from x_T ~ N(0,I) to x_0.
    For domain adaptation, we keep 'source' the same and
    ↪   gradually refine x_t.
    '''
    x_t = torch.randn(shape, device=device)
    for i in reversed(range(self.n_steps)):
```

```
            x_t = self.p_sample(model, source, x_t, i,
            ↪  guidance_scale=guidance_scale)
        return x_t

# ---------------------------------------------------------------
# 5) Training and evaluation routines
# ---------------------------------------------------------------
def train_one_epoch(model, diffusion, optimizer, dataloader,
↪  device):
    '''
    A single training epoch for the domain adaptation diffusion
    ↪  model.
    We sample a random t, forward diffusing the *target* image,
    ↪  while
    conditioning on the *source* image. The model predicts the
    ↪  noise.
    '''
    model.train()
    loss_sum = 0
    for source_imgs, target_imgs in dataloader:
        source_imgs = source_imgs.to(device)
        target_imgs = target_imgs.to(device)

        # Sample random t
        t = torch.randint(0, diffusion.n_steps,
        ↪  (source_imgs.size(0),), device=device).long()

        # Create random noise
        noise = torch.randn_like(target_imgs)

        # Forward diffuse the target image at step t
        x_t = diffusion.q_sample(target_imgs, t, noise=noise)

        # Predict the noise, conditioning on source_imgs
        noise_pred = diffusion.predict_noise(model, source_imgs,
        ↪  x_t, t)

        # L2 loss to match the real noise
        loss = nn.functional.mse_loss(noise_pred, noise)

        optimizer.zero_grad()
        loss.backward()
        optimizer.step()

        loss_sum += loss.item()

    return loss_sum / len(dataloader)

def evaluate_model(model, diffusion, dataloader, device):
    '''
    Evaluate average L2 error of noise prediction on a validation
    ↪  set.
    '''
```

```python
    model.eval()
    loss_sum = 0
    with torch.no_grad():
        for source_imgs, target_imgs in dataloader:
            source_imgs = source_imgs.to(device)
            target_imgs = target_imgs.to(device)

            t = torch.randint(0, diffusion.n_steps,
            ↪   (source_imgs.size(0),), device=device).long()
            noise = torch.randn_like(target_imgs)
            x_t = diffusion.q_sample(target_imgs, t, noise=noise)

            noise_pred = diffusion.predict_noise(model, source_imgs,
            ↪   x_t, t)
            loss = nn.functional.mse_loss(noise_pred, noise)
            loss_sum += loss.item()
    return loss_sum / len(dataloader)

def sample_and_save(model, diffusion, source_imgs, device, epoch,
↪   guidance_scale=1.0):
    '''
    Use the reverse diffusion process to adapt source_imgs into the
    ↪   target domain.
    We sample random noise as a starting point for the target side,
    ↪   then
    iteratively refine it using p_sample_loop.
    Each source image is processed individually for demonstration.
    '''
    model.eval()
    os.makedirs("adapted_results", exist_ok=True)

    with torch.no_grad():
        for i in range(len(source_imgs)):
            source = source_imgs[i].unsqueeze(0).to(device)
            # shape for the target domain
            shape = (1, 3, source.shape[2], source.shape[3])

            adapted = diffusion.p_sample_loop(model, source, shape,
            ↪   device, guidance_scale=guidance_scale)
            # The output is in [-1,1], clamp and convert to [0,1]
            ↪   range
            adapted = (adapted.clamp(-1.0, 1.0) + 1) * 0.5

            grid = torchvision.utils.make_grid(adapted, nrow=1)
            plt.figure(figsize=(3,3))
            plt.axis("off")
            plt.imshow(grid.permute(1, 2, 0).cpu().numpy())
            plt.savefig(f"adapted_results/
            epoch_{epoch}_img_{i}_gs_{guidance_scale}.png")
            plt.close()

# -----------------------------------------------------------
# 6) Main function: set up dataset, model, diffusion, and train
```

```
# --------------------------------------------------------------
def main():
    set_seed(42)
    device = torch.device("cuda" if torch.cuda.is_available() else
    ↪   "cpu")

    # Example transforms, normalization to [-1,1]
    transform = transforms.Compose([
        transforms.Resize((128,128)),
        transforms.ToTensor(),
        transforms.Normalize((0.5, 0.5, 0.5),
                             (0.5, 0.5, 0.5))
    ])

    # Replace 'source_dir' and 'target_dir' with real folders
    train_source_dir = "data/train/source"
    train_target_dir = "data/train/target"
    val_source_dir   = "data/val/source"
    val_target_dir   = "data/val/target"

    train_dataset = PairedDomainDataset(train_source_dir,
    ↪   train_target_dir, transform=transform)
    val_dataset   = PairedDomainDataset(val_source_dir,
    ↪   val_target_dir, transform=transform)

    train_loader = DataLoader(train_dataset, batch_size=4,
    ↪   shuffle=True)
    val_loader   = DataLoader(val_dataset, batch_size=4,
    ↪   shuffle=False)

    # Initialize the conditional U-Net
    model = ConditionUNet(in_channels=6, out_channels=3,
    ↪   base_channels=64).to(device)

    # Diffusion process
    diffusion = Diffusion(n_steps=200, beta_schedule='linear')

    # Optimizer
    optimizer = optim.Adam(model.parameters(), lr=1e-4)

    # Train for a few epochs (example: 5)
    epochs = 5
    for epoch in range(epochs):
        train_loss = train_one_epoch(model, diffusion, optimizer,
        ↪   train_loader, device)
        val_loss = evaluate_model(model, diffusion, val_loader,
        ↪   device)
        print(f"Epoch [{epoch+1}/{epochs}] - Train Loss:
        ↪   {train_loss:.4f}, Val Loss: {val_loss:.4f}")

        # Let's sample a small batch of source images from the val
        ↪   dataset to preview adaptation
        sample_batch = []
```

```
      for source_imgs, _ in val_loader:
          sample_batch = source_imgs[:2]  # take a couple of
          ↪   images
          break

      sample_and_save(model, diffusion, sample_batch, device,
      ↪   epoch, guidance_scale=1.0)
      sample_and_save(model, diffusion, sample_batch, device,
      ↪   epoch, guidance_scale=2.0)

    print("Training complete! Check the 'adapted_results' folder for
    ↪   adapted images.")

if __name__ == "__main__":
    main()
```

Key Implementation Details:

- **Forward Diffusion:** We implement `q_sample` to corrupt the target-domain image step by step using a linear beta schedule. The fraction of noise injected depends on `betas[t]` and cumulative products of `alphas`.

- **Reverse Diffusion:** The function `p_sample_loop` iteratively calls `p_sample` to denoise from random noise back to a target-like image. The source image is concatenated with the noised target at each step for conditioning.

- **ConditionUNet Architecture:** The `ConditionUNet` takes 6 channels as input (3 for the source, 3 for the noised target) and predicts 3 channels of noise. This merges the source domain information with the partially noised target image to guide adaptation.

- **Training Objective:** We compare the network's predicted noise against the actual noise with MSE loss, encouraging the model to learn how to remove noise in a way that aligns with the target domain, given the source domain context.

- **Data Handling:** `PairedDomainDataset` pairs source and target images. In practice, you can extend this to unpaired data by creating separate datasets or by implementing a matching strategy.

- **Sampling and Visualization:** `sample_and_save` demonstrates how to create adapted images from source domain inputs by reversing the diffusion from random initialization. The guidance scale (`guidance_scale`) modulates how strongly the denoising process is influenced by the predicted noise, allowing for style or fidelity adjustments.

Chapter 29

Adversarial Example Generation for Robustness

Diffusion-based adversarial attacks can probe model vulnerabilities by creating small perturbations that cause misclassification, while remaining visually imperceptible. Common usage is in testing the robustness of image classifiers. We begin by taking an input image or data point and apply partial forward noise. The diffusion network is trained under constraints that shift the data distribution enough to fool the classifier. Key steps: (1) training a diffusion model on the original dataset, (2) incorporating a classifier's gradient into the sampling process, (3) adjusting the reverse diffusion steps to maximize classifier error while minimizing perceptibility, and (4) producing adversarial examples. An innovative variant sets up a min-max procedure, where the diffusion model injects subtle changes and a reconstructor tries to detect or neutralize them, leading to more sophisticated attacks and improved defensive strategies.

Python Code Snippet

```
import os
import random
import math
import torch
```

```python
import torch.nn as nn
import torch.optim as optim
import torch.nn.functional as F
from torch.utils.data import DataLoader
import torchvision
import torchvision.transforms as transforms
import matplotlib.pyplot as plt

# ----------------------------------------------------------------
# 1) Set random seed for reproducibility
# ----------------------------------------------------------------
def set_seed(seed=42):
    random.seed(seed)
    torch.manual_seed(seed)
    if torch.cuda.is_available():
        torch.cuda.manual_seed_all(seed)


# ----------------------------------------------------------------
# 2) Simple CNN Classifier for MNIST
# ----------------------------------------------------------------
class ClassifierCNN(nn.Module):
    '''
    A small CNN for classification on MNIST.
    Two convolution layers + two fully connected layers.
    '''
    def __init__(self, num_classes=10):
        super(ClassifierCNN, self).__init__()
        self.conv1 = nn.Conv2d(1, 32, kernel_size=3, padding=1)
        self.conv2 = nn.Conv2d(32, 64, kernel_size=3, padding=1)
        self.pool = nn.MaxPool2d(2)
        self.fc1 = nn.Linear(64*7*7, 128)
        self.fc2 = nn.Linear(128, num_classes)

    def forward(self, x):
        # x shape: [B,1,28,28]
        x = F.relu(self.conv1(x))
        x = self.pool(F.relu(self.conv2(x)))   # shape [B,64,14,14]
        x = x.view(x.size(0), -1)              # shape [B,64*14*14]
        x = F.relu(self.fc1(x))
        x = self.fc2(x)
        return x

def train_classifier(model, dataloader, optimizer, device):
    model.train()
    total_loss = 0
    correct = 0
    total = 0
    for images, labels in dataloader:
        images, labels = images.to(device), labels.to(device)
        optimizer.zero_grad()
        outputs = model(images)
        loss = F.cross_entropy(outputs, labels)
        loss.backward()
```

297

```
            optimizer.step()
            total_loss += loss.item() * images.size(0)
            _, predicted = outputs.max(1)
            correct += predicted.eq(labels).sum().item()
            total += labels.size(0)
        avg_loss = total_loss / total
        accuracy = 100. * correct / total
        return avg_loss, accuracy

def evaluate_classifier(model, dataloader, device):
    model.eval()
    total_loss = 0
    correct = 0
    total = 0
    with torch.no_grad():
        for images, labels in dataloader:
            images, labels = images.to(device), labels.to(device)
            outputs = model(images)
            loss = F.cross_entropy(outputs, labels)
            total_loss += loss.item() * images.size(0)
            _, predicted = outputs.max(1)
            correct += predicted.eq(labels).sum().item()
            total += labels.size(0)
        avg_loss = total_loss / total
        accuracy = 100. * correct / total
        return avg_loss, accuracy


# -----------------------------------------------------------
# 3) Create a simple U-Net for diffusion denoising
# -----------------------------------------------------------
class DoubleConv(nn.Module):
    '''
    A helper module that performs two convolutions (each followed by
    ↪ ReLU)
    to reduce block boilerplate in the U-Net.
    '''

    def __init__(self, in_channels, out_channels):
        super(DoubleConv, self).__init__()
        self.conv = nn.Sequential(
            nn.Conv2d(in_channels, out_channels, 3, padding=1),
            nn.ReLU(inplace=True),
            nn.Conv2d(out_channels, out_channels, 3, padding=1),
            nn.ReLU(inplace=True)
        )

    def forward(self, x):
        return self.conv(x)


class UNet(nn.Module):
    '''
    A simplified U-Net architecture with down-sampling (encoder)
    and up-sampling (decoder) blocks, plus skip connections.
    '''
```

298

```python
def __init__(self, in_channels=1, out_channels=1,
↪ base_channels=64):
    super(UNet, self).__init__()

    # Down-sampling (encoder)
    self.down1 = DoubleConv(in_channels, base_channels)
    self.down2 = DoubleConv(base_channels, base_channels*2)
    self.down3 = DoubleConv(base_channels*2, base_channels*4)

    self.pool = nn.MaxPool2d(2)

    # Bottleneck
    self.bottleneck = DoubleConv(base_channels*4,
    ↪ base_channels*8)

    # Up-sampling (decoder)
    self.up1 = nn.ConvTranspose2d(base_channels*8,
    ↪ base_channels*4, kernel_size=2, stride=2)
    self.conv_up1 = DoubleConv(base_channels*8, base_channels*4)

    self.up2 = nn.ConvTranspose2d(base_channels*4,
    ↪ base_channels*2, kernel_size=2, stride=2)
    self.conv_up2 = DoubleConv(base_channels*4, base_channels*2)

    self.up3 = nn.ConvTranspose2d(base_channels*2,
    ↪ base_channels, kernel_size=2, stride=2)
    self.conv_up3 = DoubleConv(base_channels*2, base_channels)

    # Final output
    self.final_conv = nn.Conv2d(base_channels, out_channels,
    ↪ kernel_size=1)

def forward(self, x):
    # Encoder
    x1 = self.down1(x)
    x2 = self.pool(x1)

    x2 = self.down2(x2)
    x3 = self.pool(x2)

    x3 = self.down3(x3)
    x4 = self.pool(x3)

    # Bottleneck
    b = self.bottleneck(x4)

    # Decoder
    x = self.up1(b)
    x = torch.cat([x, x3], dim=1)   # skip connection
    x = self.conv_up1(x)

    x = self.up2(x)
    x = torch.cat([x, x2], dim=1)
```

299

```python
        x = self.conv_up2(x)

        x = self.up3(x)
        x = torch.cat([x, x1], dim=1)
        x = self.conv_up3(x)

        # Final
        out = self.final_conv(x)
        return out


# --------------------------------------------------------------
# 4) Define beta schedule and main Diffusion class
# --------------------------------------------------------------
def make_beta_schedule(schedule_name, n_timestep, start=1e-4,
↪   end=2e-2):
    '''
    Creates a beta schedule for the diffusion process.
    We use a linear schedule as a straightforward example.
    '''
    if schedule_name == "linear":
        return torch.linspace(start, end, n_timestep)
    else:
        raise NotImplementedError("Only 'linear' schedule is
        ↪   implemented here.")


class Diffusion:
    '''
    A class that encapsulates:
    1) The forward noising process: q(x_t | x_0)
    2) The reverse denoising process: p(x_{t-1} | x_t)
    3) Utility for training and sampling, including an adversarial
    ↪   version.
    '''

    def __init__(self, n_steps=1000, beta_schedule='linear'):
        self.n_steps = n_steps
        self.betas = make_beta_schedule(beta_schedule, n_steps)
        self.alphas = 1.0 - self.betas
        self.alpha_cumprod = torch.cumprod(self.alphas, dim=0)
        self.alpha_cumprod_prev = torch.cat([torch.tensor([1.0]),
        ↪   self.alpha_cumprod[:-1]], dim=0)

        # Posterior variance term for p(x_{t-1} | x_t, x_0)
        self.posterior_variance = self.betas * (1.0 -
        ↪   self.alpha_cumprod_prev) / (1.0 - self.alpha_cumprod)

    def q_sample(self, x_start, t, noise=None):
        '''
        Forward diffusion: Adds noise to x_start at step t.
        x_t = sqrt(alpha_cumprod[t]) * x_start + sqrt(1 -
        ↪   alpha_cumprod[t]) * noise
        '''
        if noise is None:
            noise = torch.randn_like(x_start)
```

```python
        sqrt_alpha_cumprod_t =
        ↪  self.alpha_cumprod[t].sqrt().unsqueeze(-1).
        unsqueeze(-1).unsqueeze(-1)
        sqrt_one_minus_alpha_cumprod_t = (1 -
        ↪  self.alpha_cumprod[t]).sqrt().unsqueeze(-1).
        unsqueeze(-1).unsqueeze(-1)
        return sqrt_alpha_cumprod_t * x_start +
        ↪  sqrt_one_minus_alpha_cumprod_t * noise

    def predict_noise(self, model, x_t, t):
        '''
        Use the UNet model to predict the noise added at step t.
        For simplicity, we pass the raw x_t to the model (omitting
        ↪  time embedding).
        '''
        return model(x_t)

    def p_sample(self, model, x_t, t, guidance_scale=1.0):
        '''
        One reverse diffusion step: p(x_{t-1} | x_t).
        The model predicts the noise e_t, and we compute the mean of
        ↪  p(x_{t-1} | x_t, x_0).
        We also demonstrate a "guidance_scale" that scales the
        ↪  predicted noise for more/less variation.
        '''
        betas_t = self.betas[t]
        alpha_t = self.alphas[t]
        alpha_cumprod_t = self.alpha_cumprod[t]
        alpha_cumprod_prev_t = self.alpha_cumprod_prev[t]

        # Model-predicted noise
        e_t = model(x_t) * guidance_scale

        # Reconstruct x_0:
        sqrt_recip_alpha_t = (1.0 / alpha_t).sqrt()
        x_0_hat = (x_t - (1.0 - alpha_t).sqrt() * e_t) *
        ↪  sqrt_recip_alpha_t

        # Coefficients
        coef1 = ((alpha_cumprod_prev_t).sqrt() * betas_t) / (1.0 -
        ↪  alpha_cumprod_t)
        coef2 = ((1.0 - alpha_cumprod_prev_t) * alpha_t.sqrt()) /
        ↪  (1.0 - alpha_cumprod_t)

        mean = coef1 * x_0_hat + coef2 * x_t

        posterior_var = self.posterior_variance[t]
        if t > 0:
            noise = torch.randn_like(x_t)
        else:
            noise = torch.zeros_like(x_t)

        x_prev = mean + noise * posterior_var.sqrt()
```

```
    return x_prev

def p_sample_adversarial(self, model, classifier, x_t, t, y,
↪   step_size=0.1):
    '''
    A reverse diffusion step that also includes a gradient-based
    ↪   adversarial update
    to push the classifier toward misclassification.
    1) Standard p_sample to get x_{t-1}.
    2) Adversarial gradient step to maximize classifier error on
    ↪   x_{t-1}.
    '''
    # 1) Standard diffusion step
    x_prev = self.p_sample(model, x_t, t, guidance_scale=1.0)

    # 2) Adversarial gradient step
    # We want to push x_prev to confuse the classifier about
    ↪   label y.
    x_prev.requires_grad_()
    # The classifier expects normalized data in [-1,1],
    # which we already have, but let's pass x_prev directly.
    outputs = classifier(x_prev)
    # Minimizing cross-entropy => correct classification; we
    ↪   want to maximize it => misclassification
    loss = F.cross_entropy(outputs, y)

    # We do gradient ASCENT on cross-entropy => multiply by -1.
    loss = -loss
    loss.backward()

    with torch.no_grad():
        x_prev = x_prev + step_size * x_prev.grad.sign()
        x_prev = torch.clamp(x_prev, -1.0, 1.0)

    return x_prev.detach()

def p_sample_loop_adversarial(self, model, classifier, shape,
↪   device, y, step_size=0.1):
    '''
    Repeatedly apply p_sample_adversarial to go from x_T ~
    ↪   N(0,I) to x_0,
    creating adversarial examples that confuse the classifier.
    '''
    x_t = torch.randn(shape, device=device)
    for i in reversed(range(self.n_steps)):
        x_t = self.p_sample_adversarial(model, classifier, x_t,
        ↪   i, y, step_size=step_size)
    return x_t

def p_sample_loop(self, model, shape, device,
↪   guidance_scale=1.0):
    '''
```

```
    Repeatedly apply p_sample to go from x_T ~ N(0,I) to x_0
    ↳ (standard generation).
    '''
    x_t = torch.randn(shape, device=device)
    for i in reversed(range(self.n_steps)):
        x_t = self.p_sample(model, x_t, i,
        ↳ guidance_scale=guidance_scale)
    return x_t


# ------------------------------------------------------------------
# 5) Training routines for the diffusion model
# ------------------------------------------------------------------
def train_diffusion_one_epoch(model, diffusion, optimizer,
↳ dataloader, device):
    model.train()
    loss_sum = 0
    for images, _ in dataloader:
        images = images.to(device)

        # Sample a random timestep
        t = torch.randint(0, diffusion.n_steps, (images.size(0),),
        ↳ device=device).long()

        noise = torch.randn_like(images)
        x_t = diffusion.q_sample(images, t, noise=noise)

        # Predict the noise with the model
        noise_pred = diffusion.predict_noise(model, x_t, t)

        loss = F.mse_loss(noise_pred, noise)

        optimizer.zero_grad()
        loss.backward()
        optimizer.step()

        loss_sum += loss.item()
    return loss_sum / len(dataloader)


def evaluate_diffusion(model, diffusion, dataloader, device):
    model.eval()
    loss_sum = 0
    with torch.no_grad():
        for images, _ in dataloader:
            images = images.to(device)
            t = torch.randint(0, diffusion.n_steps,
            ↳ (images.size(0),), device=device).long()
            noise = torch.randn_like(images)
            x_t = diffusion.q_sample(images, t, noise=noise)

            noise_pred = diffusion.predict_noise(model, x_t, t)
            loss = F.mse_loss(noise_pred, noise)
            loss_sum += loss.item()
    return loss_sum / len(dataloader)
```

303

```
# ---------------------------------------------------------------
# 6) Utility: sample images/adversarial examples and save
# ---------------------------------------------------------------
def sample_and_save(model, diffusion, device, epoch,
↪   guidance_scale=1.0):
    model.eval()
    with torch.no_grad():
        sample_batch_size = 16
        generated = diffusion.p_sample_loop(model,
        ↪   (sample_batch_size, 1, 28, 28), device, guidance_scale)
        generated = (generated.clamp(-1.0, 1.0) + 1) * 0.5  # from
        ↪   [-1,1] to [0,1]
        grid = torchvision.utils.make_grid(generated, nrow=4)
        os.makedirs("results", exist_ok=True)
        plt.figure(figsize=(6,6))
        plt.axis("off")
        plt.imshow(grid.permute(1, 2, 0).cpu().numpy())

        ↪   plt.savefig(f"results/epoch_{epoch}_gs_{guidance_scale}.png")
        plt.close()

def sample_adversarial_and_save(model, classifier, diffusion,
↪   device, epoch, step_size=0.1):
    '''
    Generate adversarial samples that target random labels
    to demonstrate misclassification attempts.
    '''
    model.eval()
    classifier.eval()
    with torch.no_grad():
        sample_batch_size = 16
        # Pick random labels to target (untargeted means we want to
        ↪   produce 'any' incorrect label,
        # but we must still pass some reference label. We'll just
        ↪   sample from dataset.)
        # In practice, you can keep the original label or pick a
        ↪   random label to fully mislead.
        random_labels = torch.randint(0, 10, (sample_batch_size,),
        ↪   device=device)

        # Use p_sample_loop_adversarial
        adv_samples = diffusion.p_sample_loop_adversarial(
            model, classifier, (sample_batch_size, 1, 28, 28),
            device, random_labels, step_size=step_size
        )

        adv_samples = (adv_samples.clamp(-1.0, 1.0) + 1) * 0.5
        grid = torchvision.utils.make_grid(adv_samples, nrow=4)
        os.makedirs("results", exist_ok=True)
        plt.figure(figsize=(6,6))
        plt.axis("off")
        plt.imshow(grid.permute(1, 2, 0).cpu().numpy())
```

304

```python
        plt.savefig(f"results/
        adversarial_epoch_{epoch}_step_{step_size}.png")
        plt.close()

# ----------------------------------------------------------------
# 7) Main function: train classifier, train diffusion, generate
# ↪   adversarial examples
# ----------------------------------------------------------------
def main():
    set_seed(42)
    device = torch.device("cuda" if torch.cuda.is_available() else
    ↪   "cpu")

    # MNIST dataset
    transform = transforms.Compose([
        transforms.ToTensor(),
        transforms.Normalize((0.5,), (0.5,))
    ])
    train_dataset = torchvision.datasets.MNIST(root='data',
    ↪   train=True, download=True, transform=transform)
    test_dataset = torchvision.datasets.MNIST(root='data',
    ↪   train=False, download=True, transform=transform)

    train_loader = DataLoader(train_dataset, batch_size=64,
    ↪   shuffle=True)
    test_loader = DataLoader(test_dataset, batch_size=64,
    ↪   shuffle=False)

    # 1) Train or load a classifier
    classifier = ClassifierCNN().to(device)
    clf_optimizer = optim.Adam(classifier.parameters(), lr=1e-3)

    print("Training classifier (1 epoch for demonstration)...")
    train_loss, train_acc = train_classifier(classifier,
    ↪   train_loader, clf_optimizer, device)
    print(f"Classifier train loss: {train_loss:.4f}, train acc:
    ↪   {train_acc:.2f}%")

    val_loss, val_acc = evaluate_classifier(classifier, test_loader,
    ↪   device)
    print(f"Classifier val loss: {val_loss:.4f}, val acc:
    ↪   {val_acc:.2f}%")

    # 2) Prepare diffusion model
    diffusion_model = UNet(in_channels=1, out_channels=1,
    ↪   base_channels=64).to(device)
    diffusion = Diffusion(n_steps=200, beta_schedule='linear')
    diff_optimizer = optim.Adam(diffusion_model.parameters(),
    ↪   lr=1e-4)

    # Minimal training loop for diffusion
    print("Training diffusion model (2 epochs for
    ↪   demonstration)...")
```

```
epochs = 2
for epoch in range(epochs):
    train_loss = train_diffusion_one_epoch(diffusion_model,
    ↪   diffusion, diff_optimizer, train_loader, device)
    val_loss = evaluate_diffusion(diffusion_model, diffusion,
    ↪   test_loader, device)
    print(f"Epoch [{epoch+1}/{epochs}] - Diffusion Train Loss:
    ↪   {train_loss:.4f}, Val Loss: {val_loss:.4f}")

    sample_and_save(diffusion_model, diffusion, device, epoch,
    ↪   guidance_scale=1.0)

# 3) Generate adversarial examples using the diffusion process
print("Generating adversarial examples with diffusion +
↪   classifier gradient...")
sample_adversarial_and_save(diffusion_model, classifier,
↪   diffusion, device, epoch="final", step_size=0.1)

print("Done! Check the 'results' folder for generated images and
↪   adversarial examples.")

if __name__ == "__main__":
    main()
```

Key Implementation Details:

- **Forward Diffusion:** We implement `q_sample` to corrupt each input image with noise, according to a linear schedule of `betas[t]`.

- **Reverse Diffusion (Sampling):** The function `p_sample` removes noise step by step, using the model's predicted noise.

- **Adversarial Steps:** We introduce `p_sample_adversarial` to include a gradient ascent step on the classifier's cross-entropy loss, pushing the generated image to confuse the classifier.

- **UNet Architecture:** The UNet, provided in `UNet`, handles denoising by learning multi-scale features and skip connections.

- **Classifier Integration:** We define a small CNN (`ClassifierCNN`) to test adversarial attacks; the gradient from this classifier is incorporated into the diffusion sampling.

- **Training Pipeline:** The script trains the classifier briefly, then trains the diffusion model, and finally generates adversarial examples by merging both procedures.

Chapter 30

Reflection and Haze Removal in Photographs

This chapter targets clearing reflections from glass surfaces or haze from outdoor scenes. Common use cases include enhancing clarity in camera shots or surveillance footage. Construction relies on training a diffusion model to remove reflection or haze patterns. We gather pairs of hazy/reflected images alongside clean versions (often produced through synthetic augmentation). A forward noise process is applied to the clean images, and a UNet is trained to denoise them, with partial conditioning on the hazy or reflected input. Implementation steps: (1) simulating reflection or haze in a controlled manner, (2) injecting noise in the forward direction on the clean target, (3) concatenating the degraded input into the diffusion network, (4) training the model to reconstruct the clean scene by predicting the noise, and (5) sampling on real images to remove haze or reflections. A novel extension uses a specialized reflection/haze map to guide the diffusion, focusing denoising on problematic regions.

Python Code Snippet

```
import os
import random
import math
```

```python
import torch
import torch.nn as nn
import torch.optim as optim
from torch.utils.data import DataLoader, Dataset
import torchvision
import torchvision.transforms as transforms
import matplotlib.pyplot as plt

# ------------------------------------------------------------------
# 1) Set seed for reproducibility
# ------------------------------------------------------------------
def set_seed(seed=42):
    random.seed(seed)
    torch.manual_seed(seed)
    if torch.cuda.is_available():
        torch.cuda.manual_seed_all(seed)


# ------------------------------------------------------------------
# 2) Data handling: simulate haze/reflection + load clean images
# ------------------------------------------------------------------
class ReflectionHazeDataset(Dataset):
    """
    A demonstration dataset that loads MNIST digits as 'clean'
    ↪  images
    and artificially adds haze-like or reflection-like artifacts
    to create a 'degraded' image.
    """
    def __init__(self, train=True, transform=None):
        super().__init__()
        self.dataset = torchvision.datasets.MNIST(
            root='data',
            train=train,
            download=True,
            transform=transform
        )
        self.transform = transform

    def __len__(self):
        return len(self.dataset)

    def __getitem__(self, idx):
        img, _ = self.dataset[idx]
        # img is the "clean" image (1 x 28 x 28)
        # We'll simulate haze/reflection via an additive or overlay
        ↪  approach
        degraded = self.simulate_reflection_haze(img)
        return degraded, img

    def simulate_reflection_haze(self, clean_img):
        """
        Simple synthetic approach: apply random blur or lighten
        ↪  certain areas.
```

```
      This yields a 'degraded' version that mimics haze or
      ↪  reflection.
      """
      # Convert to a simple tensor we can manipulate
      # clean_img is already a tensor in [0,1], or [-1,1] if
      ↪  normalized
      # We'll do something subtle, like a random alpha blend of a
      ↪  blurred version
      # or a bright overlay to mimic reflection.
      degraded = clean_img.clone()

      # Randomly decide haze vs. reflection
      mode = random.choice(["haze", "reflection"])

      if mode == "haze":
          # Add a small constant or blur to lighten
          haze_amount = 0.2
          degraded = torch.clamp(degraded + haze_amount, 0, 1)
      else:
          # Reflection; overlay bright lines or shapes
          # We'll draw a random white stripe
          x_start = random.randint(0, degraded.shape[1] - 1)
          thickness = random.randint(1, 3)
          degraded[:, x_start:x_start+thickness] = 1.0

      return degraded

# ------------------------------------------------------------------
# 3) U-Net implementation for partial conditioning (degraded + x_t
↪  as input)
# ------------------------------------------------------------------
class DoubleConv(nn.Module):
    """
    A helper module that performs two consecutive conv+ReLU
    ↪  operations.
    """
    def __init__(self, in_channels, out_channels):
        super(DoubleConv, self).__init__()
        self.net = nn.Sequential(
            nn.Conv2d(in_channels, out_channels, kernel_size=3,
            ↪  padding=1),
            nn.ReLU(inplace=True),
            nn.Conv2d(out_channels, out_channels, kernel_size=3,
            ↪  padding=1),
            nn.ReLU(inplace=True)
        )

    def forward(self, x):
        return self.net(x)

class UNet(nn.Module):
    """
    A simplified U-Net architecture.
```

```
Here, the input has 2 channels:
- Channel 0: x_t (noisy version of the clean image)
- Channel 1: degraded image (hazy/reflected)
Output has 1 channel: predicted noise.
"""
def __init__(self, in_channels=2, out_channels=1,
↪   base_channels=64):
    super(UNet, self).__init__()

    # Encoder (downsampling)
    self.down1 = DoubleConv(in_channels, base_channels)
    self.pool1 = nn.MaxPool2d(kernel_size=2)
    self.down2 = DoubleConv(base_channels, base_channels*2)
    self.pool2 = nn.MaxPool2d(kernel_size=2)

    self.down3 = DoubleConv(base_channels*2, base_channels*4)
    self.pool3 = nn.MaxPool2d(kernel_size=2)

    # Bottleneck
    self.bottleneck = DoubleConv(base_channels*4,
↪   base_channels*8)

    # Decoder (upsampling)
    self.up1 = nn.ConvTranspose2d(base_channels*8,
↪   base_channels*4, kernel_size=2, stride=2)
    self.conv_up1 = DoubleConv(base_channels*8, base_channels*4)

    self.up2 = nn.ConvTranspose2d(base_channels*4,
↪   base_channels*2, kernel_size=2, stride=2)
    self.conv_up2 = DoubleConv(base_channels*4, base_channels*2)

    self.up3 = nn.ConvTranspose2d(base_channels*2,
↪   base_channels, kernel_size=2, stride=2)
    self.conv_up3 = DoubleConv(base_channels*2, base_channels)

    # Final output
    self.final_conv = nn.Conv2d(base_channels, out_channels,
↪   kernel_size=1)

def forward(self, x):
    """
    x has shape [B, 2, H, W], combining x_t and degraded_image.
    """
    # Downsample
    d1 = self.down1(x)
    p1 = self.pool1(d1)

    d2 = self.down2(p1)
    p2 = self.pool2(d2)

    d3 = self.down3(p2)
    p3 = self.pool3(d3)
```

```
        # Bottleneck
        b = self.bottleneck(p3)

        # Upsample
        up1 = self.up1(b)
        cat1 = torch.cat([up1, d3], dim=1)
        up1c = self.conv_up1(cat1)

        up2 = self.up2(up1c)
        cat2 = torch.cat([up2, d2], dim=1)
        up2c = self.conv_up2(cat2)

        up3 = self.up3(up2c)
        cat3 = torch.cat([up3, d1], dim=1)
        up3c = self.conv_up3(cat3)

        out = self.final_conv(up3c)
        return out


# -------------------------------------------------------------------
# 4) Diffusion schedule (beta) and forward diffusion logic
# -------------------------------------------------------------------
def make_beta_schedule(schedule_name, n_timestep, start=1e-4,
↪   end=2e-2):
    """
    Creates a beta schedule for the diffusion process.
    We use a simple linear schedule here.
    """
    if schedule_name == "linear":
        return torch.linspace(start, end, n_timestep)
    else:
        raise NotImplementedError("Currently only 'linear' schedule
        ↪   is supported.")


class Diffusion:
    """
    Encapsulates the forward and reverse diffusion processes.
    1) Forward: q(x_t | x_0)
    2) Reverse: p(x_{t-1} | x_t), using a UNet to predict noise.
    """
    def __init__(self, n_steps=200, beta_schedule='linear'):
        self.n_steps = n_steps
        self.betas = make_beta_schedule(beta_schedule, n_steps)   #
        ↪   shape [n_steps]
        self.alphas = 1.0 - self.betas
        self.alpha_cumprod = torch.cumprod(self.alphas, dim=0)   #
        ↪   product of alphas up to step t
        self.alpha_cumprod_prev = torch.cat([torch.tensor([1.0]),
        ↪   self.alpha_cumprod[:-1]], dim=0)

        # Posterior variance for q(x_{t-1} | x_t, x_0)
        self.posterior_variance = self.betas * (1.0 -
        ↪   self.alpha_cumprod_prev) / (1.0 - self.alpha_cumprod)
```

312

```python
def q_sample(self, x_start, t, noise=None):
    """
    Forward diffusion: x_t = sqrt(\alpha_cumprod_t)*x_0 +
    ↪    sqrt(1-\alpha_cumprod_t)*noise
    """
    if noise is None:
        noise = torch.randn_like(x_start)

    sqrt_alpha = self.alpha_cumprod[t].sqrt().view(-1,1,1,1)
    sqrt_one_minus_alpha = (1.0 -
    ↪    self.alpha_cumprod[t]).sqrt().view(-1,1,1,1)

    return sqrt_alpha * x_start + sqrt_one_minus_alpha * noise

def predict_noise(self, model, x_t, degrade_img, t):
    """
    Use the UNet model to predict noise. The input to the model
    ↪    is [x_t, degrade_img].
    """
    # Concat along channel dimension
    model_input = torch.cat([x_t, degrade_img], dim=1)    # shape
    ↪    [B, 2, H, W]
    e_t = model(model_input)
    return e_t

def p_sample(self, model, x_t, degrade_img, t):
    """
    One reverse diffusion step using the model's noise
    ↪    prediction.
    p(x_{t-1} | x_t).
    """
    betas_t = self.betas[t]
    alpha_t = self.alphas[t]
    alpha_cumprod_t = self.alpha_cumprod[t]
    alpha_cumprod_prev_t = self.alpha_cumprod_prev[t]

    # Predict the noise
    e_t = self.predict_noise(model, x_t, degrade_img, t)

    # Estimate x_0 from x_t and e_t
    sqrt_recip_alpha_t = (1.0 / alpha_t).sqrt()
    x_0_hat = (x_t - (1.0 - alpha_t).sqrt() * e_t) *
    ↪    sqrt_recip_alpha_t

    # Calculate the mean of the posterior q(x_{t-1} | x_t,
    ↪    x_0_hat)
    coef1 = (alpha_cumprod_prev_t.sqrt() * betas_t) / (1.0 -
    ↪    alpha_cumprod_t)
    coef2 = ((1.0 - alpha_cumprod_prev_t) * alpha_t.sqrt()) /
    ↪    (1.0 - alpha_cumprod_t)
    mean = coef1 * x_0_hat + coef2 * x_t
```

```python
        # Sample x_{t-1}
        if t > 0:
            var = self.posterior_variance[t]
            noise = torch.randn_like(x_t)
            x_prev = mean + noise * var.sqrt()
        else:
            # At t=0, no noise is added
            x_prev = mean

        return x_prev

    def p_sample_loop(self, model, degrade_img, shape, device):
        """
        Reverse diffusion: sample from x_T ~ N(0,I) back to x_0.
        degrade_img is concatenated for each step as conditioning.
        """
        x_t = torch.randn(shape, device=device)
        for i in reversed(range(self.n_steps)):
            x_t = self.p_sample(model, x_t, degrade_img, i)
        return x_t

# --------------------------------------------------------------------
# 5) Training and evaluation routines
# --------------------------------------------------------------------
def train_one_epoch(model, diffusion, optimizer, dataloader,
↪   device):
    model.train()
    total_loss = 0
    for degraded, clean in dataloader:
        degraded = degraded.to(device)
        clean = clean.to(device)
        batch_size = clean.shape[0]

        # Randomly pick a step t for each image
        t = torch.randint(0, diffusion.n_steps, (batch_size,),
        ↪   device=device).long()

        # Sample noise
        noise = torch.randn_like(clean)

        # Forward diffuse the clean image to get x_t
        x_t = diffusion.q_sample(clean, t, noise=noise)

        # Predict noise
        noise_pred = diffusion.predict_noise(model, x_t, degraded,
        ↪   t)

        # L2 loss
        loss = nn.functional.mse_loss(noise_pred, noise)

        optimizer.zero_grad()
        loss.backward()
        optimizer.step()
```

314

```python
            total_loss += loss.item()

    return total_loss / len(dataloader)

def evaluate_model(model, diffusion, dataloader, device):
    model.eval()
    total_loss = 0
    with torch.no_grad():
        for degraded, clean in dataloader:
            degraded = degraded.to(device)
            clean = clean.to(device)
            batch_size = clean.shape[0]

            t = torch.randint(0, diffusion.n_steps, (batch_size,),
            ↪   device=device).long()
            noise = torch.randn_like(clean)
            x_t = diffusion.q_sample(clean, t, noise)

            noise_pred = diffusion.predict_noise(model, x_t,
            ↪   degraded, t)
            loss = nn.functional.mse_loss(noise_pred, noise)
            total_loss += loss.item()
    return total_loss / len(dataloader)

def sample_and_save(model, diffusion, degrade_img, device, epoch,
↪   idx):
    """
    Use the trained model to remove haze/reflection from degrade_img
    ↪   by
    sampling x_0 from noise while conditioning on degrade_img.
    Then plot the final result vs. degrade_img for comparison.
    """
    model.eval()
    shape = degrade_img.shape  # [B, 1, H, W]
    with torch.no_grad():
        # We'll run the reverse diffusion process
        x_0_est = diffusion.p_sample_loop(model, degrade_img, shape,
        ↪   device)
        # x_0_est in [-some, +some], we clamp to [-1,1] for viewing
        x_0_est = x_0_est.clamp(-1.0, 1.0)

        # Convert them to [0,1]
        x_0_est = (x_0_est + 1) * 0.5
        degrade_vis = (degrade_img + 1) * 0.5

        # Save the result
        grid_original = torchvision.utils.make_grid(degrade_vis,
        ↪   nrow=4)
        grid_restored = torchvision.utils.make_grid(x_0_est, nrow=4)
        os.makedirs("results_haze", exist_ok=True)

        fig, axs = plt.subplots(1, 2, figsize=(6,3))
```

315

```python
    axs[0].imshow(grid_original.permute(1,2,0).cpu().numpy(),
    ↪    cmap='gray')
    axs[0].set_title("Degraded Input")
    axs[0].axis("off")

    axs[1].imshow(grid_restored.permute(1,2,0).cpu().numpy(),
    ↪    cmap='gray')
    axs[1].set_title("Restored Output")
    axs[1].axis("off")

    plt.tight_layout()
    plt.savefig(f"results_haze/epoch_{epoch}_sample_{idx}.png")
    plt.close()

# -----------------------------------------------------------------
# 6) Main script for training and inference
# -----------------------------------------------------------------
def main():
    set_seed(42)
    device = torch.device("cuda" if torch.cuda.is_available() else
    ↪    "cpu")

    # Transforms: We rescale MNIST from [0,1] to [-1,1]
    transform = transforms.Compose([
        transforms.ToTensor(),
        transforms.Normalize((0.5,), (0.5,))
    ])

    # Datasets
    train_data = ReflectionHazeDataset(train=True,
    ↪    transform=transform)
    test_data = ReflectionHazeDataset(train=False,
    ↪    transform=transform)

    # Loaders
    train_loader = DataLoader(train_data, batch_size=64,
    ↪    shuffle=True)
    test_loader = DataLoader(test_data, batch_size=64,
    ↪    shuffle=False)

    # Model, Diffusion, Optimizer
    model = UNet(in_channels=2, out_channels=1,
    ↪    base_channels=64).to(device)
    diffusion = Diffusion(n_steps=200, beta_schedule='linear')
    optimizer = optim.Adam(model.parameters(), lr=1e-4)

    # Training
    epochs = 5
    for epoch in range(epochs):
        train_loss = train_one_epoch(model, diffusion, optimizer,
        ↪    train_loader, device)
        val_loss = evaluate_model(model, diffusion, test_loader,
        ↪    device)
```

```
    print(f"Epoch [{epoch+1}/{epochs}] - Train Loss:
    ↪  {train_loss:.4f}, Val Loss: {val_loss:.4f}")

    # Sample a few images from the test set to visualize
    ↪   reflection/haze removal
    sample_count = 2
    test_iter = iter(test_loader)
    with torch.no_grad():
        for i in range(sample_count):
            degraded_batch, _ = next(test_iter)
            degraded_batch = degraded_batch.to(device)
            sample_and_save(model, diffusion, degraded_batch,
            ↪   device, epoch, i)

    print("Training complete! Check the 'results_haze' folder for
    ↪  sample outputs.")

if __name__ == "__main__":
    main()
```

Key Implementation Details:

- **Dataset Construction:** The `ReflectionHazeDataset` simulates reflection or haze by applying simple random overlays
  or brightness changes to MNIST digits, creating a paired (degraded, clean) sample. Real-world applications would substitute actual paired data of hazy/reflected images and their
  ground-truth clean equivalents.

- **Forward Diffusion (`q_sample`):** We corrupt the clean image by adding Gaussian noise according to a linear `beta`
  schedule. At each time step t, the fraction of noise is dictated by `betas[t]` and cumulative products of `alphas`.

- **Partial Conditioning:** The UNet input has two channels:
  x_t (the noisy version of the clean image) concatenated with
  the degraded (hazy/reflected) image. By predicting noise
  while having direct access to the degraded image, the network learns to restore the underlying clean scene.

- **Reverse Diffusion (`p_sample`):** The network is used to
  estimate the added noise at each step. We compute the posterior mean of x_t-1, which, combined with the posterior
  variance, gives a new sample x_t-1.

- **Training Objective:** The loss is an `MSE` between the predicted noise and the true noise used in the forward diffusion. Minimizing this encourages the model to accurately invert the degradation and denoising processes.

- **Sampling for Reflection/Haze Removal:** In `sample_and_save`, we begin from random noise and iteratively denoise while conditioning on the degraded input, yielding a restored image. This demonstrates how the partial conditioning influences the generative process to remove reflection or haze artifacts.

Chapter 31

Neural Rendering and View Synthesis

Diffusion can be employed to render new views of a scene from limited input images. Common applications include VR and telepresence, where novel viewing angles are synthesized. The approach typically learns a scene representation—like a voxel-based or neural radiance field—then applies diffusion across spatial or ray samples. Construction involves:

- collecting multi-view images of a scene,

- representing the scene with radiance fields or layered depth images,

- defining a forward noise schedule that corrupts these representations,

- training a UNet to recover the unobserved view from partial or noisy samples,

- and sampling new viewpoints by reversing the diffusion process.

An innovative technique is to introduce a geometry-aware conditioning scheme, where predicted depth or normal maps anchor the diffusion, ensuring consistent 3D structure for each synthetic viewpoint.

Python Code Snippet

```python
import os
import random
import math
import numpy as np
import torch
import torch.nn as nn
import torch.optim as optim
from torch.utils.data import Dataset, DataLoader
import torchvision.transforms as transforms
import matplotlib.pyplot as plt

#
↪ -------------------------------------------------------------------
# 1) Setting up a synthetic multi-view rendering dataset for
↪ demonstration
#
↪ -------------------------------------------------------------------
class SyntheticMultiViewDataset(Dataset):
    """
    A mock dataset that simulates multi-view images of a scene
    along with approximate depth or geometry maps.
    For illustration, we generate random noise images and depth
    ↪ maps.
    In practice, you'd load real multi-view data plus depth/normal
    ↪ maps.
    """
    def __init__(self, num_samples=1000, image_size=64):
        super().__init__()
        self.num_samples = num_samples
        self.image_size = image_size
        self.transform = transforms.Compose([
            transforms.ToTensor(),
            transforms.Normalize((0.5,), (0.5,))
        ])

    def __len__(self):
        return self.num_samples

    def __getitem__(self, idx):
        # Generate a random "view" image (RGB) plus a "depth map"
        ↪ (1-channel)
        view_image = np.random.uniform(0, 1, (self.image_size,
        ↪ self.image_size, 3)).astype("float32")
        depth_image = np.random.uniform(0, 1, (self.image_size,
        ↪ self.image_size, 1)).astype("float32")

        # Convert to tensor and normalize
        view_image = self.transform(view_image)
        # For depth, replicate the transform except it's already
        ↪ single channel
```

320

```python
        depth_image = torch.from_numpy(depth_image).permute(2, 0, 1)
        ↪  # shape: (1,H,W)
        depth_image = (depth_image - 0.5) / 0.5  # roughly mimic the
        ↪  normalization

        return view_image, depth_image


#
↪  --------------------------------------------------------------------
# 2) Define a U-Net module that supports conditioning on geometry
↪  maps
#
↪  --------------------------------------------------------------------
class DoubleConv(nn.Module):
    """
    A two-convolution convenience block with ReLU activations.
    """

    def __init__(self, in_channels, out_channels):
        super(DoubleConv, self).__init__()
        self.conv = nn.Sequential(
            nn.Conv2d(in_channels, out_channels, 3, padding=1),
            nn.ReLU(inplace=True),
            nn.Conv2d(out_channels, out_channels, 3, padding=1),
            nn.ReLU(inplace=True)
        )

    def forward(self, x):
        return self.conv(x)


class RendererUNet(nn.Module):
    """
    A simplified U-Net that takes an (RGB + Depth) concatenated
    ↪  input,
    then predicts the noise (corruption) for the 'view' portion.

    Input channels = 4 (3 for RGB + 1 for Depth).
    Output channels = 3 (for RGB noise prediction).
    """

    def __init__(self, base_channels=64):
        super(RendererUNet, self).__init__()

        # Down-sampling (encoder)
        self.down1 = DoubleConv(4, base_channels)          # 4-ch in ->
        ↪  base
        self.down2 = DoubleConv(base_channels, base_channels*2)
        self.down3 = DoubleConv(base_channels*2, base_channels*4)

        self.pool = nn.MaxPool2d(2)

        # Bottleneck
        self.bottleneck = DoubleConv(base_channels*4,
        ↪  base_channels*8)
```

```python
        # Up-sampling (decoder)
        self.up1 = nn.ConvTranspose2d(base_channels*8,
        ↪  base_channels*4, kernel_size=2, stride=2)
        self.conv_up1 = DoubleConv(base_channels*8, base_channels*4)

        self.up2 = nn.ConvTranspose2d(base_channels*4,
        ↪  base_channels*2, kernel_size=2, stride=2)
        self.conv_up2 = DoubleConv(base_channels*4, base_channels*2)

        self.up3 = nn.ConvTranspose2d(base_channels*2,
        ↪  base_channels, kernel_size=2, stride=2)
        self.conv_up3 = DoubleConv(base_channels*2, base_channels)

        # Final output for the predicted noise in RGB: 3 channels
        self.final_conv = nn.Conv2d(base_channels, 3, kernel_size=1)

    def forward(self, x):
        """
        x has shape (B,4,H,W):
            x[:,:,0:3] -> the currently rendered or partial/noisy RGB
            x[:,:,3:4] -> the geometry (depth) map
        We return a (B,3,H,W) output that predicts the noise for the
        ↪  RGB channels.
        """
        # Encoder
        x1 = self.down1(x)   # shape: (B, base, H, W)
        x2 = self.pool(x1)
        x2 = self.down2(x2)

        x3 = self.pool(x2)
        x3 = self.down3(x3)

        x4 = self.pool(x3)

        # Bottleneck
        b = self.bottleneck(x4)

        # Decoder
        x = self.up1(b)
        x = torch.cat([x, x3], dim=1)
        x = self.conv_up1(x)

        x = self.up2(x)
        x = torch.cat([x, x2], dim=1)
        x = self.conv_up2(x)

        x = self.up3(x)
        x = torch.cat([x, x1], dim=1)
        x = self.conv_up3(x)

        # Final
        out = self.final_conv(x)
        return out
```

```
#
↪   ------------------------------------------------------------------------
# 3) Define the diffusion schedule and forward process
#
↪   ------------------------------------------------------------------------
def make_beta_schedule(schedule_name, n_timestep, start=1e-4,
↪   end=2e-2):
    """
    Constructs a beta schedule for the diffusion process.
    We'll implement a linear schedule for demonstration.
    """
    if schedule_name == "linear":
        return torch.linspace(start, end, n_timestep)
    else:
        raise NotImplementedError("Only 'linear' schedule is
        ↪   supported in this snippet.")


class ViewSynthesisDiffusion:
    """
    Handles the forward (noising) and reverse (denoising) steps for
    ↪   neural rendering.
    We only diffuse the RGB portion. Depth is used as
    ↪   geometry/conditioning input.
    """
    def __init__(self, n_steps=1000, beta_schedule='linear'):
        self.n_steps = n_steps
        self.betas = make_beta_schedule(beta_schedule, n_steps)
        self.alphas = 1.0 - self.betas
        self.alpha_cumprod = torch.cumprod(self.alphas, dim=0)
        self.alpha_cumprod_prev = torch.cat(
            [torch.tensor([1.0]), self.alpha_cumprod[:-1]], dim=0
        )
        self.posterior_variance = self.betas * (1.0 -
        ↪   self.alpha_cumprod_prev) / (1.0 - self.alpha_cumprod)

    def q_sample(self, x_start_rgb, t, noise=None):
        """
        Forward diffusion of RGB channels at step t.
        x_t = sqrt(alpha_cumprod[t]) * x_start_rgb + sqrt(1 -
        ↪   alpha_cumprod[t]) * noise
        """
        if noise is None:
            noise = torch.randn_like(x_start_rgb)
        sqrt_alpha_cumprod_t =
        ↪   self.alpha_cumprod[t].sqrt().view(-1,1,1,1)
        sqrt_one_minus_alpha_cumprod_t = (1 -
        ↪   self.alpha_cumprod[t]).sqrt().view(-1,1,1,1)
        return sqrt_alpha_cumprod_t * x_start_rgb +
        ↪   sqrt_one_minus_alpha_cumprod_t * noise

    def predict_noise(self, model, x_t_concat, t):
        """
```

```python
    Use the U-Net to predict noise. We pass in the concatenation
    ↪  of:
    - current noisy RGB (3 channels)
    - geometry/depth (1 channel)
    """
    return model(x_t_concat)

def p_sample(self, model, x_t_rgb, depth, t,
↪  guidance_scale=1.0):
    """
    Performs a single reverse diffusion step for the RGB
    ↪  portion.
    We'll incorporate 'depth' as conditioning in the input to
    ↪  the model.
    """
    betas_t = self.betas[t]
    alpha_t = self.alphas[t]
    alpha_cumprod_t = self.alpha_cumprod[t]
    alpha_cumprod_prev_t = self.alpha_cumprod_prev[t]

    # Prepare input to model: concat noisy RGB + depth
    x_t_concat = torch.cat([x_t_rgb, depth], dim=1)

    # The model predicts the noise in the RGB channels
    e_t = model(x_t_concat) * guidance_scale

    sqrt_recip_alpha_t = (1.0 / alpha_t).sqrt()
    x_0_hat = (x_t_rgb - (1.0 - alpha_t).sqrt() * e_t) *
    ↪  sqrt_recip_alpha_t

    # Posterior mean of q(x_{t-1} | x_t, x_0)
    coef1 = ((alpha_cumprod_prev_t).sqrt() * betas_t) / (1.0 -
    ↪  alpha_cumprod_t)
    coef2 = ((1.0 - alpha_cumprod_prev_t) * alpha_t.sqrt()) /
    ↪  (1.0 - alpha_cumprod_t)

    mean = coef1 * x_0_hat + coef2 * x_t_rgb

    # Sample from posterior distribution
    posterior_var = self.posterior_variance[t]
    if t > 0:
        noise = torch.randn_like(x_t_rgb)
    else:
        noise = torch.zeros_like(x_t_rgb)

    x_prev = mean + noise * posterior_var.sqrt()
    return x_prev

def p_sample_loop(self, model, depth, shape, device,
↪  guidance_scale=1.0):
    """
    Iterates backward from x_T to x_0, given random initial RGB
    ↪  noise.
```

```
    'depth' is conditioning, shape is (B,3,H,W) for the RGB
    ↪ portion.
    """
    b = shape[0]
    x_t = torch.randn(shape, device=device)
    for i in reversed(range(self.n_steps)):
        t_tensor = torch.tensor([i]*b, device=device).long()
        x_t = self.p_sample(model, x_t, depth, t_tensor,
        ↪ guidance_scale)
    return x_t

#
↪ -----------------------------------------------------------------------
# 4) Training and evaluation routines
#
↪ -----------------------------------------------------------------------
def train_one_epoch(model, diffusion, optimizer, dataloader,
↪ device):
    """
    For each batch, we randomly pick a diffusion time step 't',
    apply forward diffusion on the RGB portion, and predict the
    ↪ noise.
    """
    model.train()
    total_loss = 0
    for (view_image, depth_image) in dataloader:
        # view_image: (B, 3, H, W), depth_image: (B, 1, H, W)
        view_image, depth_image = view_image.to(device),
        ↪ depth_image.to(device)

        # Pick random diffusion step for each sample
        b = view_image.size(0)
        t = torch.randint(0, diffusion.n_steps, (b,),
        ↪ device=device).long()

        noise = torch.randn_like(view_image)
        # Forward diffuse the RGB portion
        x_t_rgb = diffusion.q_sample(view_image, t, noise=noise)

        # Concat the noisy RGB with depth for model input
        x_t_concat = torch.cat([x_t_rgb, depth_image], dim=1)   #
        ↪ shape: (B,4,H,W)

        # Predict the noise
        noise_pred = diffusion.predict_noise(model, x_t_concat, t)

        # L2 loss
        loss = nn.functional.mse_loss(noise_pred, noise)

        optimizer.zero_grad()
        loss.backward()
        optimizer.step()
```

325

```python
            total_loss += loss.item()

    return total_loss / len(dataloader)

def evaluate_model(model, diffusion, dataloader, device):
    """
    Evaluate model L2 error on a test set.
    """
    model.eval()
    total_loss = 0
    with torch.no_grad():
        for (view_image, depth_image) in dataloader:
            view_image, depth_image = view_image.to(device),
            ↪    depth_image.to(device)
            b = view_image.size(0)
            t = torch.randint(0, diffusion.n_steps, (b,),
            ↪    device=device).long()
            noise = torch.randn_like(view_image)

            x_t_rgb = diffusion.q_sample(view_image, t, noise=noise)
            x_t_concat = torch.cat([x_t_rgb, depth_image], dim=1)
            noise_pred = diffusion.predict_noise(model, x_t_concat,
            ↪    t)
            loss = nn.functional.mse_loss(noise_pred, noise)
            total_loss += loss.item()
    return total_loss / len(dataloader)

def sample_new_views(model, diffusion, depth_image, device,
↪    guidance_scale=1.0, filename_prefix="sample"):
    """
    Generate new viewpoints from noise, conditioned on a single
    ↪    depth map.
    We'll produce and save a small batch for visualization.
    """
    model.eval()
    with torch.no_grad():
        depth_image = depth_image.to(device)
        # shape for depth_image is (B,1,H,W)
        b, _, h, w = depth_image.shape

        # We sample random noise for the RGB portion
        # Then run p_sample_loop to get a synthesized view
        synthesized_rgb = diffusion.p_sample_loop(
            model,
            depth_image,
            (b, 3, h, w),
            device,
            guidance_scale=guidance_scale
        )

        # Map from [-1,1] to [0,1] for visualization
        synthesized_rgb = (synthesized_rgb.clamp(-1,1) + 1)*0.5
```

```python
        synthesized_rgb =
↪        synthesized_rgb.cpu().permute(0,2,3,1).numpy()

        # Save each image with matplotlib
        os.makedirs("results_views", exist_ok=True)
        for idx in range(b):
            img = synthesized_rgb[idx]
            plt.figure()
            plt.imshow(img)
            plt.axis("off")
            plt.savefig(f"results_views/
            {filename_prefix}_gs{guidance_scale}_idx{idx}.png")
            plt.close()


#
↪ ---------------------------------------------------------------------
# 5) Main function to orchestrate the training and synthesis
#
↪ ---------------------------------------------------------------------
def main():
    # Fix random seeds for reproducibility
    seed = 42
    random.seed(seed)
    np.random.seed(seed)
    torch.manual_seed(seed)
    if torch.cuda.is_available():
        torch.cuda.manual_seed_all(seed)

    device = torch.device("cuda" if torch.cuda.is_available() else
↪    "cpu")

    # Prepare synthetic multi-view dataset
    train_dataset = SyntheticMultiViewDataset(num_samples=500,
↪    image_size=64)
    test_dataset = SyntheticMultiViewDataset(num_samples=100,
↪    image_size=64)

    train_loader = DataLoader(train_dataset, batch_size=8,
↪    shuffle=True)
    test_loader = DataLoader(test_dataset, batch_size=8,
↪    shuffle=False)

    # Create model: 4 in-channels (3 for RGB + 1 for geometry), 3
↪    out-channels for noise
    model = RendererUNet(base_channels=64).to(device)

    # Create diffusion object with fewer steps here for quicker
↪    demonstration
    diffusion = ViewSynthesisDiffusion(n_steps=50,
↪    beta_schedule='linear')

    optimizer = optim.Adam(model.parameters(), lr=1e-4)
```

327

```
epochs = 5
for epoch in range(epochs):
    train_loss = train_one_epoch(model, diffusion, optimizer,
    ↪ train_loader, device)
    val_loss = evaluate_model(model, diffusion, test_loader,
    ↪ device)
    print(f"Epoch [{epoch+1}/{epochs}] - Train Loss:
    ↪ {train_loss:.4f}, Val Loss: {val_loss:.4f}")

    # Let's sample from the first batch of test data to see new
    ↪ views
    (test_view, test_depth) = next(iter(test_loader))

    # We'll only use the first item in that batch for
    ↪ demonstration
    test_view_0 = test_view[0:1]
    test_depth_0 = test_depth[0:1]

    # Generate new synthesized view at default guidance scale
    sample_new_views(
        model,
        diffusion,
        test_depth_0,
        device,
        guidance_scale=1.0,
        filename_prefix=f"epoch_{epoch}"
    )

    print("Training and view synthesis complete. Check
    ↪ 'results_views' folder for generated samples.")

if __name__ == "__main__":
    main()
```

Key Implementation Details:

- **Forward Diffusion:** We implement `q_sample` to corrupt only the RGB portion at each time step, while the depth/geometry map remains uncorrupted and is used as a conditioning input.

- **Reverse Diffusion (Sampling):** The function `p_sample_loop` applies the network step by step from random noise to a recovered (or newly synthesized) RGB view. We concatenate depth to the noisy RGB as an input to the U-Net.

- **UNet Architecture:** The `RendererUNet` receives four input channels (3 for RGB and 1 for depth) and outputs a 3-

channel noise prediction for the RGB portion. This approach is flexible enough to incorporate normal or other geometry maps as well.

- **Training Objective:** We directly predict and compare the added noise via a mean-squared error (MSE) loss between the network's output and the actual Gaussian noise.

- **Guidance Scale:** A factor to scale the model's predicted noise, providing a mechanism to balance fidelity and diversity in synthesized views.

- **Dataset Simulation:** The `SyntheticMultiViewDataset` generates random 2D images and depth maps for illustration. In a real application, you would load authentic multi-view image data along with corresponding geometry.

Chapter 32

Generative Design for Mechanical and Architectural Parts

This chapter addresses the creation of structural designs for mechanical parts or architectural layouts. Common use cases involve optimizing shapes for weight, strength, or aesthetic constraints. We treat CAD models, floor plans, or structural meshes as data. The forward process adds noise to these representations, while a diffusion network removes it, learning valid design patterns. Implementation details: (1) collecting design examples with known structural properties, (2) discretizing them into grids or mesh elements, (3) training a `UNet` to denoise from partial or random shape setups, (4) sampling new designs that respect constraints like building codes or stress limits, and (5) potentially refining with a structural solver that provides stress feedback. The innovative approach is an iterative design loop, where each diffusion-generated shape is re-evaluated for mechanical performance and used to guide the next generation.

Python Code Snippet

```python
import os
import random
import math
import torch
```

```python
import torch.nn as nn
import numpy as np
import matplotlib.pyplot as plt
from torch.utils.data import Dataset, DataLoader
import torch.optim as optim


# ----------------------------------------------------------------
# 1) Set random seed for reproducibility
# ----------------------------------------------------------------
def set_seed(seed=42):
    random.seed(seed)
    np.random.seed(seed)
    torch.manual_seed(seed)
    if torch.cuda.is_available():
        torch.cuda.manual_seed_all(seed)


# ----------------------------------------------------------------
# 2) Create a synthetic dataset for 2D structural design
# ----------------------------------------------------------------
class ToyStructuralDataset(Dataset):
    '''
    Generates random 2D "structural" shapes (e.g., squares, circles,
    ↪  triangles)
    on a 64x64 grid. Each sample can be viewed as a simplistic
    ↪  mechanical part.
    '''

    def __init__(self, num_samples=1000, image_size=64):
        super().__init__()
        self.num_samples = num_samples
        self.image_size = image_size
        self.samples = []
        self._generate_data()

    def _generate_data(self):
        for _ in range(self.num_samples):
            # Create a blank image using numpy
            canvas = np.zeros((self.image_size, self.image_size),
            ↪  dtype=np.float32)

            # Randomly pick a shape
            shape_type =
            ↪  random.choice(['square','circle','triangle'])

            # Random position
            cx = random.randint(self.image_size//4,
            ↪  3*self.image_size//4)
            cy = random.randint(self.image_size//4,
            ↪  3*self.image_size//4)

            # Random size
            size = random.randint(self.image_size//8,
            ↪  self.image_size//4)
```

331

```python
            if shape_type == 'square':
                x1 = max(cx - size, 0)
                x2 = min(cx + size, self.image_size)
                y1 = max(cy - size, 0)
                y2 = min(cy + size, self.image_size)
                canvas[y1:y2, x1:x2] = 1.0

            elif shape_type == 'circle':
                for y in range(self.image_size):
                    for x in range(self.image_size):
                        if (x - cx)**2 + (y - cy)**2 <= size**2:
                            canvas[y, x] = 1.0

            else:  # triangle
                # Define a simple upright triangle
                for y in range(self.image_size):
                    for x in range(self.image_size):
                        # Check if within triangle bounds
                        if y <= cy and y >= cy - size:
                            # linear interpolation of left and right
                            ↪ edges
                            left_x = int(cx - (size*(cy-y)/size))
                            right_x = int(cx + (size*(cy-y)/size))
                            if x >= left_x and x <= right_x:
                                canvas[y, x] = 1.0

            self.samples.append(canvas)

    def __len__(self):
        return self.num_samples

    def __getitem__(self, idx):
        img = self.samples[idx]
        # Expand channel: shape becomes (1, H, W)
        img = torch.from_numpy(img).unsqueeze(0)
        # We can scale to [-1,1] for convenience
        img = (img * 2.0) - 1.0
        return img, 0  # no label needed, we do unconditional
        ↪ generation

# ------------------------------------------------------------
# 3) Define a simple U-Net for 2D structural denoising
# ------------------------------------------------------------
class DoubleConv(nn.Module):
    '''
    A helper module that performs two Conv->ReLU operations in
    ↪ succession.
    '''
    def __init__(self, in_channels, out_channels):
        super(DoubleConv, self).__init__()
        self.conv = nn.Sequential(
            nn.Conv2d(in_channels, out_channels, 3, padding=1),
            nn.ReLU(inplace=True),
```

332

```python
            nn.Conv2d(out_channels, out_channels, 3, padding=1),
            nn.ReLU(inplace=True)
        )

    def forward(self, x):
        return self.conv(x)

class UNet(nn.Module):
    '''
    A simplified U-Net architecture for 2D shape generation.
    '''
    def __init__(self, in_channels=1, out_channels=1,
    ↪  base_channels=64):
        super(UNet, self).__init__()

        # Down-sampling (encoder)
        self.down1 = DoubleConv(in_channels, base_channels)
        self.down2 = DoubleConv(base_channels, base_channels*2)
        self.pool = nn.MaxPool2d(2)

        # Bottleneck
        self.bottleneck = DoubleConv(base_channels*2,
        ↪  base_channels*4)

        # Up-sampling (decoder)
        self.up1 = nn.ConvTranspose2d(base_channels*4,
        ↪  base_channels*2, kernel_size=2, stride=2)
        self.conv_up1 = DoubleConv(base_channels*4, base_channels*2)

        self.up2 = nn.ConvTranspose2d(base_channels*2,
        ↪  base_channels, kernel_size=2, stride=2)
        self.conv_up2 = DoubleConv(base_channels*2, base_channels)

        # Final output
        self.final_conv = nn.Conv2d(base_channels, out_channels,
        ↪  kernel_size=1)

    def forward(self, x):
        # Encoder
        x1 = self.down1(x)
        x2 = self.pool(x1)

        x2 = self.down2(x2)
        x3 = self.pool(x2)

        # Bottleneck
        b = self.bottleneck(x3)

        # Decoder
        x = self.up1(b)
        x = torch.cat([x, x2], dim=1)
        x = self.conv_up1(x)
```

333

```python
        x = self.up2(x)
        x = torch.cat([x, x1], dim=1)
        x = self.conv_up2(x)

        # Final
        out = self.final_conv(x)
        return out


# ----------------------------------------------------------------
# 4) Define diffusion schedule and forward process
# ----------------------------------------------------------------
def make_beta_schedule(schedule_name, n_timestep, start=1e-4,
↪    end=2e-2):
    '''
    Creates a beta schedule for the diffusion process (linear only
    ↪    here).
    '''
    if schedule_name == "linear":
        return torch.linspace(start, end, n_timestep)
    else:
        raise NotImplementedError("Only 'linear' schedule is
        ↪    implemented here.")


class Diffusion:
    '''
    A class encapsulating:
    1) The forward noising process: q(x_t | x_0)
    2) The reverse denoising process: p(x_{t-1} | x_t)
    3) Training and sampling utilities.
    '''
    def __init__(self, n_steps=200, beta_schedule='linear',
    ↪    device='cpu'):
        self.device = device
        self.n_steps = n_steps
        self.betas = make_beta_schedule(beta_schedule,
        ↪    n_steps).to(device)
        self.alphas = 1.0 - self.betas
        self.alpha_cumprod = torch.cumprod(self.alphas,
        ↪    dim=0).to(device)
        self.alpha_cumprod_prev = torch.cat([torch.tensor([1.0],
        ↪    device=device), self.alpha_cumprod[:-1]], dim=0)

        self.posterior_variance = self.betas * (1.0 -
        ↪    self.alpha_cumprod_prev) / (1.0 - self.alpha_cumprod)

    def q_sample(self, x_start, t, noise=None):
        '''
        Forward diffusion: x_t = sqrt(alpha_cumprod[t]) * x_start
                            + sqrt(1 - alpha_cumprod[t]) * noise
        '''
        if noise is None:
            noise = torch.randn_like(x_start)
        # gather() to shape the correct index dimension
```

334

```python
        sqrt_alpha_cumprod_t =
        ↪   self.alpha_cumprod[t].sqrt().view(-1,1,1,1)
        sqrt_one_minus_alpha_cumprod_t = (1 -
        ↪   self.alpha_cumprod[t]).sqrt().view(-1,1,1,1)

        return sqrt_alpha_cumprod_t * x_start +
        ↪   sqrt_one_minus_alpha_cumprod_t * noise

    def predict_noise(self, model, x_t, t):
        '''
        Use the U-Net model to predict noise, given x_t at timestep
        ↪   t.
        We reshape t into a batch dimension for broadcasting if
        ↪   needed.
        '''
        return model(x_t)

    def p_sample(self, model, x_t, t, guidance_scale=1.0):
        '''
        One reverse diffusion step: p(x_{t-1}|x_t).
        '''
        betas_t = self.betas[t]
        alpha_t = self.alphas[t]
        alpha_cumprod_t = self.alpha_cumprod[t]
        alpha_cumprod_prev_t = self.alpha_cumprod_prev[t]

        # Model's noise prediction
        e_t = model(x_t) * guidance_scale

        # Reconstruct x_0 estimate
        sqrt_recip_alpha_t = (1.0 / alpha_t).sqrt()
        x_0_hat = (x_t - (1.0 - alpha_t).sqrt() * e_t) *
        ↪   sqrt_recip_alpha_t

        # Coefficients for x_{t-1}
        coef1 = (alpha_cumprod_prev_t.sqrt() * betas_t) / (1.0 -
        ↪   alpha_cumprod_t)
        coef2 = ((1.0 - alpha_cumprod_prev_t) * alpha_t.sqrt()) /
        ↪   (1.0 - alpha_cumprod_t)

        mean = coef1 * x_0_hat + coef2 * x_t

        # Posterior variance
        posterior_var = self.posterior_variance[t]

        if t > 0:
            noise = torch.randn_like(x_t)
        else:
            noise = torch.zeros_like(x_t)  # no noise at t=0
        x_prev = mean + noise * posterior_var.sqrt()
        return x_prev

    def p_sample_loop(self, model, shape, guidance_scale=1.0):
```

```python
        ' ' '
        Perform full reverse diffusion from x_T ~ N(0,I) to x_0.
        ' ' '
        x_t = torch.randn(shape, device=self.device)
        for i in reversed(range(self.n_steps)):
            x_t = self.p_sample(model, x_t, i, guidance_scale)
        return x_t


# -------------------------------------------------------------
# 5) Training and evaluation routines
# -------------------------------------------------------------
def train_one_epoch(model, diffusion, optimizer, dataloader,
↪   device):
    model.train()
    loss_sum = 0
    for images, _ in dataloader:
        images = images.to(device)
        # Sample a random t
        t = torch.randint(0, diffusion.n_steps, (images.size(0),),
        ↪   device=device).long()

        noise = torch.randn_like(images)
        x_t = diffusion.q_sample(images, t, noise)

        noise_pred = diffusion.predict_noise(model, x_t, t)

        loss = nn.functional.mse_loss(noise_pred, noise)
        optimizer.zero_grad()
        loss.backward()
        optimizer.step()

        loss_sum += loss.item()
    return loss_sum / len(dataloader)

def evaluate_model(model, diffusion, dataloader, device):
    model.eval()
    loss_sum = 0
    with torch.no_grad():
        for images, _ in dataloader:
            images = images.to(device)
            t = torch.randint(0, diffusion.n_steps,
            ↪   (images.size(0),), device=device).long()
            noise = torch.randn_like(images)
            x_t = diffusion.q_sample(images, t, noise)
            noise_pred = diffusion.predict_noise(model, x_t, t)
            loss = nn.functional.mse_loss(noise_pred, noise)
            loss_sum += loss.item()
    return loss_sum / len(dataloader)

def sample_and_save(model, diffusion, device, epoch,
↪   guidance_scale=1.0, sample_count=16):
    model.eval()
    with torch.no_grad():
```

336

```python
        generated = diffusion.p_sample_loop(
            model,
            (sample_count, 1, 64, 64),
            guidance_scale=guidance_scale
        )
        # Move images from [-1,1] to [0,1]
        generated = (generated.clamp(-1.0, 1.0) + 1.0)*0.5

        # Create a grid
        grid_edge = int(math.sqrt(sample_count))
        fig, axs = plt.subplots(grid_edge, grid_edge, figsize=(5,5))
        idx = 0
        for i in range(grid_edge):
            for j in range(grid_edge):
                axs[i,j].imshow(generated[idx][0].cpu().numpy(),
                ↪   cmap='gray', vmin=0, vmax=1)
                axs[i,j].axis('off')
                idx += 1

        os.makedirs("results_structural", exist_ok=True)
        plt.savefig(f"results_structural/
        epoch_{epoch}_gs_{guidance_scale}.png")
        plt.close()


# ----------------------------------------------------------------
# 6) Main: load data, initialize model, diffusion, and train
# ----------------------------------------------------------------
def main():
    set_seed(42)
    device = torch.device("cuda" if torch.cuda.is_available() else
    ↪   "cpu")

    # Create training and testing sets of random 2D shapes
    train_dataset = ToyStructuralDataset(num_samples=2000,
    ↪   image_size=64)
    test_dataset = ToyStructuralDataset(num_samples=500,
    ↪   image_size=64)

    train_loader = DataLoader(train_dataset, batch_size=64,
    ↪   shuffle=True)
    test_loader = DataLoader(test_dataset, batch_size=64,
    ↪   shuffle=False)

    # Initialize our UNet
    model = UNet(in_channels=1, out_channels=1,
    ↪   base_channels=32).to(device)

    # Diffusion with 200 steps, linear schedule
    diffusion = Diffusion(n_steps=200, beta_schedule='linear',
    ↪   device=device)

    # Optimizer
    optimizer = optim.Adam(model.parameters(), lr=1e-4)
```

```
epochs = 3
for epoch in range(epochs):
    train_loss = train_one_epoch(model, diffusion, optimizer,
    ↪  train_loader, device)
    val_loss = evaluate_model(model, diffusion, test_loader,
    ↪  device)
    print(f"Epoch [{epoch+1}/{epochs}] - Train Loss:
    ↪  {train_loss:.4f}, Val Loss: {val_loss:.4f}")

    # Sample a few shapes
    sample_and_save(model, diffusion, device, epoch,
    ↪  guidance_scale=1.0, sample_count=16)
    sample_and_save(model, diffusion, device, epoch,
    ↪  guidance_scale=2.0, sample_count=16)

print("Training complete! Check the 'results_structural' folder
↪  for generated samples.")

if __name__ == "__main__":
    main()
```

Key Implementation Details:

- **Forward Diffusion:** We implement `q_sample` to corrupt each structural image with Gaussian noise, governed by linearly spaced `betas`. This simulates increasingly noisy shapes.

- **Reverse Diffusion (Sampling):** The function `p_sample_loop` iteratively applies reverse diffusion steps, starting from random noise. At each step, the model predicts noise to be removed, producing progressively refined 2D shapes.

- **U-Net Architecture:** The `UNet` has a downsampling path (encoder) and upsampling path (decoder) with skip connections. This design captures both global layout and fine detail of structural forms.

- **Training Objective:** We directly compare the model's predicted noise with the actual Gaussian noise injected, using mean-squared error (MSE) loss for simplicity.

- **Synthetic Shape Dataset:** A `ToyStructuralDataset` yields various geometric forms (squares, circles, triangles) in a 64×64 grid, providing an illustrative representation of mechanical or architectural parts.

- **Guidance Parameter:** We introduce `guidance_scale` to demonstrate how scaling the predicted noise can enhance or reduce variability in the generated designs.

- **Iterative Design Pipeline:** In practice, each generated shape could be tested with structural solvers for constraints like stress or weight, and then refined by retraining or re-sampling the diffusion model.

Chapter 33

Multimodal Generation with Diffusion for Audio-Visual Synthesis

Finally, we explore combining audio and visuals into a single diffusion framework. Common applications include generating video clips with synchronized music or adding soundtracks to silent footage. Construction starts by treating each modality (video frames, audio spectrograms) as separate channels or streams, applying a forward noise process across both modalities in parallel. A cross-modal UNet or transformer-based architecture is then trained to denoise them jointly, using attention or feature fusion to align audio-visual cues. Key steps: (1) collecting paired video and audio data, (2) scaling or encoding them into a shared latent space, (3) applying noise that corrupts both streams simultaneously, (4) training the network to restore coherence between image frames and audio track, and (5) sampling new audio-visual sequences by reversing the diffusion from random seeds or partial inputs. An innovative design adds semantic conditioning—for instance, specifying an emotional or narrative theme that guides both the visuals and the sound toward a cohesive style.

Python Code Snippet

```python
import os
import random
import math
import torch
import torch.nn as nn
from torch.utils.data import Dataset, DataLoader
import torch.optim as optim
import matplotlib.pyplot as plt
import numpy as np

# ----------------------------------------------------------------
# 1) Set random seed for reproducibility
# ----------------------------------------------------------------
def set_seed(seed=42):
    random.seed(seed)
    np.random.seed(seed)
    torch.manual_seed(seed)
    if torch.cuda.is_available():
        torch.cuda.manual_seed_all(seed)

# ----------------------------------------------------------------
# 2) Create a toy dataset that returns combined audio-visual data
#    as a single 4-channel tensor: first 3 channels = "video frame",
#    last 1 channel = "audio spectrogram" for demonstration.
# ----------------------------------------------------------------
class ToyAudioVisualDataset(Dataset):
    """
    A synthetic dataset where each sample is a (4, H, W) tensor:
      - The first 3 channels mimic a 'video frame' (RGB).
      - The last channel mimics an 'audio spectrogram'.
    Values are randomly generated for demonstration purposes only.
    """
    def __init__(self, length=500, height=64, width=64):
        super().__init__()
        self.length = length
        self.height = height
        self.width = width

    def __len__(self):
        return self.length

    def __getitem__(self, idx):
        # Generate random "video" (3-channel) + "audio" (1-channel)
        x = torch.rand(4, self.height, self.width) * 2 - 1  # Data
        ↪   in [-1, 1]
        return x, 0  # No label needed; returning 0 for consistency

# ----------------------------------------------------------------
# 3) Define a simple U-Net that can handle multiple input channels
#    and produce the same number of output channels.
```

341

```python
# --------------------------------------------------------------
class DoubleConv(nn.Module):
    """
    A helper module that performs two convolutions (each followed by
    ↪ ReLU)
    to reduce boilerplate in the U-Net blocks.
    """
    def __init__(self, in_channels, out_channels):
        super(DoubleConv, self).__init__()
        self.conv = nn.Sequential(
            nn.Conv2d(in_channels, out_channels, 3, padding=1),
            nn.ReLU(inplace=True),
            nn.Conv2d(out_channels, out_channels, 3, padding=1),
            nn.ReLU(inplace=True)
        )

    def forward(self, x):
        return self.conv(x)

class AudioVisualUNet(nn.Module):
    """
    A simplified U-Net architecture to process 4-channel
    audio-visual input and produce 4-channel output.
    """
    def __init__(self, in_channels=4, out_channels=4,
    ↪ base_channels=64):
        super(AudioVisualUNet, self).__init__()

        # Down-sampling (encoder)
        self.down1 = DoubleConv(in_channels, base_channels)
        self.pool1 = nn.MaxPool2d(2)

        self.down2 = DoubleConv(base_channels, base_channels*2)
        self.pool2 = nn.MaxPool2d(2)

        # Bottleneck
        self.bottleneck = DoubleConv(base_channels*2,
        ↪ base_channels*4)

        # Up-sampling (decoder)
        self.up2 = nn.ConvTranspose2d(base_channels*4,
        ↪ base_channels*2, kernel_size=2, stride=2)
        self.conv_up2 = DoubleConv(base_channels*4, base_channels*2)

        self.up1 = nn.ConvTranspose2d(base_channels*2,
        ↪ base_channels, kernel_size=2, stride=2)
        self.conv_up1 = DoubleConv(base_channels*2, base_channels)

        # Final output
        self.final_conv = nn.Conv2d(base_channels, out_channels,
        ↪ kernel_size=1)

    def forward(self, x):
```

```
        # Encoder
        x1 = self.down1(x)
        x2 = self.pool1(x1)

        x2 = self.down2(x2)
        x3 = self.pool2(x2)

        # Bottleneck
        b = self.bottleneck(x3)

        # Decoder
        x = self.up2(b)
        x = torch.cat([x, x2], dim=1)   # skip connection
        x = self.conv_up2(x)

        x = self.up1(x)
        x = torch.cat([x, x1], dim=1)
        x = self.conv_up1(x)

        out = self.final_conv(x)
        return out


# ----------------------------------------------------------------
# 4) Diffusion schedule and forward process adapted to
#    multimodal data (4-channels).
# ----------------------------------------------------------------
def make_beta_schedule(schedule_name, n_timestep, start=1e-4,
↪   end=2e-2):
    """
    Creates a beta schedule for the diffusion process.
    We use a linear schedule as a straightforward example.
    """
    if schedule_name == "linear":
        return torch.linspace(start, end, n_timestep)
    else:
        raise NotImplementedError("Only 'linear' schedule is
        ↪   implemented here.")


class MultiModalDiffusion:
    """
    A class that encapsulates:
    1) The forward noising process for audio-visual data
    2) The reverse denoising process
    3) Utility for training and sampling
    """
    def __init__(self, n_steps=1000, beta_schedule='linear'):
        self.n_steps = n_steps
        self.betas = make_beta_schedule(beta_schedule, n_steps)
        self.alphas = 1.0 - self.betas
        self.alpha_cumprod = torch.cumprod(self.alphas, dim=0)
        self.alpha_cumprod_prev = torch.cat(
            [torch.tensor([1.0]), self.alpha_cumprod[:-1]], dim=0
        )
```

343

```python
        # Posterior variance for p(x_{t-1} | x_t, x_0)
        self.posterior_variance = self.betas * (1.0 -
        ↪   self.alpha_cumprod_prev) \
                                / (1.0 - self.alpha_cumprod)

    def q_sample(self, x_start, t, noise=None):
        """
        Forward diffusion: Adds noise to x_start at step t
        x_t = sqrt(alpha_cumprod[t]) * x_start + sqrt(1 -
        ↪   alpha_cumprod[t]) * noise
        """
        if noise is None:
            noise = torch.randn_like(x_start)
        sqrt_alpha_cumprod_t =
        ↪   self.alpha_cumprod[t].sqrt().unsqueeze(-1).
        unsqueeze(-1).unsqueeze(-1)
        sqrt_one_minus_alpha_cumprod_t = (1 -
        ↪   self.alpha_cumprod[t]).sqrt().unsqueeze(-1).
        unsqueeze(-1).unsqueeze(-1)
        return sqrt_alpha_cumprod_t * x_start +
        ↪   sqrt_one_minus_alpha_cumprod_t * noise

    def predict_noise(self, model, x_t, t):
        """
        Use the AudioVisualUNet model to predict the noise in x_t.
        """
        return model(x_t)

    def p_sample(self, model, x_t, t, guidance_scale=1.0):
        """
        One reverse diffusion step: p(x_{t-1} | x_t).
        The model predicts the noise e_t, and we compute
        the mean of p(x_{t-1} | x_t, x_0).
        """
        betas_t = self.betas[t]
        alpha_t = self.alphas[t]
        alpha_cumprod_t = self.alpha_cumprod[t]
        alpha_cumprod_prev_t = self.alpha_cumprod_prev[t]

        e_t = model(x_t) * guidance_scale  # simplistic "guidance"

        sqrt_recip_alpha_t = (1.0 / alpha_t).sqrt()
        # Reconstruct x_0 from x_t and predicted noise
        x_0_hat = (x_t - (1.0 - alpha_t).sqrt() * e_t) *
        ↪   sqrt_recip_alpha_t

        coef1 = ((alpha_cumprod_prev_t).sqrt() * betas_t) / (1.0 -
        ↪   alpha_cumprod_t)
        coef2 = ((1.0 - alpha_cumprod_prev_t) * alpha_t.sqrt()) /
        ↪   (1.0 - alpha_cumprod_t)

        mean = coef1 * x_0_hat + coef2 * x_t
```

```python
        posterior_var = self.posterior_variance[t]
        if t > 0:
            noise = torch.randn_like(x_t)
        else:
            noise = torch.zeros_like(x_t)

        x_prev = mean + noise * posterior_var.sqrt()
        return x_prev

    def p_sample_loop(self, model, shape, device,
    ↪   guidance_scale=1.0):
        """
        Repeatedly apply p_sample from x_T ~ N(0, I) down to x_0.
        """
        x_t = torch.randn(shape, device=device)
        for i in reversed(range(self.n_steps)):
            x_t = self.p_sample(model, x_t, i,
            ↪   guidance_scale=guidance_scale)
        return x_t


# ----------------------------------------------------------------
# 5) Training, evaluation, and sample utility
# ----------------------------------------------------------------
def train_one_epoch(model, diffusion, optimizer, dataloader,
↪   device):
    """
    A single training epoch for the audio-visual diffusion model.
    We sample a random t, forward diffuse the input, and predict the
    ↪   noise.
    """
    model.train()
    total_loss = 0
    for data, _ in dataloader:
        data = data.to(device)

        # Sample a random time step
        t = torch.randint(0, diffusion.n_steps, (data.size(0),),
        ↪   device=device).long()

        # Create random noise for the entire 4-channel input
        noise = torch.randn_like(data)

        # Forward diffuse the real data at step t
        x_t = diffusion.q_sample(data, t, noise=noise)

        # Predict the noise with the model
        noise_pred = diffusion.predict_noise(model, x_t, t)

        # L2 loss (MSE) to match the real noise
        loss = nn.functional.mse_loss(noise_pred, noise)

        optimizer.zero_grad()
        loss.backward()
```

```python
        optimizer.step()

        total_loss += loss.item()

    return total_loss / len(dataloader)

def evaluate_model(model, diffusion, dataloader, device):
    """
    Quick evaluation that reports average L2 error on a set.
    """
    model.eval()
    total_loss = 0
    with torch.no_grad():
        for data, _ in dataloader:
            data = data.to(device)
            t = torch.randint(0, diffusion.n_steps, (data.size(0),),
            ↪    device=device).long()
            noise = torch.randn_like(data)

            x_t = diffusion.q_sample(data, t, noise=noise)
            noise_pred = diffusion.predict_noise(model, x_t, t)
            loss = nn.functional.mse_loss(noise_pred, noise)
            total_loss += loss.item()
    return total_loss / len(dataloader)

def sample_and_save(model, diffusion, device, epoch,
↪    guidance_scale=1.0):
    """
    Samples a batch of audio-visual data from the diffusion model
    and saves an example image for the 'video' and a spectrogram for
    ↪    the 'audio'.
    """
    model.eval()
    with torch.no_grad():
        sample_batch_size = 4  # small batch for illustration
        shape = (sample_batch_size, 4, 64, 64)  # 4 channels,
        ↪    height=64, width=64
        generated = diffusion.p_sample_loop(model, shape, device,
        ↪    guidance_scale)

        # The first 3 channels are the "video image", last channel
        ↪    is "audio spectrogram"
        # We'll just visualize the first sample in the batch
        generated = generated.clamp(-1.0, 1.0)
        video_sample = generated[0, :3]  # shape: (3, 64, 64)
        audio_sample = generated[0, 3].unsqueeze(0)  # shape: (1,
        ↪    64, 64)

        # Normalize to [0,1] for visualization
        video_norm = (video_sample + 1) * 0.5
        audio_norm = (audio_sample + 1) * 0.5

        # Ensure directory
```

```
        os.makedirs("multimodal_results", exist_ok=True)

        # Plot and save the "video frame"
        plt.figure(figsize=(4,4))
        # permute to H,W,C for matplotlib
        plt.imshow(video_norm.permute(1,2,0).cpu().numpy())
        plt.axis('off')
        plt.savefig(f"multimodal_results/
        epoch_{epoch}_gs_{guidance_scale}_video.png")
        plt.close()

        # Plot and save the "audio spectrogram"
        plt.figure(figsize=(4,4))
        plt.imshow(audio_norm[0].cpu().numpy(), cmap='magma',
        ↪  aspect='auto')
        plt.axis('off')
        plt.savefig(f"multimodal_results/
        epoch_{epoch}_gs_{guidance_scale}_audio.png")
        plt.close()

# --------------------------------------------------------------
# 6) Main script: load synthetic data, initialize model, and train
# --------------------------------------------------------------
def main():
    set_seed(42)
    device = torch.device("cuda" if torch.cuda.is_available() else
    ↪  "cpu")

    # Create synthetic dataset
    train_dataset = ToyAudioVisualDataset(length=500, height=64,
    ↪  width=64)
    val_dataset = ToyAudioVisualDataset(length=100, height=64,
    ↪  width=64)

    train_loader = DataLoader(train_dataset, batch_size=8,
    ↪  shuffle=True)
    val_loader = DataLoader(val_dataset, batch_size=8,
    ↪  shuffle=False)

    # Create AudioVisualUNet
    model = AudioVisualUNet(in_channels=4, out_channels=4,
    ↪  base_channels=64).to(device)

    # Define the multi-modal diffusion process with fewer steps for
    ↪  demonstration
    diffusion = MultiModalDiffusion(n_steps=100,
    ↪  beta_schedule='linear')

    # Optimizer
    optimizer = optim.Adam(model.parameters(), lr=1e-4)

    # Train for a few epochs
    epochs = 3
```

347

```
for epoch in range(epochs):
    train_loss = train_one_epoch(model, diffusion, optimizer,
    ↪    train_loader, device)
    val_loss = evaluate_model(model, diffusion, val_loader,
    ↪    device)
    print(f"Epoch [{epoch+1}/{epochs}] - Train Loss:
    ↪    {train_loss:.4f}, Val Loss: {val_loss:.4f}")

    # Generate samples at the end of each epoch
    sample_and_save(model, diffusion, device, epoch,
    ↪    guidance_scale=1.0)
    # Optionally try a higher guidance scale:
    sample_and_save(model, diffusion, device, epoch,
    ↪    guidance_scale=2.0)

    print("Training complete! Check the 'multimodal_results' folder
    ↪    for generated samples.")

if __name__ == "__main__":
    main()
```

Key Implementation Details:

- **Forward Diffusion:** We implement `q_sample` to corrupt each 4-channel input (video + audio) at a random time step t, blending it with Gaussian noise based on the linear schedule.

- **Reverse Diffusion (Sampling):** The function `p_sample_loop` iterates from the noisiest state down to a clean sample by repeatedly calling `p_sample`, which reconstructs the original data in small steps.

- **UNet for Audio-Visual Data:** Our `AudioVisualUNet` is a 2D convolutional network operating on 4 input channels (3 for video, 1 for audio). It outputs 4 channels of predicted noise. In practice, 3D or cross-attention layers can better capture time and frequency relationships, but this example illustrates the core diffusion principle.

- **Training Objective:** We compute a mean-squared error (MSE) between the model's predicted noise and the actual noise added in the forward process, driving the network to learn effective denoising for both modalities.

- **Synthesis and Visualization:** During sampling, `sample_and_save` splits the predicted output into video and audio spectrogram portions, then saves them as separate images for inspection.

- **Guidance Scale:** The parameter `guidance_scale` scales the predicted noise, influencing the trade-off between fidelity and diversity (though this snippet uses a simplistic approach to demonstrate how simple guidance can be integrated).

www.ingramcontent.com/pod-product-compliance
Lightning Source LLC
LaVergne TN
LVHW051428050326
832903LV00030BD/2980